World Bank Economists' Forum

World Bank Economists' Forum

volume 1

Edited by

Shantayanan Devarajan
F. Halsey Rogers
Lyn Squire

The World Bank
Washington, D.C.

Cover design by Ultra Designs.

Library of Congress Cataloging-in-Publication Data

World Bank Economists' Forum / edited by Shantayanan Devarajan, F. Halsey Rogers,
Lyn Squire.
    p. cm.
Selected papers presented at the First World Bank Economists' Forum, held in
Washington DC, May 3–4, 1999.
Includes bibliographical references.
ISBN 0-8213-4833-7
    1. Economic development—Congresses. 2. Developing countries—Economic
policy—Congresses. 3. Europe, Eastern—Economic policy—Congresses. 4. Fiscal
policy—Congresses. 5. Debts, Public—Congresses. 6. Financial crises—Congresses. 7.
Labor market—Congresses. 8. Public health—Finance—Congresses. I. Devarajan,
Shantayanan, 1954– II. Rogers, F. Halsey, 1965– III. Squire, Lyn, 1946– IV. World Bank
Economists' Forum (1st : 1999 Washington, D.C.)

HD73 .W677 2001
338.9—dc21   2001023384

Contents

PART III. UNDERSTANDING AND MANAGING UNEMPLOYMENT

PART IV. PUBLIC SERVICES AND DEVELOPMENT

Preface

This volume collects nine outstanding papers presented at the first World Bank Economists' Forum, held May 3–4, 1999. Initiated by then-Chief Economist Joseph Stiglitz, the Forum was designed to showcase recent research carried out by economists throughout the Bank, especially those in operations. As this volume indicates, the Forum highlighted papers that combined analytical rigor with potential policy impact.

The inaugural Forum covered the landscape of modern development economics. This volume surveys much of that same territory: fiscal policy, capital flows, trade, decentralization, labor markets, infrastructure, health, and worker training are the main themes. The authors represent both the operational and the research sides of the Bank. The papers were selected from among the best Forum entries, which in turn had been selected for presentation at the Forum from 140 submitted abstracts. We are very grateful to those Bank staff who lent their expertise to this effort: the committee members who helped select papers for the Forum, the session chairs and discussants whose comments improved them, and the reviewers who refereed the papers nominated for inclusion here. Their names are listed on the next page.

Shantayanan Devarajan
Chief Economist
Human Development Network

F. Halsey Rogers
Senior Economist and Advisor
Office of the Chief Economist

Lyn Squire
Director
Global Development Network

Acknowledgments

We would like to express our special gratitude to the many World Bank staff who helped make the Forum and this volume possible:

Pierre-Richard Agenor
Kaushik Basu
Hana Polackova Brixi
Jan Bojo
Nisangul Ceran
Constantijn Claessens
Lionel Demery
Ishac Diwan
John Dixon
William Easterly
Gunnar Eskeland
Ahmed Galal
Alan Gelb
Cheryl Gray
Charles Griffin
Kenneth Gwilliam
Jeffrey Hammer
Robert Holzmann
Gregory Ingram
Steen Jorgensen
Masahiro Kawai
Elizabeth King
Odin Knudsen
William Magrath

William Maloney
Andrew Mason
Karen Mason
John Page
Guillermo Perry
Alexander Preker
Lant Pritchett
Martin Rama
Martin Ravallion
Jo Ritzen
Joanne Salop
Maurice Schiff
Marcelo Selowsky
Radwan Shaban
Joseph Stiglitz
Helen Sutch
David Tarr
Alfred Thieme
Zafiris Tzannatos
Dominique Van De Walle
Adam Wagstaff
Michael Walton
Debrework Zewdie
Heng-Fu Zou

Part I

Confronting Crises, Visible and Invisible

Crisis Management in Capital Markets: The Impact of Argentine Policy during the Tequila Effect

Eduardo J. J. Ganapolsky and Sergio L. Schmukler

Abstract

The Mexican financial crisis of 1994–95 had strong spillover effects on Argentina. The Argentine government successfully announced a series of policies to mitigate the contagion effects. This article studies how capital markets reacted to each policy announcement and news reports. Capital markets welcomed announcements that demonstrated a firm commitment to the currency board. The agreement with the International Monetary Fund (IMF), the dollarization of reserve deposits in the central bank, and changes in reserve requirements had a strong positive impact on market returns. After a period of higher volatility, the appointment of a new finance minister significantly decreased the variance of stock and bond returns, while lower reserve requirements increased the volatility of interest rates.

The financial crises that began in Mexico (1994) and in Thailand (1997) had strong spillover effects on other countries. The Mexican crisis affected, among others, Argentina and Brazil, as well as Malaysia, the Philippines, and Thailand. The forced flotation of the Thai baht prompted devaluations in Indonesia, Malaysia, the Philippines, and the Republic of Korea, while it provoked a much wider direct or indirect turbulence in both developed and emerging markets around the world.

The global extent of recent crises and the potential damaging consequences of being affected by contagion continue to attract attention among economists and policymakers. Most of the research concentrates on understanding the causes and consequences of financial crises. In this article, we focus on another aspect of financial crises: how crisis management might change the dynamics of contagion or spillover effects. Once a country has been affected by the spillover effects of an external crisis, what policies help resolve a crisis? On the other hand, what kinds of announcements and news events negatively impact capital markets?[1]

During the recent Mexican and Asian crises, several approaches were tried to avert the spillover effects. For instance, in the case of the Mexican crisis, Argentina's former finance minister wanted to change the markets' expectations by showing a strong commitment to defending the exchange rate peg. On March 11, 1995, *The Economist* reported the following:

> Mr. Cavallo has said that he would rather "dollarize" the economy entirely than devalue the peso.

While Argentina tried to reinforce the free convertibility of its currency during the Mexican crisis, Malaysia attempted to insulate its financial markets from speculative pressure during the Asian crisis. Accusing foreign speculators of orchestrating Malaysia's economic crisis, Malaysian Prime Minister Mahathir Mohamad (*New York Times*, September 21, 1997) said the following:

> Currency trading is unnecessary, unproductive and totally immoral. It should be made illegal.

In this article we analyze the experience of Argentina during the spillover of the Mexican crisis, dubbed the "tequila effect." Argentina presented an excellent opportunity to study crisis management. First, Argentina was arguably the country most affected by the Mexican peso devaluation on December 20, 1994, besides Mexico itself. Argentina's peg to the dollar and overall financial stability were reexamined during the tequila effect. On December 28 the central bank sold $353 million of reserves (the largest amount since the currency board was established). In the three months following the Mexican peso devaluation, the central bank sold more than one-third of its foreign exchange reserves.

---

1. In this article, "announcements" refer to policy measures undertaken by the government, like signing an agreement with the international financial community. "News" events refer to meaningful economic or political episodes— like a presidential election or the appointment of a new finance minister.

Argentina's stock market index plummeted 50 percent between December 19, 1994, and March 8, 1995. Argentine bond prices fell 36 percent, and the peso interest rate jumped from 11 percent to 19 percent during the same period. By March 11, 1995, there was great uncertainty about Argentina's fortunes, and *The Economist* reported:

> The big question to the [Latin American] region is whether recession will force the Argentines to . . . devalue.

Second, Argentina is under a currency board system, which constrains its monetary policy. At least 80 percent of the monetary base had to be backed by U.S. dollar reserves or other internationally liquid assets (not issued by the Argentine government).[2] Dollar-denominated bonds issued by the Argentine government can back the rest of the monetary base. Therefore, Argentina's policymakers needed to use alternative instruments, other than monetary policy, to revert the negative external shock.

Third, Argentina's policymakers took an active role in preventing a financial crash and a devaluation of the peso. Finally, Argentina was successful in controlling the negative transmission. During the Asian and Russian crises, Argentina's expertise in dealing with crises had already been internationally acknowledged. The financial press reports some examples:

> Argentines have an excellent experience in crisis management . . . Thailand should talk to them.
>
> William Rhodes, vice president of Citibank,
> *La Nación* (newspaper), September 23, 1997

> It was kind of strange to come from Latin America [to Asia] and try to give some advice, because for years it was the reverse.
>
> Miguel Kiguel, Argentina's finance undersecretary,
> *Dow Jones International*, September 23, 1997

> Cavallo steps in to advise Moscow.
>
> *Financial Times*, August 31, 1998

---

2. In 1995 more than 80 percent of the monetary base was backed by international assets. The Convertibility Law allows international reserves to be at least two-thirds of the monetary base.

In this article, we study Argentina's crisis management by analyzing how different policy announcements and news affected Argentina's stock market index, Brady bond prices, and peso-deposit interest rates. Among the announcements and news received by the markets, we found the following: The central bank lowered reserve requirements—on U.S. dollar deposits and on peso deposits—to assist troubled institutions and to reactivate the economy. Peso deposits in the central bank were automatically converted into U.S. dollars to give reassurance to the currency board. Rediscounts were limited. The central bank charter was reformed to gain more flexibility to act as a lender of last resort. An agreement with the IMF was reached. A fiduciary fund for bank capitalization was issued to support weak institutions, and a deposit insurance was established. Finally, President Menem was reelected, and the finance minister was replaced.

The remainder of the article is organized as follows. The next section, "Crisis Management under Contagion," describes in detail the announcements and news received by the markets. The following section, "Short-Run and Long-Run Impact of Policy Announcements and News," studies how each announcement and news report affected the short-run and long-run returns of financial variables. The penultimate section, "The Impact of Announcements and News on Volatility," focuses on how announcements and news impacted the markets' volatility. Finally, the last section summarizes the results and concludes the discussion.

Crisis Management under Contagion

Latin American capital markets have become increasingly integrated among themselves and with the rest of the world. Asset prices from different countries tend to co-move, so an external shock, such as the Mexican one, is transmitted to other countries. The high correlation of asset prices between Argentina and Mexico makes Argentina particularly sensitive to changes in Mexican prices. Many papers have argued that markets are prone to "contagion."[3] For instance, Calvo and Reinhart

---

3. "Contagion" has been defined differently across papers. At one extreme, "contagion" is understood as the spillover of shocks across countries. At the other end, under a more restrictive definition, "contagion" means the transmission of shocks unrelated to "market fundamentals." The evidence broadly suggests that there was contagion, in the restrictive sense, from Mexico to Argentina in 1994–95.

(1996), Valdés (1996), Baig and Goldfajn (1998), Frankel and Schmukler (1998), and Ganapolsky and Schmukler (1998) study the presence of "excess co-movement" between Argentina and Mexico, among other countries. Using a different approach, Eichengreen, Rose, and Wyplosz (1996) and Kaminsky and Reinhart (2000) study contagion by testing whether the probability of a crisis increases when there is a crisis somewhere else. Given the spillover effects from Mexico to Argentina, the present article studies the impact of the Argentine policy response to the contagion that originated in Mexico.

On December 19, 1994, Mexican policymakers announced a widening of the exchange rate band, starting on December 20. By December 22, the Mexican peso was allowed to float because of intense pressure in the foreign exchange market. Figure 1 plots the reaction of some Latin American capital markets after the Mexican peso devaluation. The Argentine peso came under attack and there was a run on bank deposits. During the period December 19–27, the Argentine stock market fell around 17 percent, Argentine bond prices fell 12 percent, and the Argentine peso-deposit interest rate rose 1 percentage point. To modify this trend, starting on December 28, Argentine policymakers began to send signals to the markets. A description of all the policy announcements and news the markets received follows.[4]

(1) Reserve requirements on U.S. dollar deposits were relaxed—December 28, 1994: After the devaluation of the Mexican peso, holders of the Argentine peso revised their expectations about the sustainability of the exchange rate peg. Therefore, they increased their holdings of U.S. dollars. To provide liquidity to the banks, reserve requirements on U.S. dollar deposits were lowered retroactively.[5]

(2) Reserve requirements on peso deposits were reduced—January 12, 1994: A few days after the devaluation of the Mexican peso, concerns about future defaults led depositors to withdraw their money from private banks to exchange their pesos for dollars. To alleviate the pressure from

---

4. A detailed description of the news can be found in the Argentine central bank and finance ministry regulations (Comunicaciones "A" 2293, 2307, 2315, 2317, 2338, 2350, 2298, 2308; Decreto 290/95, 286/95, and 445/95; Ley 24.485), as well as in the newspapers *Ambito Financiero* and *El Cronista Comercial*.

5. The retroactive lowering of reserve requirements was a means of alleviating the banks' financial illiquidity. Reserve requirements were calculated as a 30-day average, so that retroactive lower reserve requirements helped banks to substantially decrease the amount of cash they needed to deposit at the central bank.

FIGURE 1. EVOLUTION OF INTERNATIONAL CAPITAL MARKETS
DURING THE MEXICAN CRISIS
(all markets equal 100 on December 20, 1994)

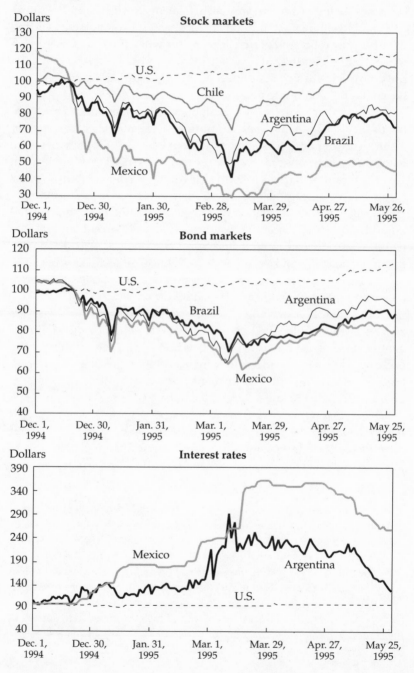

banks, reserve requirements on peso deposits were lowered retroactively to the same level on foreign currency deposits. Banks were also allowed to maintain their required reserves in either currency.

Table 1 illustrates how dollar and peso reserve requirements were modified following the Mexican peso devaluation.

(3) Bank deposits in the central bank were dollarized—January 12, 1995: To give additional support to the currency board, the central bank decided to dollarize the financial institutions' peso deposits held by the central bank. The purpose of the dollarization was to give confidence to the markets by decreasing the central bank incentives to reduce its peso-denominated debt through a devaluation of the currency.

(4) A public safety net was established—January 12, 1995: The central bank constituted a fund to help institutions by purchasing their nonperforming loans. All banks gave 2 percent of their deposits to establish the $700 million fund (administered by Banco Nación). The fund provided a safety net to the system. By mid-1997, the nonperforming loans were paid back to Banco Nación, and the shareholders (the banking sector) recovered their initial capital.

(5) The use of rediscounts was limited—February 3, 1995: Before the convertibility plan, rediscounts were frequently used to alleviate illiquidity problems faced by financial institutions. However, they could have been channeled to speculation during financial stress. Moreover, rediscounts could have been used to take advantage of the differential between the rediscount rate and the interbank rates. This differential usually increases during crises. To avoid an undesired use of rediscounts, the central bank established some limits on how financial institutions could take advantage of them. Banks were forbidden to use rediscounts

TABLE 1. RESERVE REQUIREMENTS
(percent)

	Argentine pesos			U.S. dollars		
Period	Checking account	Savings account	Time deposit	Checking account	Savings account	Time deposit
Aug. ?, 1993–Dec. 15, 1994	43	43	3	43	43	3
Dec. 16, 1994–Dec. 31, 1994	43	43	3	35	35	1
Jan. 1, 1995–Jan. 15, 1995	35	35	1	35	35	1
Jan. 16, 1995–Jan. 31, 1995	30	30	1	30	30	1
Feb. 1, 1995–Feb. 28, 1995	32	32	1	32	32	1
Mar. 1, 1995–Jul. 31, 1995	33	33	2	33	33	2

to buy back their debt, and they were only allowed to use rediscounts to return deposits.

(6) Modification of the central bank charter—February 27, 1995: The central bank acquired more flexibility to assist troubled financial institutions. First, the time limit for financial assistance was extended from 30 to 120 days. Second, financial assistance could exceed the net worth of financial institutions. Finally, the central bank could decide how to use the assets acquired from troubled institutions.

(7) Relaxation of reserve requirements—March 10, 1995: As another instrument to lower reserve requirements, the Argentine central bank allowed private banks to use 50 percent of their cash as reserve requirements. Through this mechanism, minimum reserve requirements did not need to be modified, but actual reserve requirements changed. After May 31, 1995, this 50 percent returned gradually to zero. An increase in this measure implies lower reserve requirements.

(8) Announcement of an agreement with the IMF (to be signed four days later)—March 10, 1995: The Argentine government signed an agreement with the IMF. Under this agreement Argentina accepted to be monitored by the IMF. At the same time, the Argentine government gained access to international credit for roughly $7 billion.

(9) Creation of a fiduciary fund for bank capitalization—March 28, 1995: A fund was established to help troubled financial institutions, by giving them additional credit. The fund was also meant to restructure the fragile financial system by purchasing nonperforming loans, which were going to be sold later on. The fund was established by issuing a bond, with the help of $500 million committed by the World Bank. Bondholders, the finance ministry, and the central bank managed the fund.

(10) Establishment of deposit insurance—April 4, 1995: To give confidence to the financial sector, a deposit insurance system was established. The insurance is administered by a private institution (SEDESA). The central bank, the finance minister, and commercial banks participate in SEDESA's board. The financial institutions absorb the cost of the fund. Each bank pays between 0.03 and 0.06 percent of its deposits, according to its risks. The insurance covers up to $10,000 for each person who holds money in a checking account, savings account, or time deposit up to 90 days. Furthermore, the insurance covers up to an additional $10,000 per person for deposits of at least 90 days. The deposit insurance does not cover deposits that receive an interest rate of 2 percentage points higher than the interest rate published by the central bank. Any deposits that receive extra incentives beyond the interest rate are also exempted from the insurance.

(11) President Menem was reelected—May 15, 1995: Even though the economy was in a deep recession, President Menem was reelected. His political campaign was based on the need to maintain price stability and to continue with the economic reforms.

(12) Finance minister Domingo Cavallo was replaced by central bank president Roque Fernández —July 26, 1997: After several weeks of political turmoil between the finance minister and other political sectors, President Menem decided to change his finance minister. He appointed central bank president Roque Fernández as the new finance minister.

Short-Run and Long-Run Impact
of Policy Announcements and News

This section studies the impact of the announcements and news (described above) on the return of Argentina's financial variables. Several papers have looked at the effect of announcements and news on capital markets. Some of these papers used the event study methodology to measure the impact of announcements—like earning announcements—on equity prices. This methodology investigates whether returns are abnormally high across firms after certain announcements. A description of the event study methodology can be found in Campbell, Lo, and MacKinlay (1997).

Another set of papers focused on the effect of macroeconomic announcements on capital markets. These papers studied how the release of information is transmitted to the markets and what types of news affect the markets. For example, Hardouvelis (1988) found that exchange rates and interest rates respond primarily to monetary news. Harvey and Huang (1991) studied foreign exchange markets and attributed the increased volatility to macroeconomic news announcements. Elmendorf, Hirschfeld, and Weil (1992) showed, from another perspective, that major historic news affects bond price movements, but they explained only a small fraction of those movements. Berry and Howe (1994) found a significant relationship between public information and trading volume on the New York Stock Exchange. Mitchell and Mulherin (1994) found that the number of announcements by Dow Jones and the stock market activity are directly related—even though the relationship is weak (as found in other studies). Edison (1996) found that dollar exchange rates systematically react to news about real economic activity, but exchange rates do not tend to react systematically to news on inflation. Edison also found that U.S. interest rates respond to both types of news, although the response is very small.

Melvin and Yin (1998) studied the effect of public information arrival on the volatility of the mark-to-dollar and yen-to-dollar exchange rates. They found mixed evidence on the role of public information on the evolution of foreign exchange markets. Jones, Lamont, and Lumsdaine (1996) found that conditional volatility and excess returns on daily bond prices are higher on (predetermined) announcement days. This might be because of trading or the information-gathering process. Ederington and Lee (1993) found similar results.

In this article, we investigate the role of announcements and news in modifying the negative dynamics triggered by the Mexican peso devaluation. We were not able to follow the same methodology used in previous papers. There were not enough experiences to evaluate the same type of announcements on several occasions. Moreover, we were not interested in the intraday effect of news, which is the focus of several papers. Here, we modeled the daily behavior of the stock market index, Brady bond prices, and the interest rate. Then we searched for structural breaks to determine whether the changes in regime coincide with the days the markets received news. We also performed out-of-sample forecasts to evaluate how markets would have behaved without announcements. Finally, we introduced two dummy variables per announcement or news to quantify their effect on each market. A related methodology was used, following this paper, in Baig and Goldfajn (1998) and Kaminsky and Schmukler (1999).

Modeling Argentina's Financial Variables

Separate models were estimated for each variable, controlling for the behavior of domestic and foreign factors. The regressors included variables believed to explain each market—namely, past changes of the endogenous variable and past changes of other Argentine financial variables. We also controlled for other countries' financial variables to account for spillover effects and for changes in the international financial environment.[6] The variables used in this article are described in appendix A.

---

6. As part of the foreign variables, we constructed a Latin American stock market index and a bond index, including Brazil, Chile, and Mexico. These three countries are the ones that affect Argentina the most. The indexes were weighted by the relative sizes of each country.

Unit root tests indicated that almost all variables are nonstationary. Augmented Dickey-Fuller tests rejected the hypothesis of nonstationarity for the financial sector reserves and the interest rate. Given that the domestic variables might be linked to the external variables by a stationary linear long-run relationship, we also tested for cointegration, following Johansen (1991). We failed to find cointegration, so we decided to work with models in first differences. The variables found to be $I(0)$, integrated of order zero, are included in levels.

The type of models we worked with follows:

$$\Delta Y_t^{Argentina} = \alpha + \sum_{l=1}^{L_1} \gamma_{1l} \Delta Y_{t-1}^{Argentina} + \sum_{f=1}^{F_1} \sum_{j=0}^{L_2} \gamma_{2j} \Delta Z_{f,t-j} + \sum_{f=1}^{F_2} \sum_{j=1}^{L_3} \kappa_{fj} \Delta X_{f,t-j} + \varepsilon_t.$$

$Y_t^{Argentina}$ stands for the endogenous Argentine financial variable: the stock market index, Brady bond prices, and the peso-deposit interest rate. Z_t stands for the foreign variable: the Mexican exchange rate and Brady bond prices, an index of Latin American bond prices, and the U.S. T-bill price.

Each model has F_2 exogenous variables X_f, for which there exist daily data, including reserves in the financial system, interbank interest rates (call rates), and deposits. Lagged values of these variables were assumed to be predetermined. Domestic variables were lagged, although we also estimated the contemporaneous relationship using two-stage least squares. In the case of the foreign variables, contemporaneous values were also included, since they were believed to be exogenously determined. We followed the general-to-specific methodology to determine the number of lags for each variable. We first included several lags and then excluded most of the insignificant ones. The estimations are reported in the section below, "Measuring the Impact of Each Announcement and News Report," where dummy variables are included. All the variables in the regressions are logarithms.

How Did Capital Markets React?

After determining the correct model for each variable, we evaluated how capital markets reacted during the crisis. We investigated whether the announcements and news released during the crisis helped reduce the external spillovers. In this section, we performed our analysis without introducing any dummy variable. First, we looked at the days on which the markets reacted unexpectedly. Our interest lay in whether those days coincided with policy announcements. Second, we looked at how the markets would have behaved without any announcements or news.

To search for the days of unexpected reaction, we computed recursive least squares. This methodology estimates an initial model and re-estimates the model repeatedly, using larger subsamples in every repetition. In each estimate a "one-step ahead" forecast was computed. The residuals were scaled such that the variance was constant.

The residuals of the different models were plotted in figure 2 for the period December 19, 1994, to mid-1995. Most of the residuals lie within the (±2 standard deviation) confidence interval, except during the periods of announcements. In fact, the residuals fall outside the bands on the days of major announcements. For instance, the residuals suggest that the stock and bond markets rose while the interest rate decreased on the day in which the government announced that deposits were dollarized. When news about the imminent agreement with the IMF became public, our estimates yield a positive reaction of the stock and bond markets, and an increase in the interest rate. The results from the recursive least squares are, in general, consistent with table 2, which displays the percent change in each financial variable on the announcement days.[7]

As another way to shed light on how news affected the markets, we performed out-of-sample forecasts. To compute the forecasts, we estimated each of the models up to the day before any announcements were made (December 27, 1994). Then we calculated out-of-sample forecasts for the following six-month period. The purpose of these forecasts is to show how the variables would have behaved if the markets had not received any announcements or news (namely, if the government had remained inactive after the crisis).

The out-of-sample forecasts are plotted in figure 3. The graphs display the actual and forecasted values of the stock market index, Brady bonds, and interest rate. The plots show that the actual values outperform the forecasted ones. In other words, once the crisis had started, the capital markets would have performed much worse if the government had not taken an active role. The stock market and the bond markets

---

7. During March 1 and 2 the residuals for the stock and bond models fall below the lower band, whereas the residuals for the interest rate models lie above the upper band. On March 3, the reverse happens. This last example shows that not all changes in the residuals can be clearly identified with particular announcements. During those days, the debate about the future of the convertibility plan intensified in the media, but no particular news was released.

FIGURE 2. RECURSIVE OLS RESIDUALS

Stock market recursive residuals

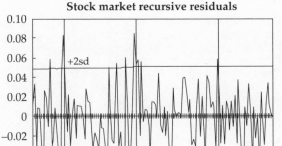

Days showing instability:

December:	27
January:	2, 10, 12
February:	16, 17, 24
March:	1, 2, 3, 10, 13, 14, 16
April:	10
May:	17

Bond price recursive residuals

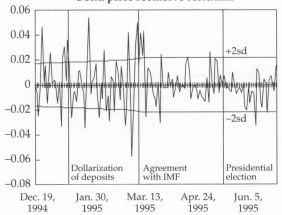

Days showing instability:

December:	21, 23, 27, 30
January:	10, 11, 13, 17 27, 31
February:	8, 13, 16
March:	1, 2, 3, 7, 8, 9, 10, 14, 16, 17, 29, 30
April:	20
May:	9

Interest rate recursive residuals

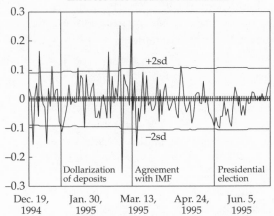

Days showing instability:

December:	21, 27
January:	2, 5, 13, 26
February:	1, 21
March:	1, 2, 3, 10, 15
April:	20

TABLE 2.   REACTION OF CAPITAL MARKETS ON DAYS
OF ANNOUNCEMENTS AND NEWS
(*percent change in prices*)

Announcement and news	Bonds	Stocks	Interest rate
Dec. 28, 1994: Reserve requirements in dollars were relaxed.	0.00	−0.15	5.97
Jan. 12, 1995: Bank deposits in the central bank were dollarized.	15.94	10.40	0.52
Jan. 31, 1995: Reserve requirements were increased.	10.65	7.07	5.69
Feb. 3, 1995: Rediscounts were limited.	1.49	−0.80	−0.34
Feb. 27, 1995: The central bank charter was modified.	−0.47	−5.24	6.69
Feb. 28, 1995: Reserve requirements were increased.	−0.47	−1.26	−0.61
Mar. 10, 1995: An agreement with the IMF was announced.	9.30	12.83	32.82
Mar. 28, 1995: A fiduciary fund was created.	0.48	1.53	−3.63
Apr. 12, 1995: A deposit insurance scheme was established.	0.23	0.77	0.52
May 15, 1995: President Menem was reelected.	2.43	1.81	−3.39
Average Dec. 20, 1994 to May 12, 1995	*2.44*	*3.21*	*7.29*
Jul. 26, 1996: Finance minister was replaced.	−0.57	−4.10	−1.63
Average Apr. 25, 1996 to Jul. 25, 1996	*0.62*	*1.07*	*2.11*

would not have recovered as they did, and the interest rate would have remained higher.

To sum up, figure 2 and table 2 suggest that the dollarization of deposits and the agreement with the IMF, among other announcements, had a positive impact on capital markets. Figure 3 suggests that the announcements jointly had a very positive effect on the capital markets. The rest of the article measures the short-run and long-run effects of each policy announcement and news event.

Measuring the Impact of Each Announcement and News Report

To measure the short-run and long-run effects on capital markets, we constructed two dummy variables for each announcement and news event. We read all major Argentine newspapers to determine the days in which the markets received new information. The dummy variables take the values 0 or 1. The short-run dummy variable is defined as follows: $D^{sr}_{k,a} = 1$ and $D^{sr}_{k,a+1} = 1$, where a is the day the announcement was released, while k defines the announcement. The short run includes both

FIGURE 3. OUT-OF-SAMPLE FORECAST: DEC. 27, 1994–JUN. 30, 1995

(The forecasts exclude the effects of all the announcements and news)

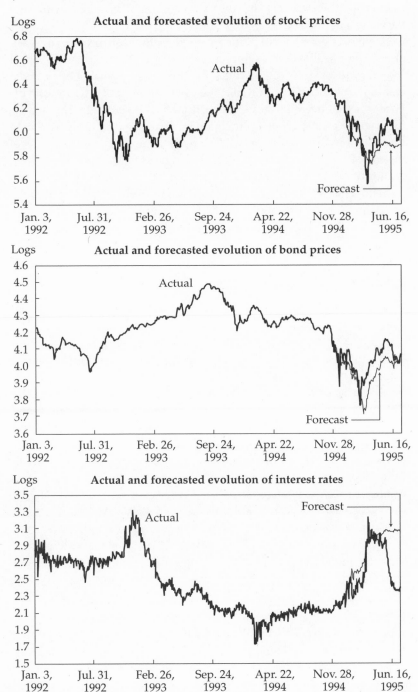

the day of, and the day after, the announcement, to account for the moment the news appeared in the printed press and because some announcements were made after the markets closed. The long-run dummy variable is defined as $D_{k,t}^{lr} = 1$ for all $t \geq a$.[8]

Some exceptions were made in the definition of the dummy variables. The variable deposit guarantee was equal to 1 during the period March 19 to April 13. At that time, the press was reporting on both the creation of a fiduciary fund and the establishment of a deposit insurance scheme. It would have been difficult to disentangle the two effects, so we included both of them in the deposit guarantee variable. In the case of reserve requirements, we used the actual requirement level instead of a dummy variable. We included two quantitative (rather than qualitative) variables—reserve requirements and cash in banks—to measure changes in the reserve requirement policy.

The models we estimated are the following:

$$\Delta Y_t^{Argentina} = \alpha + \Phi'D_t + \sum_{l=1}^{L_1} \gamma_{1l} \Delta Y_{t-1}^{Argentina} + \sum_{f=1}^{F_1} \sum_{j=0}^{L_2} \gamma_{2j} \Delta Z_{f,t-j} + \sum_{f=1}^{F_2} \sum_{j=1}^{L_3} \kappa_{fj} \Delta X_{f,t-j} + \varepsilon_t.$$

As mentioned before, $Y_t^{Argentina}$ stands for the three Argentine financial variables we study.

In all the regressions, our interest focuses on the estimates of Φ. These estimates are the coefficient of D_{kt}^{sr} and D_{kt}^{lr}, which stand for the short-run and long-run effect of announcements and news, and for the impact of different reserve requirement levels. When ϕ_k is statistically different from 0, we interpret the corresponding announcement and news to have a significant impact in explaining the dependent variable.

Table 3 displays the estimation results, with heteroskedastic consistent standard errors. The lags that repeatedly appeared to be statistically insignificant across specifications have been excluded. The reported results are robust to many specifications, except when noted. The results for each model can be summarized as follows.

(1) Stock market index: Three dummy variables were always significant and positive. The agreement with the IMF was statistically significant both in the short run and in the long run. The size of the coefficients was also large relative to the other variables. The short-run effect of the

---

8. Since our specifications calculated the impact on the returns of the variables, a short-term effect implies a long-term shift on the level of the variables.

agreement had an estimated impact of around 7 percent. The dollar-ization of deposits was the third variable that always appeared signifi-cant in the short-run behavior of the stock market index. On the other hand, the rediscount policy and the reform of the central bank charter had negative effects on stock market prices. These last two policy mea-sures, which implied more discretionary power to the central bank (re-laxing the rules imposed by the currency board), were followed by a negative market reaction.

Among the other exogenous variables, we found that the Mexican stock market index was highly correlated with the Argentine stock mar-ket index. The Mexican exchange rate also affected the Argentine stock market index. A devaluation in Mexico had a negative effect on Argen-tine stocks. U.S. bond prices were significant and positively correlated with the stock market index.

(2) Brady bond prices: The three dummy variables that were statisti-cally significant and positive in the stock market equation had the same effect on bond prices. In other words, the agreement with the IMF had a positive short-run and long-run impact on bond prices, and the dollarization of deposits had a positive short-run effect.

Other announcements and news also turned out to be significant in the equation for bond prices. Lower reserve requirements positively affected bond prices. The finance ministry had predicted that lower re-serves would have a stimulating effect on the economy—the bond mar-ket appears to have immediately reacted to that prediction. The deposit guarantee and the fiduciary fund for bank capitalization had a nega-tive effect on bond prices, although this effect disappeared under some specifications. This announcement implied a new contingent debt for the government. The rediscount policy positively affected bond prices in the short run. Lastly, the presidential election had a mild positive short-run effect on bond prices under a number of specifications. The change of finance minister had a negative short-term effect on bond prices.

Among the exogenous variables, Mexican Brady bond prices were positively correlated with the Argentine ones. U.S. bond prices and liq-uid reserves of the financial system were also significantly related to changes in Argentine bond prices.

(3) Interest rate: Some announcements and news were consistently significant across the interest rate regressions. Among them, reserve requirements were statistically significant. The estimations showed that the greater the cash that banks are able to use, the lower the interest rate. The dollarization of deposits also lowered the peso interest rate in

TABLE 3. THE IMPACT OF ANNOUNCEMENTS AND NEWS: OLS ESTIMATES—HETEROSKEDASTIC-CONSISTENT STANDARD ERRORS

Dependent variable: Stock market index			Dependent variable: Brady bond prices			Dependent variable: Interest rates		
Independent variable	Coefficient	t-statistic	Independent variable	Coefficient	t-statistic	Independent variable	Coefficient	t-statistic
Constant	0.003	0.291	Constant	0.008	1.748***	Constant	-0.071	-2.579*
Arg. stocks (-1)	0.021	0.650	Arg. bonds (-1)	-0.023	-0.799	Arg. bonds (-1)	-0.342	-2.079**
Arg. stocks (-2)	-0.100	-2.633*	Arg. bonds (-2)	-0.077	-1.141	Arg. bonds (-2)	-0.374	-2.386**
Mex. stocks	0.326	6.874*	Arg. bonds (-3)	-0.106	-3.011*	Arg. bonds (-3)	-0.201	-1.284
Mex. stocks (-1)	0.125	2.921*	Arg. reserves fin. system (-1)#	-0.011	-2.324**	Arg. bonds (-4)	-0.238	-1.980**
Mex. exchange rate	-0.149	-3.146*	Mex. bonds	0.776	19.216*	Arg. deposits (-1)	-0.507	-1.707***
Mex. exchange rate (-1)	-0.095	-2.357**	Mex. bonds (-1)	0.095	1.976**	Arg. deposits (-2)	-0.038	-0.115
Mex. exchange rate (-2)	-0.114	-2.763*	Mex. bonds (-2)	0.067	1.029	Arg. interest rate (-1)	-0.693	-9.650*
U.S. bonds	0.258	1.870***	Mex. bonds (-3)	0.135	2.711*	Arg. interest rate (-2)	-0.362	-5.811*
			Mex. bonds (-4)	-0.017	-0.593	Arg. interest rate (-3)	-0.143	-2.719*
			Mex. bonds (-5)	0.068	2.144**	Arg. interest rate (-4)	-0.051	-1.157
			U.S. bonds	0.193	3.148*	Arg. call rate (-1)#	0.020	1.446
			U.S. bonds (-1)	0.066	2.610*	Arg. call rate (-2)#	0.012	0.688
						Arg. call rate (-3)#	0.022	1.155
						Arg. call rate (-4)#	-0.025	-1.859***
						Latin Am. bonds	0.128	0.883
						Latin Am. bonds (-1)	0.124	0.722
						Latin Am. bonds (-2)	0.284	1.555
						Latin Am. bonds (-3)	-0.229	-1.319
						Latin Am. bonds (-4)	0.259	1.897***

Variable			Variable			Variable	
Reserve requirements	-0.000	-0.377	Reserve requirements	-0.000	-1.759***	Reserve requirements	0.001	0.775
Cash in banks	0.000	0.041	Cash in banks	0.000	0.593	Cash in banks	-0.001	-2.094**
Dollarization	0.003	0.657	Dollarization	-0.003	-0.543	Dollarization	0.008	0.494
Dollarization SR	0.045	7.758*	Dollarization SR	0.023	3.384*	Dollarization SR	-0.118	-6.791*
Rediscounts	-0.013	-1.399	Rediscounts	-0.003	-0.505	Rediscounts	-0.011	-0.557
Rediscounts SR	-0.015	-1.932***	Rediscounts SR	0.011	2.522**	Rediscounts SR	0.029	1.675****
Central bank charter	-0.004	-0.345	Central bank charter	-0.003	-0.414	Central bank charter	0.038	1.267
Central bank charter SR	-0.030	-3.589*	Central bank charter SR	-0.010	-1.429	Central bank charter SR	0.039	1.254
Agreement IMF	0.030	2.824*	Agreement IMF	0.022	2.252**	Agreement IMF	-0.039	-0.981
Agreement IMF SR	0.067	7.541*	Agreement IMF SR	0.020	2.159**	Agreement IMF SR	0.115	2.302**
Deposits guarantee	-0.011	-1.359	Deposits guarantee	-0.018	-2.298**	Deposits guarantee	0.032	1.865****
Deposits guarantee SR	-0.008	-1.293	Deposits guarantee SR	-0.003	-0.717	Deposits guarantee SR	0.006	0.568
President re-election	-0.006	-1.006	President re-election	-0.002	-0.602	President reelection	-0.014	-1.065
President re-election SR	-0.011	-1.547	President re-election SR	0.010	2.625*	President reelection SR	-0.053	-4.212*
Finance minister change	0.001	0.458	Finance minister change	0.001	1.130	Finance minister change	-0.002	-0.768
Finance minister change SR	-0.011	-1.066	Finance minister change SR	-0.004	-3.050*	Finance minister change SR	-0.016	-2.495**
Adjusted R-squared	0.149		Adjusted R-squared	0.566		Adjusted R-squared	0.351	
SE of regression	0.022		SE of regression	0.009		SE of regression	0.039	
Log likelihood	3482		Log likelihood	4058		Log likelihood	1904	
F-statistic	11.50		F-statistic	58.45		F-statistic	17.01	

SR: short run, *, (**), [***]: Significant at the 1, (5), [10] percent confidence level.

Note: All variables are first differences, except the ones marked with (#) and the announcement variables.

the short run. On the other hand, the agreement with the IMF raised the interest rate in the short run—as if the markets perceived that the agreement implied a tighter monetary policy.[9] However, the long-run effect was negative (although it is only significant in some specifications). Two other variables were sometimes significant. The reform of the central bank charter and the deposit insurance variable seemed to raise the interest rate, while the presidential election was negatively correlated with the interest rate in the short run.

We also controlled for the overnight interest rate, total deposits, and bond prices, which have the correct sign and are statistically significant. As a foreign variable, we controlled for the index of Latin American bonds.

As mentioned before, the reported results were robust to various specifications. We estimated the above models using different lag structures. We also estimated the contemporaneous relationship among the Argentine financial variables using two-stage least squares. Moreover, we estimated the models using seemingly unrelated regressions, since there was potential cross-correlation among the equations.

The Impact of Announcements and News on Volatility

In the previous sections we analyzed the impact of news on the first moments of the variables. However, the residuals from the previous models showed some clustering in volatility. There were periods in which volatility was low and periods where volatility was high (particularly in the aftermath of the Mexican devaluation). These residuals suggest that the variance was not constant over time. Therefore, we estimated the behavior of the variance using generalized autoregressive conditional heteroskedasticity (GARCH) models.

The models we estimated have the following specifications:

$$\Delta Y_t^{Argentina} = \alpha + \Phi'D_t + \sum_{l=1}^{L_1} \gamma_{1l} \Delta Y_{t-1}^{Argentina} + \sum_{f=1}^{F_1} \sum_{j=0}^{L_2} \gamma_{2j} \Delta Z_{f,t-j}$$

$$+ \sum_{f=1}^{F_2} \sum_{j=1}^{L_3} \kappa_{fj} \Delta X_{f,t-j} + \varepsilon_t,$$

---

9. Even though a strict currency board implies the inability to set monetary policy, the Argentine arrangement lets the central bank use bonds as part of its reserves. Therefore, some degree exists in which to pursue monetary policy. Also, the central bank can affect reserve requirements.

where ε_t is $i.i.d.$ $N(0, \sigma_t^2)$ and $\sigma_t^2 = \omega + \Psi'D_t + \sum_{p=1}^{L_4} \tau_{1p}\varepsilon_{t-p}^2 + \sum_{j=1}^{L_5} \tau_{2j}\sigma_{t-j}^2$.

In each model the variance at t depends on four elements: a constant term ω, exogenous factors given by the news variables D_t, past variances σ_{t-j}^2, and past shocks to volatility given by ε_{t-p}^2.

GARCH models had one main advantage over the models used previously. These models enabled us to test whether the announcements and news had an impact on volatility. In other words, we were able to estimate whether financial variables became more or less stable after the markets receive new information. By explicitly specifying the variance of ε_t, GARCH models also yielded efficient estimates of the parameters α, Φ, γ, and κ.

We computed GARCH estimates assuming and not assuming normally distributed errors. The quasimaximum likelihood estimations—which compute consistent covariances (following Bollerslev and Wooldridge 1992)—are displayed in table 4. The specifications GARCH (1,1) and GARCH (2,2) seemed to capture the variability in the variance; no further lags appeared significant. We excluded all variables that repeatedly turned out to be nonsignificant in the estimations, since the large number of parameters made the convergence difficult. Therefore, we chose to work only with parsimonious specifications.

GARCH estimation results can be summarized as follows. The volatility of the stock market and bond market behaved in a similar way. They were affected mainly by one exogenous variable—the change of minister, which decreased the long-run volatility in the stock and bond markets. In the interest rate equation, more variables appeared to be statistically significant. The agreement with the IMF decreased the volatility. The two variables that capture reserve requirements were statistically significant and had the expected negative sign. A decrease in reserve requirements increased the volatility of the interest rate, although it increased bond prices and reduced the interest rate. Lower reserve requirements enabled banks to charge lower deposit rates, but at the same time, banks were less able to absorb shocks, which are transmitted more to interest rates.[10]

---

10. Several papers, including Edwards and Végh (1997), explain how reserve requirements can affect deposit interest rates.

TABLE 4. THE IMPACT OF ANNOUNCEMENTS AND NEWS ON CAPITAL MARKETS: GARCH ESTIMATES—ROBUST STANDARD ERRORS

Dependent variable: Stock market index

Independent variable	Coefficient	t-statistic
Constant	0.001	1.824***
Arg. stocks (–1)	0.045	1.701***
Arg. stocks (–2)	–0.085	–3.043*
Mex. stocks	0.367	10.674*
Mex. stocks (–1)	0.129	3.548*
Arg. interest rate (–1)	–0.645	17.881*
Mex. exchange rate	–0.140	–3.773*
Mex. exchange rate (–1)	–0.078	–1.588
Mex. exchange rate (–2)	–0.126	–2.608*
U.S. bonds	0.228	2.582*

Dependent variable: Brady bond prices

Independent variable	Coefficient	t-statistic
Constant	0.004	2.052**
Arg. bonds (–1)	0.030	1.037
Arg. bonds (–2)	0.009	0.307
Arg. bonds (–3)	–0.095	–3.521*
Arg. reserves fin. system (–1) #	–0.005	–1.213
Mex. bonds	0.798	24.563*
Mex. bonds (–1)	0.038	0.990
Mex. bonds (–2)	–0.052	–1.292
Mex. bonds (–3)	0.176	4.123*
U.S. bonds	0.165	4.612*
U.S. bonds (–1)	0.091	3.357*

Dependent variable: Interest rates

Independent variable	Coefficient	t-statistic
Constant	–0.058	–6.173*
Arg. bonds (–1)	–0.064	–0.571
Arg. bonds (–2)	–0.186	–1.824***
Arg. deposits (–1)	–0.352	–2.011**
Arg. interest rate (–2)	–0.407	–10.748*
Arg. interest rate (–3)	–0.185	–5.080*
Arg. interest rate (–4)	–0.104	–3.276*
Arg. call rate (–1)#	0.031	6.073*
Latin Am. bonds	0.084	0.866
Latin Am. bonds (–1)	0.075	0.642
Latin Am. bonds (–2)	0.093	0.766
Latin Am. bonds (–3)	–0.141	–1.526

Model 1		
Dollarization SR	0.043	3.868*
Rediscounts SR	−0.033	−5.453*
Central bank charter SR	−0.052	−3.404*
Agreement IMF SR	0.077	8.486*
Variance equation		
Constant	0.000	3.050*
ARCH (1)	0.109	2.904*
ARCH (2)	0.136	3.818*
GARCH (1)	0.027	0.122
GARCH (2)	0.673	3.461*
Finance minister change	−0.000	−2.001***
Adjusted R-squared	0.142	
SE of regression	0.022	
Log likelihood	3736	
F-statistic	14.18	

Model 2		
Reserve requirements	−0.000	−1.909**
Dollarization SR	0.004	0.287
Agreement IMF SR	0.038	2.152**
Deposits guarantee	−0.002	−1.733***
Constant	0.000	2.756*
ARCH (1)	0.010	0.564
ARCH (2)	0.181	3.251*
GARCH (1)	0.159	1.698***
GARCH (2)	0.601	6.419*
Finance minister change	−0.000	−2.123***
Adjusted R-squared	0.538	
SE of regression	0.009	
Log likelihood	4231	
F-statistic	73.05	

Model 3		
Cash in banks	−0.000	−2.708*
Dollarization SR	−0.107	−4.280*
President reelection SR	−0.058	−2.407**
Constant	0.001	3.006*
ARCH (1)	0.133	3.840*
GARCH (1)	0.782	17.531*
Reserve requirements	−0.000	−2.561*
Cash in banks	0.000	2.382***
Agreement IMF	−0.000	−3.093*
Adjusted R-squared	0.306	
SE of regression	0.041	
Log likelihood	2119	
F-statistic	22.80	

SR: short run, *, (**), [***]: Significant at the 1, (5), [10] percent confidence level.
Note: All variables are first differences, except the ones marked with (#) and the announcement variables.

The GARCH models yielded the following results for the announcement variables in the first-moment equations. The model for the stock market showed that most of the variables that appeared significant in the ordinary least squares estimation remained significant here. In the model for bond prices, the significant announcement variables were reserve requirements, the agreement with the IMF, the deposit guarantee, and the fiduciary fund. In the interest rate equation, reserve requirements, the dollarization of deposits, and the presidential election remained statistically significant.

Summary of Results and Conclusions

Argentina was hit hard by the Mexican peso devaluation of December 20, 1994. In response to the spillover effects, Argentine policymakers pursued an active policy to manage the crisis by trying to send the right signals to the markets. Monetary policy has been constrained because of the currency board system (under which 80 percent of the monetary base needed to be backed by international reserves). Nevertheless, Argentina successfully prevented a financial crash without abandoning its peg to the dollar.

This article analyzed Argentina's crisis management during the tequila effect. We showed that Argentina's capital markets seemed to have performed better than if no active policies had been taken. We also estimated the impact of each policy announcement and news events on the Argentine capital markets. We studied their impacts on the short-run and long-run returns and on the markets' volatility. We worked with the stock market index, Brady bond prices, and the interest rate.

Our results showed that the agreement with the IMF was one of the most significant announcements the markets received. Both the stock and bond market returns reacted positively. The interest rate increased in the short run, while its volatility decreased. These reactions suggest that the markets perceived the agreement as being beneficial in the long run, but with a short-run tightening of domestic credit. We believe that the agreement with the IMF not only implied additional funding for the country, but also signaled to markets that sound policies were going to be adopted. In addition, the agreement gave international support to the way the government was dealing with the crisis. The impact of this announcement was significant even after controlling for changes in foreign markets. Mexico's financial agreement with the IMF and with the United States was announced around the same time, which positively affected the entire region.

Among the other announcements, the dollarization of deposits also had a positive effect on stock market and bond market returns. At the same time, the dollarization decreased the interest rate. Lower reserve requirements increased bond prices (perhaps because they provided a stimulus to the economy) and reduced the interest rate. However, they seem to have increased the volatility of the interest rate.[11] The fiduciary fund for bank capitalization and the deposit insurance scheme seem to have pushed bond prices downward and to have increased the interest rate. This increase in interest rates was partly expected, since the banking sector finances the deposit insurance. The presidential election decreased the interest rate and increased the value of Brady bonds. When significant, the reform of the central bank charter had a negative effect on capital markets, increasing the interest rate and reducing the value of stocks and bonds. The effect of the rediscount policy is ambiguous. This variable negatively affects stock prices and interest rates, while it positively affects bond prices.

The change of minister calmed down the stock and bond markets, as estimated in the GARCH models. The markets' nervousness about what was going to occur the day after Mr. Cavallo left the finance ministry appear now to have been unjustified. The stock and bond markets calmed down when the new minister was appointed, but the short-run effect on bond prices was negative. Higher reserve requirements and the agreement with the IMF seemed to decrease the volatility of interest rates.

To conclude, the capital markets recovered when they received signals that Argentina's conditions had room to improve and that Argentina was consolidating its currency board. There was a differentiation in returns between Argentina and Mexico. The markets welcomed the signals that demonstrated a strong commitment to the existing exchange rate peg and economic program. In this sense, the agreement with the IMF, the dollarization of deposits, and the reelection of President Menem were welcomed by the markets. On the other hand, measures like the reform of the central bank charter—which gave more discretionary power to the central bank—appear to have had a negative effect. It is likely that the previous government's proposal, after the Brazilian devaluation in 1999, to fully dollarize the economy was based on the type

---

11. During early 1995, there was a public discussion about the potential costs and benefits of lowering reserve requirements. Our estimates clearly reflect this tradeoff.

of market reactions we found in this article. The markets welcomed any move toward dollarization.

The reaction of the Argentine capital markets stand in sharp contrast to what happened in Asia. For instance, a tightening of the monetary policy sent good signals to the markets in Argentina, while the reaction in Asia was mixed (as shown in Kaminsky and Schmukler 1999). Moreover, Indonesia, Korea, the Philippines, Russia, and Thailand signed agreements with the IMF (for much larger amounts than $7 billion). However, the markets in these countries did not recover immediately after those agreements were signed. Future research might shed light on the circumstances in which certain policies work. For example, does the situation of the banking sector condition the success of a tight monetary policy (as discussed in Goldfajn and Gupta 1998)? Do the agreements with the international financial community need to be signed simultaneously, as was the case with Argentina and Mexico? Do countries need to show some commitment to confront the crisis besides calling on the IMF, as Argentina did? Do policymakers need to signal to markets that they really support the agreements?

Appendix A: Data Description

This appendix describes the series used in the paper. The data sources were the central bank of Argentina and Bloomberg. The listed series cover the period January 2, 1992, to July 10, 1997, except as indicated.

We worked with the following series:

1. Stock Markets
Argentina: Merval index
Brazil: Bovespa index
Chile: IPSA index
Mexico: IPC index
United States: Dow Jones index
Latin America: We have constructed a stock market index, including Brazil, Chile, and Mexico. The index is weighted by the relative GDP of each country.

2. Bond Markets
Argentina: Discount bond price index
Brazil: Discount bond price index
Mexico: Discount bond price index
United States: U.S. Treasury price index (maturity November 2021)

Latin America: We have constructed a bond market index, including Brazil and Mexico. The index is weighted by the relative GDP of each country.

Argentina's bond index started on September 24, 1992; Brazil's on June 28, 1993; and Mexico's and the United States' on January 2, 1992.

3. Money Markets
Argentina: Time deposits interest rate in pesos, 30 to 59 days
Mexico: Time deposits rate in pesos, 60 days
United States: T-bill rate in U.S. dollars, 1 month
The Mexican data started on September 29, 1992, Argentine interbank (call) interest rate on January 28, 1992, and the others on January 2, 1992.

4. Argentine Financial System
Fulfillment of reserve requirements (stock) and stock of international reserves held by the central bank. Both series ended in June 25, 1997.

5. Mexican exchange rate (pesos per U.S. dollar)

References

Baig, Taimur, and Ilan Goldfajn. 1998. "Financial Market Contagion in the Asian Crisis." International Monetary Fund Working Paper 98/155.

Berry, Thomas, and Kith Howe. 1994. "Public Information Arrival." *The Journal of Finance* XLIX (4): 1331–46.

Bollerslev, Tim, and Jeffrey M. Wooldridge. 1992. "Quasi-Maximum Likelihood Estimation and Inference in Dynamic Models with Time Varying Covariances." *Econometric Reviews* 11: 143–72.

Calvo, Sara, and Carmen Reinhart. 1996. "Capital Flows to Latin America: Is There Evidence of Contagion Effects?" In Guillermo Calvo, Morris Goldstein, and Edward Hochreiter, eds., *Private Capital Flows to Emerging Markets*. Washington, D.C.: Institute for International Economics.

Campbell, John, Andrew Lo, and A. Craig MacKinlay. 1997. *The Econometrics of Financial Markets.* Princeton, N.J.: Princeton University Press.

Ederington, Lois, and Jae Ha Lee. 1993. "How Markets Process Information: News Releases and Volatility." *The Journal of Finance* XLVIII (4): 1161–91.

Edison, J. Hali. 1996. "The Reaction of Exchange Rates and Interest Rates to News Releases." International Finance Discussion Paper 570, Federal Reserve Board.

Edwards, Sebastian, and Carlos Végh. 1997. "Banks and Macroeconomic Disturbances under Predetermined Exchange Rates." *Journal of Monetary Economics* 40 (2): 239–78.

Eichengreen, B., A. Rose, and C. Wyplosz. 1996. "Contagious Currency Crises." NBER Working Paper 5681, National Bureau of Economic Research, Cambridge, Mass..

Elmendorf, Douglas, Mary Hirschfeld, and David Weil. 1992. "The Effect of News on Bond Prices: Evidence from the United Kingdom, 1900–1920." Working Paper 4234, National Bureau of Economic Research, Cambridge, Mass.

Engel, Charles, and Jeffrey Frankel. 1984. "Why Interest Rates React to Money Announcements: An Explanation from the Foreign Exchange Market." *Journal of Monetary Economics* 13: 31–9.

Frankel, Jeffrey A., and Sergio L. Schmukler. 1998. "Crisis, Contagion, and Country Funds: Effects on East Asia and Latin America." In Reuven Glick, ed., *Managing Capital Flows and Exchange Rates: Lessons from the Pacific Basin.* Cambridge, U.K.: Cambridge University Press.

Ganapolsky, Eduardo, and Sergio Schmukler. 1998. "Crisis Management in Argentina during the 1994–95 Mexican Crisis." Policy Research Working Paper 1951, World Bank, Washington, D.C.

Goldfajn, Ilan, and Poonam Gupta. 1998. "Does Monetary Policy Stabilize the Exchange Rate." Working Paper, International Monetary Fund, Washington, D.C.

Hardouvelis, Gikas. 1988. "Economic News, Exchange Rates and Interest Rates." *Journal of International Money and Finance* 7: 23–5.

Harvey, Campbell, and Roger Huang. 1991. "Volatility in the Foreign Currency Futures Market." *The Review of Financial Studies* 4 (3): 543–69.

Johansen, Søren. 1991. "Estimation and Hypothesis Testing of Cointegration Vectors in Gaussian Vector Autoregressive Models." *Econometrica* 59:1551–80.

Jones, Charles, Owen Lamont, and Robin Lumsdaine. 1996. "Public Information and the Persistence of Bond Market Volatility." Working Paper 5446, National Bureau of Economic Research, Cambridge, Mass.

Kaminsky, Graciela, and Carmen Reinhart. 2000. "On Crises, Contagion, and Confusion." *Journal of International Economics* 51 (1): 145–68.

Kaminsky, Graciela, and Sergio Schmukler. 1999. "What Triggers Market Jitters? A Chronicle of the Asian Crisis." *Journal of International Money and Finance* 18: 537–60.

Melvin, Michael, and Xixi Yin. 1998. "Public Information Arrival, Exchange Rate Volatility, and Quote Frequency." Working Paper, Arizona State University.

Mitchell, Mark, and J. Harold Mulherin. 1994. "The Impact of Public Information on the Stock Market." *The Journal of Finance* XLIX 3: 923–50.

Valdés, Rodrigo. 1996. "Emerging Markets Contagion: Evidence and Theory." Unpublished manuscript, Massachusetts Institute of Technology.

Fiscal Policy, Hidden Deficits, and Currency Crises

Homi Kharas and Deepak Mishra

Abstract

Budget deficits, as conventionally measured, suffer from many measurement and methodological problems. Researchers who have used these conventional deficits to explain currency crises, therefore, unsurprisingly, have found little evidence of any systematic link between the two. We provide an alternative definition of budget deficit and show that there is a close association between the number of currency crises and our measure of deficit.

If asked to pick a single concept that best measures the fiscal situation of an economy, many of us would pick "budget deficit," but budget deficit, as conventionally measured, suffers from many problems. These problems, which are mostly measurement-related and methodological in nature and more severe in developing than in industrial countries, arise because of a variety of reasons. These range from complicated budgetary accounting practices to noninclusion of corporate and bank restructuring expenses, incurred during financial crises, into the budget. Not many attempts have been made in the literature to find out how

The authors are grateful to Hana Polackova Brixi, Sara Calvo, Michael Dooley, William Easterly, Indermit Gill, Santiago Herrera, Ashoka Mody, Saumya Mitra, Guillermo Perry, John Williamson, participants of the Economists' Forum 1999, and an anonymous referee for many insightful comments.

much difference it would make to the reported budget deficit if some or all these problems are taken into account. As a consequence, conventional budget deficits are rarely found to be useful to explain macroeconomic issues, be they the inflationary impact of budget deficit or discussion of long-term growth.

The deficiency of the conventional budget deficit to accurately reflect the fiscal position of an economy is most evident in the currency-crisis literature. One of the long-standing explanations of currency crises is that they result from profligate fiscal policies (Krugman 1979). A natural implication of this hypothesis is that the collapse of a fixed exchange rate is preceded by large and persistent budget deficits.[1] Even the most ardent critics of this hypothesis agree that many currency crises in the developing countries during the 1970s and 1980s, and some of the recent crises, like Brazil's devaluation in 1999, have been driven primarily by indefensible fiscal policies. Surprisingly, however, the large body of empirical work aimed at explaining currency crises has found little evidence of any systematic link between currency crises and reported budget deficits.[2]

The lack of evidence has regrettably been interpreted as a rejection of Krugman's model. We, however, argue that the evidence should be interpreted as yet another reason why "budget deficit" as conventionally measured is in need of a fix. The following two observations have led us to make such a claim.

First, we empirically confirm the importance of looking beyond the reported budget deficit in assessing the fiscal situation in a country, especially in developing countries. We do so by providing an alternative definition of budget deficit that is referred to as the actuarial budget deficit. Unlike the conventional deficit, which is a flow concept, actuarial deficit is computed using stock variables and is defined as the change in the stock of public debt and the money base (that is, total stock of government liabilities). The quantitative difference between the actuarial and the conventional deficits is called the hidden deficit. Using

---

1. Krugman's (1979) model has been extended in several directions to show that collapse of the peg may be preceded by deterioration of economic fundamentals, including loose monetary policy, bank failures, and an appreciation of the real exchange rate. For a recent review of the literature, see Flood and Marion (1997).

2. For example, see Kaminsky, Lizondo, and Reinhart (1997) and Frankel and Rose (1996).

data from 32 countries, from 1980–97, we show that the average hidden deficits are relatively large in developing countries as compared to industrial countries, and in some countries are larger than even their conventional budget deficits. Second, we demonstrate empirically that there is a close link between the number of currency crises and hidden and actuarial deficits. This link is nonexistent if one uses conventional deficits in place of actuarial deficits.

The concept of hidden deficits and its association with currency crises has important policy implications. First, an increase in hidden deficits is found to affect the expectations of market participants in the same way as an increase in visible deficits of the same amount, so any attempt on the part of the policymaker to keep the visible deficits small by running large hidden deficits is futile. Second, while designing policies to reduce the likelihood of currency crises, one should bear in mind that currency crises may be caused by past hidden deficits, as well as by current and prospective hidden deficits.[3] Although it is difficult to distinguish these two cases, recent research shows that policymakers, using nonperforming loans of the banking system and movement of bank shares, may be able to deduce the approximate size of prospective hidden deficits. Third, hidden deficits, when averaged over a long period, say 20–30 years, provide a crude approximation of how much contingent claims and capital gains and losses the government is likely to absorb in the long run. Therefore, an efficient intertemporal budgetary allocation calls for making provision in the budget every year for an amount equal to its long-run average hidden deficit, so that the country can meet future contingent claims and capital gains and losses without resorting to sharp changes in the tax rate or sudden contraction in government expenditure, or both.

It is important to point out that, while actuarial deficit is a better indicator to measure the fiscal position of the economy than the conventional deficit, it does have limitations. First, it provides a precise measurement of the fiscal situation only of the past years and not of the future years, because it does not take into account existing, unrealized contingent liabilities of the government. Second, the government's assets are not taken into account when computing hidden deficits, and therefore the numbers generated here may slightly overstate the actual fiscal constraints of the government.

---

3. For a discussion of prospective deficits, see Burnside, Eichenbaum, and Rebelo (1998).

The rest of the article is organized as follows. In the section "The Problems with Conventional Budget Deficits," we elaborate on the problems associated with the concept of budget deficit as conventionally measured, with special reference to developing countries. In the section "An Alternative Definition of Budget Deficit," we introduce the concept of actuarial budget deficit and show that it is significantly different, often considerably higher in magnitude, from conventional budget deficit. In the section "Links with Currency Crises," we provide cross-country evidence linking hidden deficits to currency crises and discuss how the two are potentially linked. The section "Institutional Implications and Concluding Remarks," discusses the institutional implications of these new concepts of budget deficits in terms of budgetary accounting practices and managing debt and budgetary risks and the conclusion.

The Problems with Conventional Budget Deficits

We begin with a simple textbook definition of budget deficit. *Conventional deficit* is defined on a cash basis as the difference between total government cash outlays and total government receipts:[4]

$$D_t^c = r_t B_{t-1} + (G_t - T_t) + (H_t - H_{t-1}) \tag{1}$$

where D_t^c is the conventional budget deficit in period t; G_t and T_t are the government expenditure and tax revenue, respectively; B_t is the stock of government's debt (foreign plus domestic) in period t; and H_t is the base money.

The problems associated with the above concept of budget deficits are well known. Blejer and Cheasty (1991) note that "conventional measures of the fiscal (*budget*) deficit miscalculate the public sector's true budget constraint and give a misleading picture of the economy's fiscal stance."[5] The miscalculation to which they refer primarily arises from the following two factors.

One, it is measured using flow variables. Eisner and Pieper (1984) have pointed out that budget flows do not distinguish between current and capital accounts, and thus measures of surpluses and deficits may

---

4. The monetary authority (that is, the central bank) is treated as part of the government.

5. Easterly (1998) and Brixi (1998) provide much anecdotal evidence in which governments comply with ceilings on budget deficits by switching to hidden liability accumulation.

be inconsistent with changes in the real value of net debt. In particular, all gains and losses in the capital account arising from fluctuations in relative prices (real exchange rate, domestic inflation, change in cross-currency exchange rate) are excluded from budgetary accounts even when they affect the total stock of government debt.

Two, in practice, conventional budget deficits are often calculated without full inclusion of expenses incurred by the government on realized contingent liabilities.[6] In a recent paper, Daniel, Davis, and Wolfe (1997) argue that the standard government finance statistics (GFS)–based system of the International Monetary Fund (IMF) inadequately captures the fiscal cost of most bank assistance operations.[7] They closely examine how bank restructuring (bailout) expenses are accounted for in the budget and find that, in many countries, noncash operations are completely excluded from the budget. Though we are not aware of any studies looking at how corporate restructuring expenses are accounted for in the computation of the budget, it is likely that such expenses are also not fully included in the budget deficit. Another important item that is likely to be excluded from the flow definition of budget deficit is quasi-fiscal cost associated with sterilization of capital inflows.

Several economists have, therefore, proposed that budget deficit be measured as a change in net worth of the government. While theoretically appealing, and considered the right conceptual measure of deficit by many (for example, Buiter 1985; Eisner 1984; Easterly 1998), this approach also suffers from measurement and definitional problems.[8] For example, despite the use of a forward-looking framework to compute net worth, it does not include the existing, unrealized contingent liabilities as part of its calculation.[9]

---

6. It is, of course, well known that conventional budget deficit completely excludes contingent claims that are likely to be made on the government in the future.

7. Note that the GFS is the prime source for data on budget deficit for developing countries.

8. See Blejer and Cheasty (1991). It should, however, be mentioned that Easterly (1998) takes a positive step by empirically testing this concept for developing countries. His paper, however, does not provide an operational estimate of "net worth." Rather, it tests the implications of a fiscal model with net worth.

9. According to the international accounting standards, contingent liabilities do not have to be reported in the balance sheet and net worth calculation, unless their realization is probable.

To our knowledge, there have been no studies that look at net worth measures for the public sectors of developing countries. Intuitively, we believe that the deficiencies of the conventional measures of the budget deficit are even more severe in developing countries than in industrial countries.[10] This is because public investment in developing countries is a significantly higher share of total public spending than in industrial countries, and thus the failure to differentiate between current and capital spending is more misleading. Second, because developing countries borrow in foreign currencies, and in a variety of foreign currencies reflecting donor government aid programs, they are especially vulnerable to capital gains and losses stemming from exchange-rate changes. Last, as recent crisis events have shown, the contingent liabilities assumed by developing country governments can be very large. For example, some estimates put the cost to the public sector of Indonesia's 1997–98 financial crisis at 50 percent or more of GDP.[11]

An Alternative Definition of Budget Deficit

We propose an alternative approach to measure fiscal balance of a country, which we call the actuarial budget deficit. It is defined as the change in the total stock of government liabilities, that is,

$$D_t^a = (B_t - B_{t-1}) + (H_t - H_{t-1}) \tag{2}$$

where D_t^a is the actuarial budget deficit in period t. Theoretically speaking, equations (1) and (2) should yield similar numbers, but as shown later, in practice, a wide gap exists between the actuarial and conventional deficits. Hidden deficit (D_t^h) is defined as

$$D_t^h = D_t^a - D_t^c \tag{3}$$

---

10. Apart from the conceptual issues noted below, developing countries also have less standardized accounting practices that make the cross-country comparability of deficits particularly problematic. Kotlikoff (1989) shows how easy it is for governments to manipulate the deficit figure while maintaining the same fiscal policy. Easterly (1998) presents empirical evidence suggesting that much of the observed change in deficits associated with adjustment programs is indeed a fiscal illusion.

11. The latest cost estimate of bank recapitalization, announced by the finance minister, Bambang Subianto, on July 15 is Rp 550 trillion ($73 billion). The ratings agency Standard and Poors estimates that the cost could run to $87 billion, which is 19 percent higher than the official estimate (see EIU 1999).

Before we compare the numbers generated from equations (1) and (2), one caveat is in order. We use gross debt rather than net debt in the estimation of actuarial deficit. We do so for two reasons. The first reason is one of practicality. It is known that public assets are hard to measure, and even financial assets, such as directed credit, are often not worth their face value. The general experience with public assets has been that they do not yield commercial rates of return, and even the privatization returns are small when averaged over long periods. Perhaps for this reason, there is a tradition of not including assets in practical applications, such as EMU convergence criteria.[12] The second reason concerns the public policy choice of the government. In many countries, asset accumulation is a secondary implication of policy, not a driver of spending. For example, if a country's objective is to maintain a fixed exchange rate with low inflation, the country may sterilize foreign capital inflows, building up both foreign exchange reserves and domestic debt at the same time. The asset, though, is then a by-product of such a policy decision, and it is not tied to the liability, so while the asset can be used up to defend the exchange rate, the liability would remain. In this scenario, the change in gross debt is the price for maintaining a fixed exchange rate regime.

Using equations (1) through (3), we compute conventional, actuarial, and hidden deficits for 32 countries.[13] Data from the *World Development Indicators* (*WDI*) are used, except for transition countries (that is, Czech Republic, Hungary, Poland, and Russia), the data for which are obtained from "Datastream."[14] WDI reports the ratios—that is, B_t / Y_t and D_t^c / Y_t— where Y_t is the economy's GDP in period t. Using the data on Y_t we reconvert the series into levels. The data on base money, H_t, is obtained from the International Financial Statistics. All the variables are then scaled by nominal exchange rate and expressed in current U.S. dollars.[15]

---

12. European Monetary Institute 1998.

13. We could find continuous long-time series data for the 1980–97 period (for transition countries, 1992–97) for only 32 countries. They are Argentina, Australia, Austria, Bahrain, Brazil, Chile, Cyprus, Czech Republic, Finland, Hungary, India, Indonesia, Israel, Jordan, Korea, Malaysia, Mauritius, Mexico, Norway, Pakistan, Philippines, Poland, Spain, Sri Lanka, South Africa, Sweden, Thailand, Tunisia, Turkey, Uruguay, the United States, and Republica Bolivariana de Venezuela.

14. Data are for the central government only, except for the transition countries, where general government data are used.

15. The use of the exchange rate as the deflator rather than an index of domestic price level was motivated by two factors. First, use of the dollar value

FIGURE 1.   AVERAGE HIDDEN DEFICITS FOR INDUSTRIAL COUNTRIES

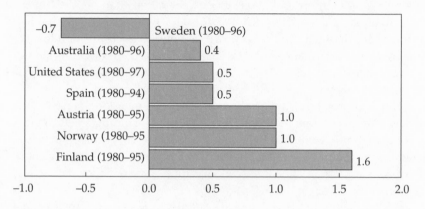

The magnitude of the average hidden deficits, as shown in figure 1, ranges from a maximum of 1.6 percent of GDP per year in Finland to a minimum of –0.7 percent in Sweden. These numbers are small compared to their corresponding average conventional deficits reported during the same period, that is, 4.6 percent in Finland and 5.4 percent in Sweden. Note, however, that the Nordic countries, Finland and Norway, which experienced financial crises in 1992–93, are also the countries in which the hidden deficits are relatively larger compared to other industrial countries.[16]

In contrast to the industrial countries, the developing countries have extremely large hidden deficits or surpluses. Figure 2 below shows that in 16 out of 25 developing countries, the average hidden deficit (or surplus) exceeds 1.5 percent per year. This is significantly higher compared to the 1 out of 7 for industrial countries.

(at current prices) facilitated intercountry comparisons. Second, it proved useful to get around the problem of dealing with episodes of hyperinflation in some of our sample countries, where it has been observed that use of the domestic price index introduces significant noise to the data. The exchange rate used to convert base money into dollars is obtained from the International Financial Statistics (line *rf*, that is, the average value of the period).

16. It is important to note that governments in industrial countries are involved in financial bailouts and other such activities as well, but either they include these expenses within their budgets, or their capital gains and losses offset some of the extrabudgetary expenditures or both, resulting in smaller hidden deficits than in developing countries.

FIGURE 2. AVERAGE HIDDEN DEFICITS FOR DEVELOPING COUNTRIES

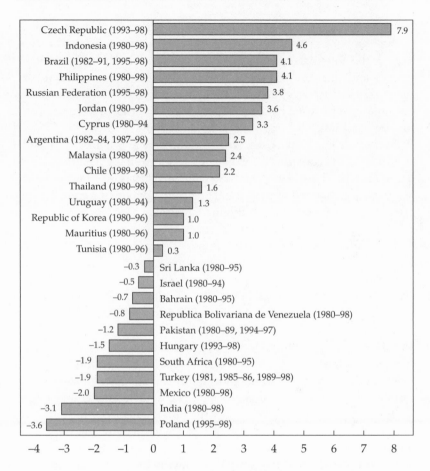

There can be many potential reasons why some countries, like India, Mexico, and Poland have large negative hidden deficits. First, the country may have received generous debt forgiveness (for example, Poland), used its privatization revenue to retire debt (for example, Mexico), obtained large amount of aids and grants from multilateral and bilateral donors to finance its budget (for example, India), or its capital gains because of a favorable change in prices (high inflation or large appreciation of the real exchange rate, or both) may have more than offset its off-budgetary expenses.[17]

---

17. See Dooley (1999) and Kharas and Mishra (forthcoming) for more discussion about this.

Links with Currency Crises

In this section, we first show that actuarial deficits are more closely linked to the number of currency crises than conventional deficits. Then we explore the potential channels that can explain the link between hidden deficits and currency crises. Specifically, we distinguish between currency crises caused by realization of past contingent liabilities versus currency crises caused by the prospect of large current and future contingent liabilities.

To identify currency crises, we use Kaminsky and Reinhart's (1999) methodology to construct a currency-crisis index. It is a weighted average of nominal depreciation rate and change in reserves, where weights are chosen such that the conditional volatilities of both the components are equal. The year in which the index exceeds a certain threshold is taken as the crisis year.[18]

The scatter plots between the number of currency crises and two alternative definitions of deficits, as shown in figure 3, reveal that the actuarial deficit is more closely associated with the number of currency crises than the conventional deficit. The correlation coefficient between number of crises and conventional deficit is only 0.15, while with respect to actuarial deficits it is 0.55. The coefficients of the exponential and the linear (not shown) trends are found to be significant with respect to actuarial deficits and not with respect to conventional deficits.

The evidence from the scatter plots is further strengthened when more formal examination of this relationship is conducted using regression analysis. Assuming that only successful, but not unsuccessful, speculative attacks are observed and that the occurrence of two crises is a worse outcome than the occurrence of one crisis, we estimate an *ordered*, limited, dependent variable model using the following log likelihood function:

$$\lambda(\beta, \theta) =$$
$$\sum_{i \ni y_i = 0} \log (Pr(y_i = 0 \,|\, x_i, \beta, \theta)) + \sum_{i \ni y_i = 1} \log (Pr(y_i = 1 \,|\, x_i, \beta, \theta)) + \ldots +$$
$$\sum_{i \ni y_i = 5} \log (Pr(y_i = 5 \,|\, x_i, \beta, \theta))$$

---

18. Readers are referred to Kaminsky and Reinhart (1999) and Eichengreen, Rose, and Wyplosz (1995) for details on how to construct such an index.

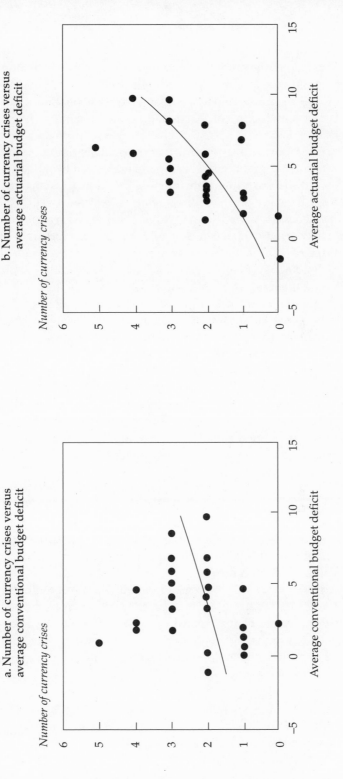

FIGURE 3. SCATTER PLOTS BETWEEN ALTERNATIVE DEFINITIONS OF DEFICITS AND NUMBER OF CRISES

a. Number of currency crises versus average conventional budget deficit

b. Number of currency crises versus average actuarial budget deficit

Note: Correlation (conventional deficit, number of crises) = 0.15; correlation (actuarial deficit, number of crises) = 0.55.

where y denotes the number of currency crises, x the explanatory variables (in our case four variables: average deficits, real exchange rate, loss of reserves, and number of banking crises), θ the threshold values, and β the slope coefficient. Note that y is an integer, and in our case, ranges from 0 to 5.

The error terms are assumed to have normal distribution, so we estimate an ordered probit model using the maximum likelihood estimation procedure. The results from the cross-section regressions are shown in table 1. First we estimate three bivariate regressions, in which the number of currency crises a country has experienced is regressed separately on conventional deficit, actuarial deficit, and hidden deficit. The first three rows of table 1 report the results from these regressions. It shows that average conventional deficit is not statistically significant in explaining the number of currency crises, while actuarial and hidden deficits are significant at 1 and 10 percent levels, respectively. The next three columns report the results from the multivariate regressions where three additional regressors are included, namely change in real exchange rate, number of banking crises, and change in reserves as a percentage of GDP.[19] Again, the conventional deficit is not significant, although the actuarial and hidden deficits are significant in explaining the number of currency crises. The last three columns in table 1 give two diagnostic tools that can be interpreted as goodness-of-fit tests. They show that the log likelihood and pseudo-R square are bigger when actuarial or hidden deficits, rather than conventional deficits, are included in the regression.

Identical sets of regressions were estimated assuming that the error terms have logistic or exponential distribution. The results from these regressions, not reported here, continue to validate the main hypothesis of the article, that is, the actuarial and hidden deficits are statistically significantly linked to the number of currency crises, but the conventional deficit is not.

The obvious question that arises from our empirical findings is how hidden deficits and the number of currency crises may be linked. There are two potential linkages. One, in times of economic weakness, past government promises or contingent liabilities may be called upon, resulting in a buildup of hidden deficits that would put pressure on the

---

19. These variables are chosen because previous studies have shown that they are important in explaining currency crises. For example, see Sachs, Tornell, and Velasco (1996) and Kaminsky and Reinhart (1999).

TABLE 1. RESULTS FROM CROSS-COUNTRY CROSS-SECTION REGRESSIONS
(method: ordered probit; number of countries included = 28; dependent variable = number of currency crises between 1980 and 1997 [range from 0 to 5])

	Explanatory variables						Diagnostic statistics	
Equation	Conventional deficit	Actuarial deficit	Hidden deficit	Number of banking crises	Change in RER	Change in reserve	Log likelihood	Pseudo-R^2 (LR index)
1	0.093 (1.155)	—	—	—	—	—	-41.04	0.02
2	—	0.216*** (2.755)	—	—	—	—	-37.77	0.09
3	—	—	0.140* (1.771)	—	—	—	-40.12	0.04
4	0.074 (0.874)	—	—	0.039 (1.090)	0.062 (1.343)	-0.281 (-1.146)	-38.85	0.07
5	—	0.375*** (3.751)	—	0.649** (2.068)	0.157*** (2.838)	-0.433* (-1.667)	-31.01	0.26
6	—	—	0.346*** (3.118)	0.577* (1.877)	0.129** (2.431)	-0.681** (-2.403)	-33.37	0.20

Note: The numbers in parentheses are the z-statistics. Also, *, **, and *** denote that the estimate is significant at 10, 5, and 1 percent level respectively.
— Not available.

exchange rate. Since these realized contingent claims are generally not included in the conventional deficit, one will not observe any increase in the latter. According to this channel, large hidden deficits are likely to *precede* currency crises, which is consistent with the Krugman (1979) proposal.

There can be a second link, which has been proposed by Burnside, Eichenbaum, and Rebelo (1998). Using the experience of East Asian countries, they argue that, while these countries had budget surpluses prior to the currency crisis in 1997, they also had large prospective deficits. Although they did not distinguish between visible and hidden deficits, but as we have argued before, most of these prospective deficits, when realized, are treated by the governments as extrabudgetary items and therefore, according to this channel, sharp increases in hidden deficits are likely to *follow* currency crises.

It is not easy to distinguish whether a currency crisis was triggered by the realization of past contingent claims or the prospect of contingent liabilities coming due in the future. Burnside, Eichenbaum, and Rebelo (1998) are one of the first to attempt to estimate the size of prospective deficits for Thailand and Korea, using data on total nonperforming bank loans and estimated liabilities from nonbank foreign borrowing as a proxy for future government liabilities.

We make two additional observations here that link hidden deficits to the East Asian currency crisis. First, while East Asian countries did have small visible deficits, and, in a few cases, surpluses, prior to the crisis they actually had large hidden deficits during the 1992–96 period, as shown in table 2. While we do not claim that the East Asian countries tripped into the crisis solely because of these hidden deficits, the numbers in table 2 do provide further evidence that Krugman's first generation currency-crisis model is not completely irrelevant to the East Asian case. The researchers, however, need to pay attention to actuarial deficits and not to conventional deficit for such evidence.

TABLE 2. AVERAGE ACTUARIAL, CONVENTIONAL, AND HIDDEN
DEFICITS FOR EAST ASIAN COUNTRIES (1992–96)

Country	Average actuarial	Average conventional	Average hidden
Indonesia	2.4	−0.9	3.3
Korea, Rep. of	1.0	−0.2	1.2
Malaysia	4.9	−0.7	5.6
Philippines	8.9	0.1	8.8
Thailand	1.1	−2.4	3.5

Second, an examination of the fiscal balance of the East Asian countries during the postcrisis period shows that most bank and corporate restructuring expenses are not being fully included into the budget and thus hidden deficits are on the rise. For example, in Thailand, while central government's debt has increased from 22 percent of GDP in 1997 to more than 46 percent of GDP in 1999 (see figure 4), the visible budget deficits have been less than 5 percent for both 1998 and 1999. The imbalance between the change in debt stock and conventional deficits worsens if one includes the debt of the central bank and the public sector enterprises. Thus the hidden deficits have substantially increased in Thailand in the first two years following the crisis. Similarly, according to the Economist Intelligence Unit report, a total of W 76.7 trillion in public funds, more than 15 percent of country GDP, has been spent on the restructuring of domestic financial sector by end-1999 in Korea. But the conventional budget deficit has been reported to be only 3 percent in 1998 and 3.3 percent in 1999, not alarmingly large compared to the precrisis periods. Thus it clearly suggests that if the East Asian crisis was caused by prospective deficits, as argued by Burnside, Eichenbaum,

FIGURE 4.   DEBT AND DEFICIT IN THAILAND FOLLOWING
THE EAST ASIAN CRISIS

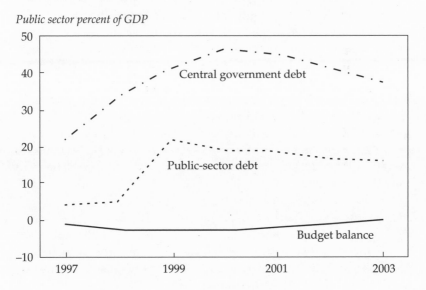

Public sector percent of GDP

Source: Economist Intelligence Unit report on Thailand, February 2000.

and Rebelo, the researchers should be looking for evidence in the actuarial and hidden deficits and not in the conventional deficit.

Institutional Implications and Concluding Remarks

One of the important objectives of the article was to bring out the limitations of conventional budget deficits so that debt managers will pay closer attention to hidden deficits. The fact that hidden deficits are more tightly linked to currency crises than are conventional deficits demonstrates that market participants tend to ignore reported deficits and make their own judgment about the actual fiscal position of the government, using techniques that are likely to be similar to the one proposed here. Any effort on the part of the policymaker, therefore, to report small visible deficits by running large hidden deficits is wasted and should not be attempted.

The evidence presented here also indicates that the debt and budget management techniques in developing countries have to be expanded well beyond the traditional concerns. Since the growth of debt has more to do with off-budget than with in-budget transactions, the sources of hidden deficits need careful monitoring and management. For transparency reasons, actuarial deficit should be reported alongside the conventional deficit in the budget.

The magnitude of average hidden deficits of most developing countries is shown to be very high and sometime higher than their corresponding magnitudes of conventional deficits. Because many of these hidden deficits are incurred during financial crises, they are initially paid by domestic and external borrowings, and finally by temporarily raising taxes or shrinking government expenditures, or both. These sudden temporary spikes in tax rates and cuts in government expenditures are likely to be associated with large deadweight losses. Therefore, budgetary allocation can be made intertemporally more efficient by keeping aside a part of government revenue every year, equal to the long-run average hidden deficits amount, to meet future contingent claims and capital gains and losses.

The literature on hidden deficits, contingent liabilities, and prospective deficits is still in its infancy. More research is called for to clearly distinguish between when a currency crisis is caused by the realization of past hidden deficits, and when it is caused by the prospect of hidden deficits in the future, in line with the work of Burnside, Eichenbaum, and Rebelo (1998). Similarly, it is important that the framework to manage contingent liabilities as proposed by Brixi (1998) and Brixi, Ghanem, and Islam (1999) be firmly integrated with the financial crisis literature to be able to find a more accurate measure of prospective hidden deficits.

References

Blejer, Mario I., and Adrienne Cheasty. 1991. "The Measurement of Fiscal Deficits: Analytical and Methodological Issues." *Journal of Economic Literature* 29(4):1644–78.

Brixi, Hana Polackova. 1998. "Contingent Liabilities: A Threat to Fiscal Stability." PREM Sector Unit (EASPR), World Bank, Washington, D.C.

Brixi, Hana Polackova, Hafez Ghanem, and Roumeen Islam. 1999. "Fiscal Adjustment and Contingent Government Liabilities: Case Studies of the Czech Republic and Macedonia." In Devarajan, Rogers, and Squire, eds., *World Bank Economists' Forum*. vol. 1. Washington, D.C.: World Bank.

Buiter, Willem H. 1985. "A Guide to Public Sector Debt and Deficits." *Economic Policy* (November).

Burnside, Craig, Martin Eichenbaum, and Sergio Rebelo. 1998. "Prospective Deficits and the East Asian Currency Crises." World Bank Policy Research Working Paper 2174, Washington, D.C.

Caprio, Gerard, Jr., and Daniela Klingebiel. 1996. "Bank Insolvencies: Cross-Country Experience." Financial Sector Strategy and Policy (FSP), World Bank, Washington, D.C.

European Monetary Institute. 1998. *Convergence Report*. March. http://www.dgep.pt/repconv98i-menu.html.

Daniel, James A., Jeffery M. Davis, and Andrew M. Wolfe. 1997. "Fiscal Accounting of Bank Restructuring." International Monetary Fund Paper on Policy Analysis and Assessments PPAA/97/5, Washington, D.C.

Dooley, Michael. 1999. "Responses to Volatile Capital Flows: Controls, Asset Liability Management and Architecture." Presented at the WTO–World Bank–IMF Conference, Washington, D.C.

Easterly, William. 1998. "When Is Fiscal Adjustment an Illusion?" World Bank Policy Research Working Paper 2109, Washington, D.C.

EIU (Economist Intelligence Unit). 1999. *Country Reports, 3rd quarter*. http://wb.eiu.com/.

Eichengreen, Barry, Andrew Rose, and Charles Wyplosz. 1995. "Exchange Market Mayhem: The Antecedents and Aftermath of Speculative Attacks." *Economic Policy* 21: 249–312.

Eisner, Robert. 1984. "Which Budget Deficit? Some Issues of Measurement and Their Implications." *American Economic Review* 74 (2): 138–43.

Eisner, Robert, and Paul J. Pieper. 1984. "A New View of the Federal Debt and Budget Deficits." *American Economic Review* 74 (1): 11–29.

Flood, Robert, and Nancy Marion. 1997. "Perspectives on the Recent Currency Crisis Literature." International Monetary Fund Working Paper WP/98/130, Washington, D.C.

Frankel, Jeffrey, and Andrew Rose. 1996. "Currency Crashes in Emerging Markets: An Empirical Treatment." *Journal of International Economics* 41 (3–4): 351–66.

Kaminsky, Graciela, Leonardo Leiderman, and Carmen M. Reinhart. 1997. "Leading Indicators of Currency Crises." International Monetary Fund Working Paper WP/97/79, Washington, D.C.

Kaminsky, Graciela, Saul Lizondo, and Carmen Reinhart. 1997. "Leading Indicators of Currency Crises." International Monetary Fund Working Paper WP/97/79, Washington, D.C.

Kaminsky, Graciela, and Carmen M. Reinhart. 1999. "The Twin Crises: The Causes of Banking and Balance of Payments Problems." *American Economic Review* 89 (3): 473–500.

Kharas, Homi. 1997. "The Philippines: Three Decades of Lost Opportunities." In Danny M. Leipziger, ed., *Lessons from East Asia*. Ann Arbor: University of Michigan Press.

Kharas, Homi, and Deepak Mishra. Forthcoming. "Public Deficits and Debt Dynamics in Developing Countries." *International Journal of Finance and Economics.*

Kotlikoff, Laurence. 1989. "Deficit Delusion." *What Determines Savings?* Cambridge, Mass., and London: MIT Press.

Krugman, Paul. 1979. "A Model of Balance of Payments Crises." *Journal of Money, Credit and Banking* 11: 311–25.

Sachs, Jeffrey D., Aaron Tornell, and Andres Velasco. 1996. "Financial Crises in Emerging Markets: The Lessons from 1995." Brookings Papers on Economic Activity 1, Brookings Institution, Washington, D.C.

World Bank. 1999. *World Development Indicators*. Washington, D.C.

Fiscal Adjustment and Contingent Government Liabilities: Case Studies of the Czech Republic and the Former Yugoslav Republic of Macedonia

Hana Polackova Brixi, Hafez Ghanem, and Roumeen Islam

Abstract

Our work in the Czech Republic and in FYR Macedonia demonstrates the importance of including contingent liabilities when assessing the magnitude of the true fiscal adjustment, and when analyzing fiscal sustainability. To the extent that explicit expenditures are shifted off-budget or replaced by the issuance of guarantees, the achieved improvement in fiscal balances is overstated. For the Czech Republic we find that adjustment may have been overstated by some 3–4 percent of GDP annually. The accumulation of contingent liabilities today is a threat to future fiscal stability. Hence, a stabilization program that is accompanied by a build-up of contingent liabilities may not be sustainable. In the case of FYR Macedonia, we found that the present fiscal equilibrium may be temporary, because the stock of existing contingent liabilities could add 2–4 percent of GDP to future deficits. Moreover, the methods used to reduce the "traditional" deficit are unlikely to be sustainable without further modification. Our work also shows that fiscal adjustment and structural reforms are closely linked. The most obvious example is that failure to improve banking sector performance can over time lead to an accumulation of implicit contingent liabilities for governments.

This article was originally issued as World Bank Policy Research Working Paper 2177 in 1999. Currencies cited in this article include the Czech crowns (CZK) and the Macedonian denars (DIN).

Faced with external and domestic pressures, governments all around the world have been lowering their fiscal deficits. At the same time, economists are increasingly coming to realize that focusing exclusively on traditional measurements of the fiscal deficit to assess the extent of fiscal adjustment that has been attained can be misleading for two reasons. First, as Selowsky (1998) points out, quantitative improvements in fiscal policy have not always been accompanied by progress in the "quality" of adjustment. Traditional deficit measures (government budget deficits on a cash basis) do not shed sufficient light on two key dimensions of "quality": sustainability and efficiency.[1] Second, governments can reduce their measured deficit without carrying out any "true" adjustment. Easterly (1999) argues that fiscal adjustment can be just an "illusion" when it lowers the budget deficit, but leaves government net worth unchanged.[2] When an outside agent forces a reduction in a government's conventional deficit, the government often responds by lowering asset accumulation or by increasing hidden or off-budget liabilities, giving the illusion of a fiscal adjustment. Fiscal adjustment of this nature may not be either sustainable or efficient. This article focuses mostly on the issue of sustainability.

Building up explicit or implicit contingent government liabilities is an important way of reducing the measured traditional fiscal deficit while avoiding difficult adjustment. Kharas and Mishra, in a separate article in this volume, show that contingent liabilities are mainly responsible for the fact that the past increases in governments' debts have significantly exceeded their reported budget deficits in most developing and emerging-market economies. Many examples of this type of government behavior exist. In Italy the railways have raised funds through the financial markets to cover their deficits for many years with government agreement and an explicit guarantee from the treasury. Yet, those operations had no impact on the measured fiscal deficit or on the measured stock of government liabilities (Glatzel 1998). Similarly, faced with the Gramm-Rudman constraint on fiscal deficits, the U.S. Con-

---

1. Efficiency is a broad concept that includes issues such as (a) where the government should spend resources, (b) what the nature of its intervention should be, and (c) how it should obtain fiscal revenues in the least distortionary manner.

2. For other examples and explanations why change in net worth is the right conceptual measure of the deficit, see Buiter (1983 and 1985) or Blejer and Cheasty (1991).

gress has reduced direct lending by $50 billion and increased loan guarantees by $178 billion, replacing budgetary outlays by explicit contingent liabilities (Rubin 1997). Implicit liabilities often arise from the financial sector. The savings and loan crisis in the United States, which eventually cost the government about $200 billion, is a notable example (Kotlikoff 1993). In many other countries, governments have used financial institutions to hide their fiscal deficits, often by asking them to extend subsidized loans to public entities (Easterly 1999).

Several factors are working to increase contingent government liabilities and fiscal risk in countries around the world: rapidly increasing volumes of private capital flows, leading to fast growth of financial systems and volatility in these flows; transformation of the state from financing of services to guaranteeing particular outcomes; and related to both of these, moral hazard in the markets and fiscal opportunism of policymakers.[3] Transition and emerging-market economies face particularly large fiscal risks. Their dependence on private foreign financing, weak regulatory and legal enforcement systems, often distorted incentive structures, opaque ownership structures, and low information disclosure elevate failures in the financial and corporate sectors. Such failures, in turn, often generate political pressures on governments to intervene through bailouts.

A first step toward controlling the expansion of contingent government liabilities and reducing fiscal risk is being able to identify and measure them. In this article, we discuss how this may be done and demonstrate how assessment of fiscal adjustment may change substantially when a broader picture of government liabilities is included. The article is based on our experience in analyzing fiscal adjustment in the Czech Republic and in the former Yugoslave Republic of (FYR) Macedonia. The Czech case provides an example of the deliberate use of guarantees and other support provided through off-budget institutions, which have reduced the (traditional) measured fiscal deficit and public debt. The Macedonian example demonstrates how ignoring implicit liabilities arising from financial sector and enterprise restructuring could lead to

---

3. The relationship between financial flows and fiscal deficits works in two ways: large capital outflows can increase implicit contingent liabilities, and large capital inflows in poorly regulated financial sectors set the stage for the accumulation of implicit contingent liabilities and even without outflows increase fiscal risk. Moreover, outflows may be prompted by the accumulation of contingent liabilities.

a serious underestimation of the extent of fiscal adjustment needed to ensure sustainability. Both case studies provide examples of how to deal with some difficult conceptual and measurement issues when trying to estimate contingent government liabilities.

The article is divided into four sections. The first section, "A Simple Framework for Identifying Government Liabilities," presents a simple framework for identifying and classifying contingent liabilities. The next two sections—"What Is the True Fiscal Deficit in the Czech Republic?" and "Is Fiscal Stabilization in FYR Macedonia Sustainable?"—describe our work in the Czech Republic and FYR Macedonia. The "Concluding Remarks" summarize our main conclusions and suggestions for future work.

A Simple Framework for Identifying Government Liabilities: The Fiscal Risk Matrix

As in Polackova (1998) government liabilities are divided into four types: direct explicit, direct implicit, contingent explicit, and contingent implicit (table 1). Government direct explicit liabilities are specific obligations that will fall due with certainty and are defined by law or contract. They are the subject of traditional fiscal analysis and include repayment of sovereign debt, expenditures based on budget law in the current fiscal year, and expenditures in the long term for legally mandated items, such as civil service salaries and pensions. Government direct implicit liabilities represent a moral obligation or political, rather than legal, burden on the government that will occur with certainty. They often arise as a presumed consequence of public expenditure policies in the longer term. For example, in a public pay-as-you-go pension scheme, in a country where the government is not legally obliged to pay future public pensions, future pensions constitute a direct (expected with certainty) or implicit (political but not legal) liability. Explicit contingent liabilities represent government's legal obligations to make a payment only if a particular event occurs. State guarantees and financing through state-guaranteed institutions are examples of this type of liability. Implicit contingent liabilities are those that are not officially recognized until a failure occurs. The triggering event, the value at risk, and the required size of the government outlay are uncertain. In most countries, the financial system represents the most serious source of implicit contingent liabilities for government. International experience indicates that markets expect the government to support the financial system far beyond its legal obligation in the aftermath of a systemic crisis, or to prevent such a crisis.

TABLE 1. THE FISCAL RISK MATRIX: EXAMPLES

Liabilities	Direct *(obligation in any event)*	Contingent *(obligation if a particular event occurs)*
Explicit Government liability as recognized by a law or contract	• Foreign and domestic sovereign borrowing (loans contracted and securities issued by central government) • Budgetary expenditures • Budgetary expenditures legally binding in the long term (civil servants' salaries and pensions)	• State guarantees for nonsovreign borrowing and obligations issued to subnational governments and public and private sector entities (development banks) • Umbrella state guarantees for various types of loans (mortgage loans, student loans, agriculture loans, small business loans) • Trade and exchange rate guarantees issued by the state • Guarantees on borrowing by a foreign sovereign state • State guarantees on private investments • State insurance schemes (deposit insurance, income from private pension funds, crop insurance, flood insurance, war-risk insurance)
Implicit A "moral" obligation of government that reflects public and interest group pressures	• Future public pensions (as opposed to civil service pensions) if not required by law • Social security schemes if not required by law • Future health care financing if not required by law • Future recurrent cost of public investments	• Default of subnational government, and public or private entity on nonguaranteed debt and other obligations • Liability clean-up in entities under privatization • Banking failure (support beyond state insurance) • Investment failure of a nonguaranteed pension fund, employment fund, or social security fund (social protection of small investors) • Default of central bank on its obligations (foreign exchange contracts, currency defense, balance of payment stability) • Bailouts following a reversal in private capital flows • Environmental recovery, disaster relief, military financing, and so forth

Note: The liabilities listed above refer to the fiscal authorities, not the central bank.
Source: Polackova (1998).

Using the Framework

So that governments may manage their resources better, volatility in the government's financing requirement and changes in overall government risk exposure resulting from off-budget activities should be considered in the design of government programs. The value of predictability is particularly high for governments that have (a) restricted access to borrowing, (b) low capacities to manage risk, and (c) low risk preference. Risk-averse governments would prefer to know their financing requirements with certainty. But when facing constraints on the cash deficit, such as deficit "targets," or when having short planning horizons, policymakers may prefer to provide off-budget support to conceal the impact on expenditures and taxpayers, as is the case with the provision of guarantees in many emerging markets.[4] The formation of reserve funds, of maximum limits on government liabilities under different scenarios for contingent liabilities, or of a hedging strategy may reduce the potential harm when contingent liabilities fall due. These measures raise other problems, however, related to overall management of reserve resources, calculations of the required amounts of contingent funds needed, and appropriate use of derivatives.

The first step in attaining fiscal stability is for policymakers to identify, classify, and understand the full range of fiscal risks. Understanding their consequences will at least encourage policymakers to avoid risks that are bound to surface in a politically meaningful time horizon. For risks that extend beyond that time frame, fiscally sound behavior may depend on coercion. Policymakers are more likely to gravitate to fiscally sound decisions if the media, the public, investors, credit-rating agencies, and multilateral institutions understand the government's fiscal performance in its entirety and if there are credible sanctions when the government exposes the state to excessive risks and attempts to conceal those risks.

The two case studies presented in the following sections attempt to use this simple framework to identify and evaluate key fiscal risks in the Czech Republic and FYR Macedonia. The Czech analysis highlights that off-budget fiscal interventions, mainly in the form of explicit guarantees and directed lending by government, have led to a rapid accumulation of government liabilities. True government net worth therefore

---

4. The provision of an explicit government guarantee is generally a first-best instrument of support only when sharing risk with another economic agent is the objective. Defining guarantees narrowly, and placing limits on the maximum exposure of government for each guarantee, as well as the overall set of guarantees provided, helps limit future government liability.

is lower than a simple evolution of fiscal deficits would indicate. Although these debts may be manageable at the present time, if government liabilities continue to grow at the rate at which they have in the past, they will present a threat to future fiscal stability. In the Macedonian case, the threat to fiscal sustainability comes from the recognition of past implicit contingent liabilities and a substantial accumulation of further such liabilities. The key issues here are that slow structural reforms can increase debt from implicit contingent liabilities. The stock of debt, and therefore also changes in net worth, resulting from the recognition of implicit contingent liabilities may vary according to both economic and political decisions made in FYR Macedonia. The effect on the debt increases will depend very much on the manner in which government decides to repay its obligations on the maturity structure and terms of the debt, which are determined upon recognition of these liabilities.

What Is the True Fiscal Deficit in the Czech Republic?

The Czech Republic has been known for balanced government budgets. In contrast to most countries, however, fiscal performance in the Czech Republic encompasses a significant amount of government activities financed outside the budgetary system. These activities generate fiscal risks. Recently these off-budget fiscal risks have become more visible as state guarantees and agencies that are either explicitly or implicitly guaranteed by the government have generated significant claims on the budget. Given the magnitude of off-budget activities, fiscal analysis in the Czech Republic needs to identify all the main activities of a fiscal nature to determine the "true" fiscal deficit. Excluding quasi-fiscal activities of the central bank, the Czech National Bank, the "hidden" part of the fiscal deficit comprises two main components: (a) net spending on programs of a fiscal nature by special, off-budget institutions (Konsolidacni Banka, Ceska Inkasni, Ceska Financni, and the National Property Fund) and (b) implied subsidies extended through state guarantees.[5] For financial relationships of these

---

5. Ceska Financni has financed two blocks of programs geared toward bank revitalization. One block, in the total amount of approximately CZK 35 billion, is financed and guaranteed by the Czech National Bank. The other, called the Stabilization Program, in the amount of about CZK 12 billion, is financed through Konsolidacni Bankia, and thus guaranteed by the government. It is only the latter block that is considered in the "true" deficit calculation. It is included as an activity of Konsolidacni Banka.

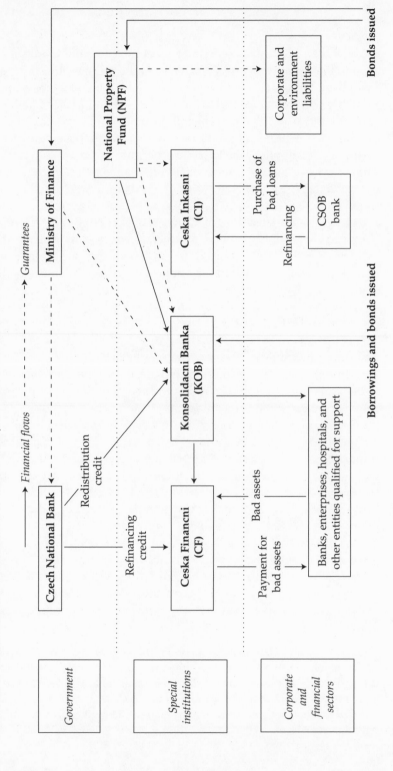

FIGURE 1. FINANCIAL RELATIONSHIPS OF SPECIAL, OFF-BUDGET INSTITUTIONS

special institutions, see figure 1. For quasi-fiscal operations of the Czech National Bank, see appendix A.

Contribution of the Off-Budget Programs to the Hidden Fiscal Deficit

For any given year, net public spending by the special off-budget institutions includes cash outlays on new programs in the form of directed credits and asset purchases, and interest expenditures.[6] This spending is adjusted for debt collection, interest revenue, and other revenue from programs. Table 2 shows the components of the "hidden" deficit. In the remainder of this section, each row of this table is described in more detail.

Until 1993, off-budget programs had mainly dealt with pretransition problems inherited by the banking sector. These programs had been financed through Konsolidacni Banka. This bank was capitalized by the National Property Fund (the privatization agency whose revenues are derived from asset sales and borrowing on domestic markets), and borrowing from the Czech National Bank.[7] In 1995, the Ministry of Finance established Ceska Inkasni, a nonbank financial institution with the mandate of cleaning up the portfolio of a state-owned bank, the CSOB. Covered by a guarantee issued by the National Property Fund, Ceska Inkasni obtained a credit from the CSOB and used this credit to purchase the CSOB's bad assets at face value.

During 1996–98 a new bank consolidation and stabilization program was launched to deal with newly emerging problems in the banking sector. To implement these programs, the Czech National Bank established Ceska Financni, another nonbank financial institution. In 1998, Ceska Financni had in its portfolio nonperforming assets purchased at face value from small- and medium-size banks (in the amount of about CZK 50 billion, which is 3 percent of GDP), which it financed by borrowing one-third from Konsolidacni Banka and two-thirds from the Czech National Bank.

The Czech National Bank has also financed other bank rescue operations, which have become the source of a further addition (CZK 161 billion, over 9 percent of GDP) to its portfolio of substandard assets in

---

6. The assets purchased through off-budget programs are of extremely low quality. Therefore, the analysis considers asset purchases to be a spending program rather than a financial transaction.

7. Debt to the Czech National Bank still constitutes about half of Konsolidacni Banka's total debt.

TABLE 2. SOURCES OF THE "HIDDEN" DEFICIT IN THE CZECH REPUBLIC, 1993–98
(billions of CZK)

	1993	1994	1995	1996	1997	1998
KOB[a]						
Net public expenditures	7.7	7.3	4.5	0.9	10.6	28.8
CI						
Net public expenditures	20.1	6.6	4.9	4.8	3.1	2.7
CF						
Net public expenditures	0.0	0.0	0.0	0.0	0.6[b]	1.8[b]
NPF						
Net public expenditures (excluding the KOB and CI)	4.2	8.2	4.3	1.9	2.0	2.6
State guarantees Implicit subsidy (risk-adjusted)	0.1	–0.4	1.3	14.9	51.5	26.7
Total (% of GDP)	*3.2*	*1.9*	*1.1*	*1.5*	*4.1*	*3.5*

a. Activities of the KOB include a credit to finance Stabilization Program of the CF. Therefore, the table includes only interest payments by the CF (which are then reported as interest income of the KOB).

b. These figures are interest payments to the KOB on credit taken by the CF from the KOB to finance the Stabilization Program. In addition, the CF paid interest of CZK 0.8 billion and CZK 2.8 billion in 1997 and 1998, respectively, to the Czech National Bank on its credit from the Czech National Bank to finance the Consolidation Program.

Note: CF stands for Ceska Financni, CI for Ceska Inkasni, KOB for Konsolidacni Banka, and NPF for National Property Fund.

Source: Ministry of Finance, the KOB, the CF, and the NPF.

1998. The government covers the risk for 12 percent of the total substandard assets held by the Czech National Bank. A further 22 percent of these assets are in the form of a credit from the Czech National Bank to Konsolidacni Banka and thus are indirectly also covered by the government. (For details, see Appendix A.)

Aside from the bank rescue operations, Konsolidacni Banka and, less directly, the National Property Fund have also financed government programs to support troubled insurance companies, public hospitals, and the Czech Railways to build infrastructure and to clean up industrial enterprises for privatization (see table 3). The National Property Fund has partly financed these programs from privatization revenues, but partly also from its debt issuance. Calculation of contributions to the "true" fiscal deficit by the National Property Fund excludes princi-

TABLE 3. PROGRAMS COVERED BY THE NATIONAL PROPERTY FUND, 1993–98

(billions of CZK)

Program	1993	1994	1995	1996	1997	1998
Financing environment rehabilitation	0	0.1	0.8	1.0	1.4	2.1
Financing the development of railway routes	0	0	0	0.1	0	0.2
Support to state-owned enterprises (including liability clean-up)	2.1	0.5	0.9	0.3	0.2	0.3
Support to agricultural businesses		6.1	1.0	0	0	0
Bond interest	2.1	1.5	1.6	0.5	0.4	0.5
National Property Fund's "hidden" fiscal deficit (excluding transfers to the KOB, CI, and CF and transfers according to state budget law)	4.2	8.2	4.3	1.9	2.0	2.9
Others, already included in "hidden" deficit calculation: Health insurance companies (through the KOB)[a]	0.0	0.0	0.0	0.8	0.4	0.4
Support to aviation companies (through the KOB)[a]	0.0	0.0	0.0	0.0	0.1	0.0
Provisions to the CI	0.0	0.0	3.4	10.3	5.5	6.0
Stabilization program of the CF (through the KOB)[a]	0.0	0.0	0.0	0.0	0.6	1.8
Others, included in the reported budget deficit: Transfers according to state budget law[a]	9.5	19.4	10.7	0.0	0.0	0.0

a. These items are excluded from the "true" deficit calculation. The National Property Fund's expenditures related to the KOB, CI, and CF are accounted for as financing items of these institutions.

Note: CF stands for Ceska Financni, CI for Ceska Inkasni, and KOB for Konsolidacni Banka.

Source: The National Property Fund's Annual Reports.

TABLE 4. GUARANTEES ISSUED, 1993–98
(face values; billions of CZK)

	1993	1994	1995	1996	1997	1998
Very high risk (90%)	0.0	0.0	0.0	10.8	51.7	31.0
High risk (30%)	0.0	0.0	0.0	16.2	20.3	0.0
Medium risk (15%)	5.0	0.0	13.3	3.0	5.8	7.8
Low risk (5%)	3.7	0.0	1.8	0.0	0.0	87.0
Total	8.7	0.0	15.1	30.0	77.8	125.8

Source: Calculation by the authors.

pal repayments and thus does not reflect the ongoing financing of pre-1993 programs by the National Property Fund. In addition, both Konsolidacni Banka and the National Property Fund have accumulated their own contingent liabilities in the form of various guarantees.[8]

The impact of guarantees on the hidden deficit is estimated as the net implicit subsidy provided through guarantees in a given year from the portfolio of guarantees issued in that year, or the potential fiscal cost of government obligations that will emerge from the guarantee in the future. If the amount of this subsidy had been transferred to a guarantee reserve fund the same year the guarantee was issued, it would have served to cover potential future claims emerging from the guarantee. The cost of default would be paid from the guarantee reserve fund and thus would not affect the budget and the deficit.

Assessment of each guarantee and its underlying project had preceded the estimation of their future fiscal costs. Projects were ranked according to their risk. Accordingly, the default risk of each guarantee was estimated. The probability of default was determined by careful consideration of each loan. Table 4 shows the amounts of guarantees issued according to their risk ranking. The implicit subsidy (risk adjusted) embedded in state guarantees is calculated by multiplying the loan amount for which a guarantee was issued by the default risk. To avoid double accounting, the net implicit subsidy, or the net contribution to the hidden deficit in a given year, is defined as the total implicit subsidy provided in a given year minus guarantee claims paid from the

---

8. Risk assessment of guarantees issued by the National Property Fund and Konsolidacni Banka is not available. Therefore, calculation of the "true" fiscal deficit includes only the implicit subsidy extended through net spending by the special institutions and through guarantees issued directly by the state, but not guarantees issued by special institutions.

TABLE 5. GUARANTEES CONTRIBUTED TO THE HIDDEN DEFICIT, 1993–98
(billions of CZK)

Program	1993	1994	1995	1996	1997	1998
Very high (90%)	0.0	0.0	0.0	9.7	46.5	27.9
High (30%)	0.0	0.0	0.0	4.9	6.1	0.0
Medium (15%)	0.7	0.0	2.0	0.4	0.9	1.2
Low (5%)	0.2	0.0	0.1	0.0	0.0	4.4
Subtotal	0.9	0.0	2.1	15.0	53.5	33.4
Budget paid out (–)	–0.8	–0.4	–0.8	–0.1	–2.0	–6.7
Total	0.1	–0.4	1.3	14.9	51.5	26.7
(as % of GDP)	*0.0*	*–0.0*	*0.1*	*1.0*	*3.1*	*1.5*

Source: Calculation by the authors.

budget and reported in the budget that year. Table 5 provides the risk-adjusted amounts of guarantees issued each year and the claims paid from the budget on guarantee defaults each year.

The Implications of the Hidden Fiscal Deficit

It turns out that the "true" fiscal deficit in the Czech Republic (table 6), though significantly higher that the deficit calculated through conventional methods, is comparable with the deficits of other Central Euro-

TABLE 6. CZECH REPUBLIC "TRUE" FISCAL DEFICIT, 1993–98
(% of GDP)

Deficits	1993	1994	1995	1996	1997	1998
Reported fiscal deficit	–0.5	–1.3	0.3	0.5	1.1	2.1
"Hidden" fiscal deficit in the special institutions (KOB, CI, CF, and NPF)	3.2	1.9	1.0	0.5	1.0	2.0
"Hidden" fiscal deficit in guarantees net hidden subsidy (risk-adjusted)	0.0	0.0	0.1	1.0	3.1	1.5
"True" fiscal deficit (including the special institutions and guarantee net hidden subsidy)	2.7	0.6	1.4	2.0	5.2	5.6

Note: KOB stands for Konsolidacni Banka; CI for Ceska Inkasni; CF for Ceska Financni; and NPF for National Property Fund.
Source: Calculation by the authors.

pean countries. Therefore, the Czech Republic's fiscal performance, contrary to the widely accepted view, is not noteworthy for its fiscal restraint. Moreover, if left to grow as in the past, the off-budget risk to future fiscal stability can increase significantly. There has been no institutional mechanism in the country mandated to keep a check on government off-budget obligations and the ensuing fiscal risk, and demands on new guarantees and further programs to be financed through various off-budget agencies are growing.

The first troubling fact implied by the above discussion is the sharp increase in the amount and risk of guarantees issued by the state. The bulk of the increase has emerged from the government's support to banks and to the Czech Railways. In 1997 and 1998 the government issued a CZK 22 billion (1.4 percent of GDP) guarantee to the Czech National Bank on some of its very risky lending for bank restructuring and a CZK 31 billion (nearly 2 percent of GDP) guarantee to a bank (the CSOB) on its claim against a Slovak financial institution (Slovenska Inkasni). To support the Czech Railways, the government issued two guarantees, each more than CZK 20 billion (about 3 percent of GDP together) with a very high default risk in 1996 and 1997 on railway modernization. The hidden cost of guarantees has already started to show as a growing claim on the budget emerging from guarantee defaults. Claims on the budget increased from about CZK 1 billion annually during 1993–96 to CZK 2 billion in 1997 and almost CZK 7 billion in 1998.[9]

Another, related, troubling fact is the rapidly increasing level of hidden public liabilities. Stocks of these liabilities have been accumulated outside the budgetary system as a result of the hidden deficits (annual flows) mainly in the form of borrowing by the special institutions to finance their government programs.[10] Table 7 shows approximate lev-

---

9. Since the guarantee claims paid from the budget have contributed to the reported deficit, the "hidden" deficit that emerges from guarantees includes only the difference between the hidden subsidy extended by the government through new guarantees and the claims mostly on guarantees issued in previous years. Unadjusted for guarantee claims, the hidden subsidy through guarantees has actually reached CZK 55 billion and CZK 32 billion in 1997 and 1998, respectively.

10. Hidden public liabilities are calculated on a gross basis. The analysis focuses on gross liabilities because the quality of directed loans extended and assets purchased through off-budget programs is extremely low and their potential value is, on average, estimated at 10 percent (3 percent for the CI, less than 10 percent in the CF, and under 20 percent in the KOB).

TABLE 7. HIDDEN PUBLIC LIABILITIES
(billions of CZK)

Sources of hidden public liabilities	1993	1994	1995	1996	1997	1998
KOB[a] net of provisions and reserves	79	81	79	70	86	98
CI net of provisions and reserves	20	27	25	17	8	7
NPF	29	33	40	22	17	15
State guarantees outstanding—adjusted for risk	3	3	6	28	74	107
Hidden public liabilities (net of provisions and reserves)	131	114	150	137	185	226
(% of GDP)	13.1	12.1	10.8	8.7	10.9	12.4
Provisions and reserves of the KOB and CI	19	24	42	59	71	84
Gross hidden public liabilities	150	168	192	196	256	310
Reported gross government debt	159	162	154	155	173	194
Reported gross government debt (% of GDP)	15.8	13.7	11.2	9.8	10.3	10.6

a. Activities of the KOB include financing of the Stabilization Program of Ceska Financni. Therefore, the table does not include Ceska Financni as a separate entity.

Note: CI stands for Ceska Inkasni, and KOB stands for Konsolidacni Banka; and NPF stands for National Property Fund.

Sources: The KOB, CI, and the NPF.

els of hidden public liabilities, excluding nonguaranteed quasi-fiscal operations of the Czech National Bank. Comparison of the figures of hidden deficits in table 2 and the resulting hidden liabilities in table 7 will illustrate the extent of cross-financing among the special institutions, and also the extent of the use of privatization revenues to partly cover the cost of off-budget programs.

Off-budget programs, such as guarantees and support extended through Konsolidacni Banka, the National Property Fund, Agriculture Support and Guarantee Fund (PGRLF) and other, possibly new, agen-

TABLE 8. ESTIMATED GUARANTEE CLAIMS ON THE BUDGET
(billions of CZK)

Guarantees outstanding in 1998	Default risk	Total claim	1999	2000	2001	2002	2003	1999–2003	1999–2030
284.8	Average 38%	107.4	3.3	4.9	5.4	33.3	3.7	50.5	97.8

Source: Calculation by the authors.

cies and guarantee funds impose a cost on taxpayers with a delay but with no discount. As it has already started to happen, past hidden deficits and servicing of the hidden government debt outside the budgetary system gradually generate claims on government budget.

One source of budget claims is state guarantees. In 1998, the government paid nearly CZK 7 billion (0.4 percent of GDP) on guarantee claims. Assuming no new state guarantees are issued, the budget may need to cover about CZK 4 billion annually in the next few years, and CZK 33 billion in 2002 if the debt of Slovenska Inkasni to the CSOB is not resolved. Table 8 builds on table 5 and, taking into account the individual guaranteed debt repayment schedule, it shows the expected guarantee claims on future budgets. Figures in table 8 are obtained by multiplying the default risk by annual scheduled payments. More conservative assumptions for default risk would increase the estimated claims on budget resources.[11]

Another source of future claims on the budget is Konsolidacni Banka. This bank experienced a loss of about CZK 14.4 billion in 1998 and over CZK 30 billion in 1999 (2 percent of GDP), which have been covered by the issue of state bonds. Assuming no new programs, the analysis of Konsolidacni Banka's asset portfolio indicates that its future losses and potential claims on the state budget are likely to stabilize in the neighborhood of about CZK 10 billion annually in 2000–02. However, new government programs that require further borrowing by Konsolidacni Banka without generating adequate revenues will further increase Konsolidacni Banka's debt service and, thus, losses.

Without further privatization revenues, the National Property Fund will need to borrow further to meet its commitment regarding Ceska Financni, Ceska Inkasni, environmental recovery, and railway devel-

---

11. Useful discussion on the measurement of the future possible fiscal cost of state guarantees can be found in Irwin and others (1997) and Mody (1996).

opment, and to cover principal repayments for its obligations.[12] To meet its obligations, analysis of the National Property Fund's commitments, excluding those vis-à-vis Konsolidacni Banka, suggests that the Fund will annually need about CZK 15 billion during 1999–2003 and about CZK 33 billion in 2004.

In the medium to long run, off-budget financing of government activities, guarantees, and other contingent liabilities surface as increases in government debt. In the Czech Republic, the expected increase in public debt by the amount of hidden public liabilities—estimated at around 12.4 percent of 1998 GDP (see table 7)—is significant, but not disastrous. What appears as disastrous is the dynamic in the rise of the hidden public liabilities. Clearly the levels of new guarantees issued and new government programs entrusted for financing to Konsolidacni Banka are not sustainable. Their continued growth at the current pace may in a few years endanger fiscal stability, and thus play against the country's objective of EU accession. The situation will appear more serious if "implicit" government liabilities were included in the deficit and debt calculations.

Moreover, off-budget programs contribute only marginally to achieving the main policy objectives of the government and, in some instances, may even undermine these objectives. What have the results been of off-budget programs in the Czech Republic? To support reforms and prevent problems from recurrence? Or just to pay for failures that are likely to occur again? A brief overview suggests that many off-budget programs, such as bailouts of banks and health insurance companies, have done the latter. Sometimes, programs that did not qualify for budgetary support (for example, an additional subsidy to Railways) did qualify for assistance outside the budget (such as a very risky guarantee extended to Railways). Moreover, often, these programs have implied that the government will help again in a case of future failures, and thus have generated moral hazard among market agents, reducing their incentives to improve productivity and competitiveness. Thus, the objective of EU accession and integration with European markets, which poses high requirements on competitiveness of banks and enterprises in the Czech economy, may have been undermined.

---

12. The initial issuance of the National Property Fund's obligations had been used mainly to capitalize Konsolidacni Banka. The following issuances by the Fund were used to cover its other commitments.

Is Fiscal Stabilization in FYR Macedonia Sustainable?

The Former Yugoslav Republic (FYR) of Macedonia's macroeconomic stabilization has often been referred to as a remarkable success. In 1992, FYR Macedonia had a general government budget deficit of 9.6 percent of GDP, and in 1993 13.4 percent of GDP. The country had little access to foreign finance, had an almost nonexistent domestic bond market, and financed its deficit through money creation. As a result, inflation reached 2,000 percent in 1992. The government adopted a stabilization program in 1994, the primary elements of which were a dramatic reduction in expenditures relative to GDP, the adoption of a fixed exchange rate, some changes in the tax system, and strengthened tax collection efforts. By 1997 the budget deficit was –0.4 percent of GDP, and the inflation rate 4 percent.

This adjustment is impressive, but is it sustainable? There are two parts of the sustainability question: (a) the traditional analysis, which focuses on whether the current pattern of expenditures and revenues, *not including contingent liabilities*, is sustainable and (b) the more complete analysis, which accounts for off-budget liabilities. Quite different answers are possible depending on which track is followed. In FYR Macedonia, the government had built a large stock of direct and contingent liabilities that has increased fiscal risks and that threatens future budgetary stability. The two main sources of contingent liabilities are those emanating from the financial sector and those from enterprise restructuring or privatization.[13]

The Macedonian government is under strong pressure to resolve the problem of the frozen foreign currency deposits it inherited from the former Yugoslavia. These are household deposits in foreign currency that were deposited in commercial banks in the former Yugoslavia that the commercial banks were required to redeposit with the National Bank of Yugoslavia. Since 1991 these deposits have been frozen, and since independence the Macedonian government has recognized these deposits as a liability of the state.

These liabilities are no longer implicit, but their fiscal effects are contingent on decisions taken by the government on the terms and structure of its debt. The government owes about DIN 1.2 billion (21 percent of GDP) toward some 770,000 foreign currency accounts held by Macedonians. The government is currently considering several options

---

13. If unreformed, the pay-as-you-go pension system could, in the long run, add a substantial amount in net liabilities to the government.

to deal with this problem. The most recently discussed solution is to swap these deposits with bonds of 15-year maturity, which would bear an interest rate of 1.5 percent. At this low interest rate and assuming no exchange risk, the debt service on these bonds would average 2.7 percent of GDP over the next 10 years.

The banking sector is an important source of implicit contingent liabilities, as past experience in FYR Macedonia has shown. Bank recapitalization and restructuring has already cost the budget more than 2 percent of GDP a year since 1995. Yet, incomplete structural reform has meant that the financial system's portfolio of bad debts has grown. It is now estimated that roughly 40 percent of the system's loans are compromised. Even after all provisions are accounted for, and after accounting for the total capital of the banking system, the total uncovered exposure (for balance sheet items) in the financial sector could be as high as 9 percent of GDP.[14]

Incomplete enterprise restructuring and labor issues, such as overdue wages, are also a potential source of budgetary pressures. Wage arrears are very high, estimated at about 15 billion DIN, or 9 percent of GDP. Typically, wage arrears and arrears in social security contributions will be paid by governments when they restructure or privatize government-owned firms (these firms may be taken over by the government as part of a restructuring program) or, in the case of FYR Macedonia, socially owned enterprises.[15] The government may explicitly pay for the wage arrears or may accept a lower price in the privatization process while asking the future employer to deal with labor issues. The total magnitude of arrears reported here includes arrears of privatized companies. The largest arrears in terms of the number of months overdue, however, are in the socially owned companies. A significant portion of the 15 billion DIN may be assumed to be wage arrears in these companies.[16] In some companies, the accumulation of arrears to workers is avoided by accumulating arrears to the government—as in the case of arrears in electricity bills of major companies.

---

14. There are reports that the government is considering taking on some debt owed to domestic banks by foreign borrowers, but the amount has not been decided yet. The above estimate refers to the cost of repaying creditors only, not to recapitalization to achieve positive net worth.

15. Socially owned companies are those that are owned by all—there are no clear owners in the sense of shareholders.

16. For some of the calculations, it is later assumed that around one-third of the total amount represents wage arrears in socially owned companies.

(Wage arrears have also been associated with arrears in tax payments—an implicit fiscal expenditure.) At the same time, enterprise adjustment will require massive layoffs. Estimates of overstaffing vary between 10 and 25 percent of the labor force. Severance costs alone are estimated at about 9 billion DIN.[17] The government of FYR Macedonia, as in other countries that had to go through such an adjustment process, has already funded severance pay for some laid-off workers.

The above discussion shows the links between structural reforms and fiscal adjustment. Problems in the enterprise and financial sectors lead to a buildup of implicit contingent liabilities, at least some of which will eventually have to be paid. Recognition of the government's contingent liabilities in the past has already created moral hazard in the financial and enterprise sectors. In the past, nonperforming loans have been removed from the balance sheet of banks and placed with a government agency, the Bank Rehabilitation Agency. Repayments on these loans, however, are minimal, and nonpaying enterprises continue to operate without undergoing bankruptcy. To limit the distortion of private sector incentives by creating further moral hazard, the government will need to find ways to limit repayment of its liabilities, particularly in the absence of legal and regulatory reform, that is, without strengthening the incentives for good performance. In cases where the net benefits from recognizing the contingent liabilities are positive, there is a need to ensure that those who benefit from implicit or explicit guarantees are required to bear some of the losses.

In addition to those three major liabilities, other sources of fiscal risk in the FYR of Macedonia include the following:

(a) The restitution of expropriated land. The Macedonian government will be giving away state-owned assets—or the equivalent value of land previously expropriated in transfer payments—to citizens. It is not possible to estimate the amount of this debt, because even the authorities do not know the value of the land covered.

(b) Guarantees provided by commercial banks for loans to enterprises (mostly from abroad). If 40 percent of these liabilities are called, and become expenses of the commercial banks, fiscal transfers may be involved.[18] Forty percent of the off-balance sheet guarantees amounts to 2.6 percent of GDP.

---

17. This is estimated by multiplying the prevailing average wage by nine months, the average length of time for which severance pay may be paid.

18. This is the percentage of nonperforming loans in the banking sector.

(c) The guarantee of DIN 35 million for the privatization of the largest bank, Stopanska.

(d) A one-time repayment of arrears to the health sector and in social payments (0.6 percent and 0.4 percent of GDP, respectively).

(e) Foreign exchange risk associated with the frozen foreign currency liabilities or the Stopanska guarantee or other sources.

(f) Pension liabilities. The Macedonian pay-as-you-go system was not in deficit in 1998, but projections under optimistic growth and employment increases indicated that, if unreformed, it can run up substantial net liabilities for the government over the long term. Recent events, such as war in the region, have changed the prognosis for the sustainability of the current system; deficits have started to appear in 1999. A further cause for worry is that changes in pension benefits are sometimes implemented in an ad hoc manner. Most recently, for example, the government announced a 10 percent increase in nominal pensions.[19]

Future Possible Impact of the Accumulated Fiscal Risks

What is the impact of contingent liabilities on fiscal sustainability in FYR Macedonia? First, a "sustainable" fiscal deficit needs to be calculated. The government cash deficit, including the deficits generated by the central bank, was used as the starting point.[20] The following assumptions were made:

(a) GDP growth rose from 1.5 percent in 1997 to 4.5 percent and is expected to rise to 5 percent in 2005.

(b) Inflation is kept at around 3 percent per year.

(c) Stabilization and financial sector reform lead to an increase in money demand, so that the monetization ratio rises from 14.5 percent in 1997 to 24 percent in 2005, the ratio of public foreign

---

19. In previous years the government had changed the indexation rule for pensions, which had resulted in a lower value for pensions. At a later stage, the Macedonian court ruled this as unconstitutional and asked the government to pay its debt (the difference in pensions because of the difference in indexation rules).

20. Profits and losses of public enterprises, as well as capital transfers, are included in the budget. To the extent that public enterprises' activities and prices differ from market values, these transfers will be net of the subsidy element embodied in these prices.

TABLE 9. ESTIMATING A SUSTAINABLE FISCAL DEFICIT

Sources of deficit financing	1997	1998	1999	2003	2005
Money creation	0.3	0.5	0.4	1.0	0.8
Foreign finance	0.1	0.3	1.6	1.3	1.5
Debt finance	0.3	1.6	3.0	2.7	3.0
Reserves	–0.2	–1.3	–1.4	–1.4	–1.5
Domestic finance	–0.3	–0.4	–0.2	–0.4	–0.4
Government borrowing from the rest of the economy	–2.3	0.0	0.5	0.5	0.5
National Bank of FYR Macedonia credit	–2.0	0.4	0.7	0.9	0.9
Public sector deficit	0.0	0.4	1.8	1.9	1.9

Source: 1997 data from the government of FYR Macedonia. Other data are Bank staff projections.

debt to GDP is kept at around 30 percent, and foreign reserves are increased to reach three months of imports.[21]

Table 9 shows a possible scenario. The sustainable deficit is estimated at around 1.5–2 percent of GDP. This is not a large number, but it is larger than the cash deficit of today.

In the absence of other adjustments, the realization of some of the fiscal risks described here could easily push the deficit beyond "sustainable" levels. The debt implied by the frozen foreign currency deposits would alone add 2.7 percent of GDP to the deficit. Suppose the uncovered exposure in the financial sector, amounting to 9 percent of GDP, and one-third of the implicit liabilities in the enterprise sectors, are paid by the government. Assume that the authorities issue two bonds. The maturity structure and interest rates assumed are 15 years at 8.9 percent (discount rate of the central bank) and 10 years at 7 percent (the rate on IBRD loans), respectively. [22] The payment of these liabilities

---

21. If inflation were 10 percent, base money could grow much faster, and revenues from the inflation tax would be higher. With a more aggressive external debt strategy, the external debt stock might grow faster, allowing a higher deficit to be financed. On the other hand, the GDP growth assumptions and assumptions regarding money demand are quite optimistic, given recent trends.

22. A previous IBRD loan included restructuring of enterprises and payment of wage arrears and severance. Even if only the social contributions due on wage arrears are recognized, they would amount to 6.3 percent of GDP. Severance payment is estimated for 15 percent of the employed (on average, this seems to be a reasonable number for the redundancy in enterprises).

would increase annual expenditures by 1 percent of GDP. A one-time payment for the Stopanska guarantee (worth DIN 35 million) would add another 1 percent of GDP. Exchange rate shifts would add to the payments the government would have to make. A 10 percent devaluation would add another 0.3 percent of GDP. If the interest rate on the bonds used to repay the frozen household deposits were to rise to 8.9 percent (the discount rate), the repayments could be 1 percent of GDP higher per year in the first six years. A 10 percent devaluation at this rate would add more than 1 percent of GDP to annual payments over a similar time frame. In other words, the fiscal deficit is in danger of being pushed to unsustainable levels because of the accumulation of contingent liabilities, even if the traditional deficit analysis indicates otherwise.

It is important to note, however, that even without the accumulation of contingent liabilities the FYR Macedonia's fiscal stance may not be sustainable. The "traditional" analysis of sustainability would highlight issues such as falling tax revenues (falling from 39 percent of GDP in 1994 to 31.2 percent of GDP in 1998), low civil service wages, and high civil service employment. Add to this a very low level of investment to GDP (1.6 percent), which country experience suggests is hardly enough to maintain the value of current investments. Put differently, deaccumulation of liabilities has been one of the major elements of the adjustment strategy, which, along with the accumulation of liabilities has affected net worth of government negatively.

When governments recognize their previously implicit contingent liabilities, payment on these debts need not have large effects on the fiscal deficit, though it may on future financing requirements. For example, noninterest-bearing bonds or bonds with very low interest rates could be used to replace implicit debt. Dealing with banking sector liabilities, for example, can be thought of in two parts: (a) making depositors whole and (b) recapitalization to enable the bank to continue functioning. While the former requires real resources from the government, the latter need not. As an example, to increase the capital of a bank, the government could take a zero interest loan from the bank and buy equity in the same bank. Depending on the interest rate and the maturity structure the government chooses for its debt, and depending also on the total value of contingent liabilities it recognizes, the fiscal effects may be starkly different. When the government recognizes losses already incurred in the financial and enterprise sectors and determines repayment terms, it will really be making a decision about how to distribute the losses within the economy. The greater the fiscal effect, the greater is the cost to general taxpayers as opposed to, for example, depositors in and shareholders of banks, workers in enterprises, and landowners in FYR Macedonia. It will need to make decisions, such as: If a bank makes poor loans and incurs losses, how much of the cost should be borne by the managers and how much by the depositors and taxpayers? By recapitalizing banks with bonds, it is merely recognizing losses that have already been incurred. The higher the interest rate on the bonds, the larger the transfer of resources from taxpayers to shareholders and depositors.[23] Moreover, the government has to weigh the moral hazard issue related to bank recapitalization with the threat of systemic risk and potentially negative effects on output in the absence of recapitalization. These are not easy decisions to make.

Unlike the case for explicit contingent liabilities, implementing fiscal planning, which would account for the potential fiscal risks associated with implicit contingent liabilities, is generally much more difficult.[24] First, implicit contingent liabilities may grow because of large macro shocks, whose magnitude and impact on the overall economy may be hard to determine. For small shocks, such as small exchange rate changes, it is generally possible to estimate, for example, effects on specific agents, such as banks. The government liability depends, however, on the uncovered exposure of banks and the creditors it wants to reimburse. Even if supervisors know the status of bank assets and capital precisely at a point in time, these values change continuously, and supervisors may not share information with the fiscal authorities.[25] Another complication arises from the fact that if governments explicitly account for the potential realization of implicit contingent liabilities, they may generate or significantly increase moral hazard, unless agents also believe ex ante that those responsible for poor credit decisions (managers or shareholders) will be forced to bear sufficiently large losses.

Fiscal authorities should recognize that (a) small open economies and emerging markets are especially prone to shocks (being relatively undiversified), and (b) banks and firms in small emerging economies will be exposed to more risk because of this susceptibility to shocks in

---

23. If bonds are continuously rolled over, the government effectively never repays the principal. In cases where this is not so, the government will have to find alternative sources of financing to repay the bonds.

24. For example, a guarantee contract can be written precisely and defined narrowly. For implicit contingent liabilities, the amount depends to a large extent on the political considerations at that particular time.

25. This is highly likely in most emerging economies, given information scarcities, lack of reliable accounting, and so forth.

the real economy, as well as financial shocks. Therefore, fiscal prudence and good debt management are very important.[26] It is more so because fiscal and monetary exchange rate outcomes are closely linked.

As contingent liabilities are accumulated, the net worth of government falls, all else being equal.[27] This tendency will be exacerbated if cash payments for interest liabilities crowd out investment or asset accumulation, which has been the case in FYR Macedonia. Therefore, the true fiscal adjustment in the Macedonian economy has been smaller than a consideration of the cash deficits may indicate. It is also true that payment for implicit contingent liabilities in FYR Macedonia has exacerbated moral hazard and can lead to a further accumulation of implicit contingent liabilities in the future, in the absence of strong reforms. It is relatively easy to change balance sheets of banks and firms, for example, without strengthening incentives for improved performance, which would prevent the further accumulation of losses.

Concluding Remarks

Our work in the Czech Republic and in FYR Macedonia demonstrates the importance of including contingent liabilities when assessing the magnitude of the true fiscal adjustment, and when analyzing fiscal sustainability. To the extent that explicit expenditures are shifted off-budget or replaced by the issuance of guarantees, the achieved improvement in fiscal balances is overstated. For the Czech Republic we find that adjustment may have been overstated by some 3–4 percent of GDP annually. The accumulation of contingent liabilities today is a threat to future fiscal stability. Hence, a stabilization program that is accompanied by a build-up of contingent liabilities may not be sustainable. In the case of FYR Macedonia, we found that the present fiscal equilibrium may be temporary, because the stock of existing contingent liabili-

---

26. Burnside and others (1999) have shown that the large prospective deficits implied by the poor health of the banking sectors in East Asian countries, such as Korea and Thailand, were an important trigger of "cause" of the loss of investor confidence.

27. In this discussion, the cost of the debt taken on by the government is implicitly assumed to be greater than the gain that might accrue, such as faster growth and restructuring, from the redistribution of claims. Such gains are possible in the case where the government is redistributing claims in the aftermath of a systemic crisis or when fundamental policy changes and incentive changes accompany the redistribution of claims.

ties could add 2–4 percent of GDP to future deficits. Moreover, the methods used to reduce the "traditional" deficit are unlikely to be sustainable without further modification. Our work also shows that fiscal adjustment and structural reforms are closely linked. The most obvious example is that failure to improve banking sector performance can over time lead to an accumulation of implicit contingent liabilities for governments.

There are three areas where further work is clearly needed. First, building on work by Claessens and Klingebiel (2000), Mody (1996), and Blejer and Schumacher (1998), governments need to develop better techniques for identifying and evaluating contingent liabilities arising from the banking system, nonbanking financial institutions, state guarantees, public enterprises, or contingent and direct liabilities of subnational governments. Second, governments need to apply techniques to manage their fiscal risks, for instance, building adequate reserve funds and hedging risk when plausible. This is likely to be best achieved as an extension of government debt management to address the overall government exposure to risks (Brixi and Mody 2000; Cohen 2000; and Cassard and Folkerts-Landau 1997). Third, benefiting from experience of countries like Canada and the Netherlands (Schick 2000), governments need to adjust their approaches to fiscal reporting, accounting, and budget management to bring their contingent liabilities under control. Today, politicians in many countries have an incentive to create more contingent liabilities: such liabilities allow them to cater to requests from different constituencies while maintaining deficit targets, and they are not subjected to the same level of scrutiny by cabinet and parliament as is direct spending. Future work could help develop alternative systems that would remove this bias for more contingent liabilities.

Appendix A
Nonstandard Operations of the Czech National Bank

Since 1993 the Czech National Bank has undertaken a large amount of nonstandard operations, most of which have been aimed at consolidating and stabilizing the banking sector. Table A1 provides a summary of the assets held by the central bank as a result of nonstandard operations by the end of 1998. The table also indicates the quality of these assets and their coverage by state guarantees and provisions.

TABLE A1. NONSTANDARD OPERATIONS OF THE CZECH NATIONAL BANK
(billions of CZK)

Asset	Amount as of December 31, 1998	Default risk	Covered by state guarantee	Provisioned
Assets purchased from banks	0.65	100%	0.27	0.4
Receivables from banks	13.01	100%	10.1	2.9
Receivables from the National Bank of Slovakia	26.1	63%	0.0	16.4
Redistribution credits to the KOB	32.5	*	0.0	0.35
Receivables from special clients	0.4	63%	0.0	0.3
Credit commitments and guarantees	51.4	34%	7.6	9.6
Ceska Financni (including the Consolidation Program and Agrobank, excluding the Stabilization Program covered by the KOB)	37.1	76%	0.0	28.0
Total	161.1	n.a.	18.0	57.9

*KOB obligations are guaranteed by the state.
Note: KOB stands for Konsolidacni Banka.
Source: Czech National Bank.

Bibliography

Blejer, Mario, and Adrienne Cheasty. 1991. "The Measurement of Fiscal Deficits: Analytical and Methodological Issues." *Journal of Economic Literature* XXIX:1644–78.

Blejer, Mario, and Liliana Schumacher. 1998. "Central Bank Vulnerability and the Credibility of Commitments: A Value-at-Risk Approach to Currency Crises." IMF Working Paper WP/98/65. Washington, D.C.

Brixi, Hana Polackova, and Ashoka Mody. 2000. "How to Manage the Risk of Contingent Liabilities: An Overview." In Hana Polackova Brixi, Allen Schick, and Sweder van Wijnbergen, eds., *Government at Risk: Contingent Liabilities and Fiscal Risk.* New York: Oxford University Press (forthcoming).

Buiter, Willem. 1983. "Measurement of the Public Sector and Its Implications for Policy Evaluation and Design." IMF Staff Papers 30:306–49. Washington, D.C.

————. 1990. *A Guide to Public Sector Debt and Deficits.* Cambridge, Mass.: MIT Press; London: Simon and Schuster International Group, Harvester Wheat Sheaf.

Cassard, Marcel, and David Folkerts-Landau. 1997. "Risk Management of Sovereign Assets and Liabilities." IMF Working Paper WP/97/166. Washington, D.C.

Claessens, Constantijn, and Daniela Klingebiel. 2000. "Fiscal Risks of the Banking System: Approaches to Measuring and Managing Contingent Government Liabilities in the Banking Sector." In Hana Polackova Brixi, Allen Schick, and Sweder van Wijnbergen, eds., *Government at Risk: Contingent Liabilities and Fiscal Risk.* New York: Oxford University Press (forthcoming).

Cohen, Daniel. 2000. "Fiscal Sustainability and Contingent Liabilities: An Analytical and Institutional Framework." In Hana Polackova Brixi, Allen Schick, and Sweder van Wijnbergen, eds., *Government at Risk: Contingent Liabilities and Fiscal Risk.* New York: Oxford University Press (forthcoming).

Easterly, William. 1999. "When Is Fiscal Adjustment an Illusion?" *Economic Policy: A European Forum* v0, n28 (April):55–76.

Glatzel, Dieter. 1998. "The Measurement of Deficit and Debt under the Maastricht Treaty: Some Statistical Considerations." In *The Challenges for Public Liability Management in Central Europe.* Washington, D.C.: World Bank.

Honohan, Patrick. 1999. *Fiscal Contingency Planning for Financial Crises.* World Bank Policy Research Working Paper 2228. Washington, D.C.

Irwin, Timothy, Michael Klein, Guillermo Perry, and Mateen Thobani, eds. 1997. *Dealing with Public Risk in Private Infrastructure.* World Bank Latin America and Caribbean Studies. Washington, D.C.: World Bank.

Kotlikoff, Laurence. 1993. *Generational Accounting.* New York: Free Press.

Mody, Ashoka. 1996. "Valuing and Accounting for Loan Guarantees." *World Bank Research Observer* 11 (February):119–42.

Polackova, Hana. 1998. *Contingent Government Liabilities: A Hidden Risk for Fiscal Stability.* World Bank Policy Research Working Paper 1989. Washington, D.C.

Rubin, Irene. 1997. *The Politics of Public Budgeting: Getting and Spending, Borrowing and Balancing.* Chatham, New Jersey: Chatham House.

Schick, Allen. 2000. "Budgeting for Fiscal Risk." In Hana Polackova Brixi, Allen Schick, and Sweder van Wijnbergen, eds., *Government at Risk: Contingent Liabilities and Fiscal Risk.* New York: Oxford University Press (forthcoming).

Selowsky, Marcelo. 1998. "Fiscal Deficits and the Quality of Fiscal Adjustment." In *The Challenges for Public Liability Management in Central Europe.* Washington, D.C.: World Bank.

World Bank. 1998. "FYR Macedonia: Country Economic Memorandum—Enhancing Growth." Report No. 18573-MK. World Bank, Poverty Reduction and Economic Management Department of Europe and Central Asia Region, Washington, D.C.

———. 1999. "Czech Republic: Dealing with Contingent Liabilities." In "Czech Republic: Toward EU Accession" World Bank Country Study. Washington, D.C.

Part II

Integration and Decentralization: Macro Effects

A Preliminary Investigation of the Impact of UEMOA Tariffs on the Fiscal Revenues of Burkina Faso

Douglas Addison

Abstract

This article demonstrates how a simple computable general equilibrium model was used to develop a rapid response, with reasonable results, to what was once an urgent policy question: the impact of the proposed Union Economique et Monétaire Ouest Africaine (UEMOA) customs union on the fiscal revenues in Burkina Faso.

At the time this was first written in early 1998, most analysis of the fiscal impact of the UEMOA proposals had been done by simply applying the proposed new tariff structure to the existing composition of imports without regard to trade diversion from the elimination of internal tariffs or trade creation from lower average tariffs. This article broadens the analysis to include not only the impacts of trade diversion and trade creation, but also the impact of changing domestic prices and internal resource allocations.

The model shows that the UEMOA regime, if it had been implemented in 1996, would have succeeded in inducing more trade between countries within the UEMOA membership. Imports into Burkina Faso from UEMOA partners would have increased by 14 percent over the actual 1996 outcome while imports from other trading partners would have decreased by almost 3 percent. Total imports would have increased by 1 percent, while total exports would have increased by 3 percent over the actual 1996 outcome.

The UEMOA regime would also have created a fiscal revenue loss of between 2.3 and 2.5 percent of GDP for Burkina Faso. This loss could be partially ameliorated by a combination of tariff exoneration reductions, increased external assistance, or increased domestic taxes. The analysis in this article finds there are significant gains (nearly 1 percent of GDP) to be made from the elimination of most exonerations and exemptions. External assistance would have to be increased by 1.3 percent of GDP if there were no other compensating measures to balance the fiscal loss. This option will militate against the improvement in export performance, however, because the increased aid flows could appreciate the real exchange rate for producers.

This analysis provided a quick response to Burkinabe policymakers and World Bank economists who wished, in early 1998, to assess the likely impact of the proposed UEMOA tariff regime on the fiscal revenues of Burkina Faso. This study was made during a time when Burkina Faso was under fiscal pressure to raise revenues or reduce expenditures. There was justifiable concern that the probable revenue losses resulting from the implementation of the UEMOA tariff structure would add an additional challenge to fiscal management. This is the focus of the article, even though there are equally important issues related to the impact of the proposed tariff regime on consumer welfare.[1]

Countries participating in the UEMOA have agreed to eliminate tariffs on trade between UEMOA members and gradually harmonize their import tariff structure. At the original time of this writing, this was to be implemented by the year 2000.[2] The proposed structure is summarized in table 1.

To provide a frame of reference, in 1996 Burkina Faso levied a weighted average tariff rate of 18 percent on imports from UEMOA countries. Imports from non-UEMOA countries faced a weighted average rate of 13.8 percent. The overall weighted average was 14.7 percent.[3] The new tariff regime, with its zero internal tariff rate and

---

1. In general, a customs union will tend to increase welfare to the extent that the average tariff rate is reduced. This gain could be eroded to the extent that consumers and firms are induced to import goods at higher prices or lower quality from union members.

2. The final assignment of goods to each category was undecided at the time this was written. In addition, surcharges (*taxe degressive de protection and taxe conjoncturelle à l'importation*) for various categories had been proposed. No agreement on these had been reached. Additional changes were also under consideration to harmonize VAT and excise structures. These are not considered here.

3. These calculations are net of all exonerations and exemptions. If import revenues from the VAT and excise taxes were added, the overall weighted average would increase to 24.8 percent. The implicit tariff rates used later in the general equilibrium analysis were slightly lower because national accounts data for imports are higher than those recorded by the customs authorities.

TABLE 1. Proposed UEMOA Import Tariff Structure
(percent)

Tariff component	Rate	Import base
Intra-UEMOA tariff (TI)	0.0	UEMOA
Common external tariff (TEC)		
Category 0 (medicines, medicinal inputs, and books)	0.0	Non-UEMOA
Category I (primary products, excluding petroleum and capital goods)[a]	5.0	Non-UEMOA
Category II (manufactured intermediate goods)	10.0	Non-UEMOA
Category III (consumer goods)[a]	20.0	Non-UEMOA
UEMOA levy on third country imports (PCS)	0.5	Non-UEMOA
ECOWAS levy on third country imports	0.5	Non-UEMOA
Statistical tax (RS)	1.0	All
Declining special protection tax (TDP)	To be determined	Non-UEMOA
Compensatory import levy (TCI)	To be determined	Non-UEMOA

Note: French names are abbreviated in parentheses.
a. Some goods that might ordinarily be considered physical capital, such as cement, are proposed to be classified as category III consumer goods.

lower common external tariff, would clearly reduce the average tariff rate and create a strong bias in favor of UEMOA suppliers. At issue is the net impact of these two forces on the government's revenues and overall fiscal position.

At the time of this writing, most analysis of the fiscal impact of the UEMOA proposals had been done by simply applying the proposed tariff structure to the existing composition of imports without regard to trade creation or trade diversion. Trade creation is defined here as the increase in the volume of imports, from union and nonunion sources, made affordable by a lower average tariff. This implies the replacement of at least some expensive, or low-quality, locally produced goods with less expensive, or higher-quality, imports. Trade diversion is defined as the reduction in import volumes from nonunion nations as a result of the discriminatory common external tariff.[4]

This article broadens the analysis to include not only the obvious impacts of trade creation and diversion on tariff collections, but also the less obvious indirect impacts on other revenues, such as the VAT, via changing domestic prices and internal resource allocations. This is

4. I followed Baldwin and Venables (1995) in their straightforward definitions of *trade creation* and *trade diversion*.

made possible through the use of a general equilibrium model.[5] The net results are richer and quite different in size from those found in previous work on Burkina Faso.

Previous Analysis

I first retraced the general strategy followed in previous work to obtain an approximation of the impact on tariff collections if the proposed tariff regime had been applied in 1996. To achieve this, I briefly examined the current structure of revenues to determine the relative importance of import duties. Next, I examined the structure of imports to learn more about how the proposed tariff would be applied. This allowed the desired calculation of the revenue impact, independently of trade creation and diversion. This initial analysis was concluded with a review of Burkina Faso's potential to substitute UEMOA suppliers for external suppliers. This helped inform the initial estimate of the revenue losses.

New Analysis

I broadened the analysis to include the issues of trade creation and diversion in the context of changing prices and real resource allocations by using a simple computable general equilibrium (CGE) model. In particular, I evaluated three options for absorbing the impact of the UEMOA regime: reducing public expenditures, raising domestic taxes, or increasing external support. I also was interested to discover by how much the lower tariffs would encourage exports because lower import duties depreciate the real internal exchange rate (for example, the ratio of prices for traded and domestic goods).

Initial Analysis of Potential Revenue Losses

In this section, I briefly examine the current structure of revenues, examine the structure of imports, and look at the issue of exonerations. These help inform a preliminary assessment of the impact of the proposed tariff changes. I conclude this section with a review of Burkina Faso's potential to substitute UEMOA suppliers for external suppliers.

---

5. This analysis is an improvement upon the previous analyses, but it remains limited. This article does not examine issues of protection, nor the impact of the customs union on real growth. Moreover, the analysis is limited only to Burkina Faso rather than all the UEMOA countries taken together.

Table 2. Revenue Composition, 1996

	Billions of CFAF	Percent of GDP	Percent of revenue
Total revenues and grants	268.8	21.97	168.10
A. Revenues	159.9	13.07	100.00
1. Direct taxes	39.5	3.23	24.73
2. Domestic indirect taxes[a]	33.8	2.76	21.15
3. Export taxes	0.0	0.00	0.00
4. Import duties	75.1	6.14	46.97
a. Tariffs	41.7	3.41	26.08
b. Chamber of commerce	0.4	0.04	0.27
c. VAT	18.4	1.50	11.51
d. Excise and other	14.6	1.19	9.11
5. Nontax revenues	11.4	0.93	7.15
B. Grants	108.9	8.90	68.10

a. Includes VAT and excise taxes levied on imports.
Source: The Burkina Faso authorities.

Composition of Revenues

In 1996, 26 percent of Burkina Faso's fiscal revenues, or 3 percent of GDP, came from import tariff receipts.[6] (See table 2.) This is the single largest source of revenue for Burkina. Almost one-quarter of this amount was generated from trade with UEMOA members. Thus, the potential impact of the proposed UEMOA customs union on Burkina Faso's revenues is quite large.

Trade Shares

If one can assign tariff rates to UEMOA and external sources by category, one can approximate the impact of the proposed new tariff regime. Based on data from the Burkinabe authorities, approximately 23 percent of Burkina Faso's imports originated from UEMOA partners in

---

6. Note that the VAT and excise taxes levied on imports can be grouped together with the VAT and excise receipts levied on domestic goods. This is necessary because both were levied after the collection of import tariff receipts—in other words, a lower tariff rate would also reduce the size of the tax base for each.

TABLE 3. COMPOSITION OF 1996 IMPORTS

		Percent of total		
Tariff category	*Billions of CFAF* *Total*	*External*	*UEMOA*	*Total*
0	16.8	6	0	6
I	77.6	23	4	27
II	109.5	27	12	39
III	79.1	22	6	28
Total	283.0	78	22	100

Source: The Burkina Faso authorities.

1996.[7] (See table 3.) The same data also show that roughly 6 percent of total imports in 1996 could have been assigned to category 0, 27 percent to category I, 39 percent to category II, and the remainder to category III. Before making our calculation, however, the complication of import duty exonerations had to be considered. This is taken up next.

Exonerations

The current level of import duty exonerations and exemptions is quite high. In 1996, they totaled CFAF 39.1 billion against tariffs levied on eligible imports of CFAF 107.9 billion. (See table 4.) In other words, 38 percent of the dutiable import base was lost to these exonerations.[8] On average, 89 percent of gross tariff receipts due were exonerated. After import tariffs are reduced, however, it is reasonable to assume that the total value of exonerations and exemptions would also be reduced in proportion, if not more aggressively. In fact, exonerations for imports specified in the *"code des investissements"* are proposed for complete elimination.

---

7. IMF Direction of Trade data for 1980–96 also put the average share of imports from UEMOA countries at 23 percent. This share may be overstated if there were sizable re-exports to Burkina Faso of Organisation for Economic Co-operation and Development (OECD) and Asian imports coming into other UEMOA countries.

8. It should be noted that total imports probably would have been lower without the exonerations. Import composition would also have been different to the extent that exonerations favor intermediate and capital goods.

TABLE 4. EXONERATIONS AND EXEMPTIONS, 1996
(billions of CFAF)

	Imports	Percent imports	Total due	Exoner- ations	Net tariff collected	Exoner- ations as share of due (%)
Exonerations	107.907	38.1	43.826	39.142	4.684	89
AEFP	18.934	6.7	6.075	4.874	1.201	80
AEFT	32.549	11.5	13.114	12.952	0.162	99
CI	30.852	10.9	14.468	11.207	3.261	78
DA	0.116	0.0	0.052	0.050	0.002	97
FEFP	0.176	0.1	0.083	0.072	0.011	87
FEFT	24.417	8.6	9.694	9.677	0.017	100
PDFP	0.523	0.2	0.193	0.161	0.032	84
PDFT	0.339	0.1	0.149	0.149	0.000	100
Other	175.170	61.9	37.030	0.000	37.030	
Total	283.077	100.0	80.856	39.142	41.714	

Note: The prefix AE is for exceptional events, CI is for imports specified in the investment code, DA is grant-financed imports, FE is for project imports financed by external loans, and PD is for diplomatic imports. The suffixes FP and FT are for partial and full exonerations, respectively.
Source: The Burkina Faso authorities.

In the approximate analysis employed below, it was assumed that exonerations and exemptions would be maintained in the same proportions to tariff collections due as shown in table 4. In other words, if an average of 89 percent of eligible tariff levies were exonerated prior to the proposed UEMOA regime, I would assume the use of that same rate for the proposed regime. (This assumption was changed later in the analysis.) It was also assumed that there were no exonerations or exemptions granted for the VAT or the excise taxes.

Approximate Impact

Under the assumptions outlined above, the proposed UEMOA regime would have resulted in a loss of CFAF 23.9 billion or 1.8 percent of GDP. The full results are shown in table 5. The weighted average tariff rate for imports from UEMOA sources, after exonerations, would have decreased from 18.0 percent to seven-tenths of one percent if the proposed regime had been put in place. The weighted average tariff rate

TABLE 5. DIRECT LOSSES TO IMPORT DUTIES, 1996
(billions of CFAF)

Actual outcome	Billions of CFAF			Tariff rates (percent of imports)	
	Gross tariff	Exoner- ations	Net tariff	Gross tariff	Net tariff
Non-UEMOA			30.09		13.8
0			0.70		4.3
I			5.96		9.1
II			11.67		15.4
III			11.75		19.3
UEMOA			11.62		18.0
0			0.02		4.0
I			1.37		11.3
II			7.18		21.3
III			3.05		16.7
Total	80.86	39.14	41.71	28.6	14.7
Simulation					
Non-UEMOA	27.43	10.10	17.32	12.6	7.9
0	0.32	0.08	0.25	2.0	1.5
I	4.56	2.11	2.45	7.0	3.8
II	9.11	2.69	6.41	12.0	8.4
III	12.55	5.22	8.21	22.0	13.4
UEMOA	0.65	0.17	0.48	1.0	0.7
0	0.01	0.00	0.00	1.0	0.9
I	0.12	0.01	0.11	1.0	0.9
II	0.34	0.07	0.27	1.0	0.8
III	0.18	0.09	0.10	1.0	0.5
Total	28.07	10.27	17.80	9.9	6.3
Gain or loss in CFAF	−52.79	28.87	23.91		
Gain or loss % of GDP	−3.9	2.1	1.8		

Note: Tariff rates are weighted by import data supplied by the Burkinabe authorities. Details on gross tariff receipts due were available only for the categories shown in table 4 at the time of this writing.
Source: Author's calculations.

for imports from non-UEMOA sources, also after exonerations, would have decreased from 13.8 percent to 7.9 percent. The weighted average tariff rate for all imports would have fallen from 14.7 percent to 6.3 percent.

This type of estimate is misleading, however, because the lower tariffs on non-UEMOA imports would create new dutiable trade, whereas the differential in rates between internal and external sources would generate trade diversion away from high-tariff, externally sourced imports.

Potential for Trade Diversion

If Burkina Faso imports the same types of goods from UEMOA and external sources, the likelihood of trade diversion is quite high. Similarly, within a single trade category, UEMOA suppliers will be more likely to find success in competing with external suppliers if the goods in question are undifferentiated commodities, such as rice or cement.

In fact, one can see that the composition of these imports varies considerably between the two sources. This is illustrated in table 6. Imports from UEMOA countries are concentrated in chemicals, and nuts and fruit. Imports from external sources are concentrated in products from countries that have a comparative advantage because of either their temperate climates, such as grains and dairy products, or their level of industrialization, such as vehicles, fuels, fertilizers, electronics, or medical supplies.

In addition to chemicals, where UEMOA suppliers already provide higher volumes, the categories where UEMOA suppliers may have the best chance of quickly substituting for external suppliers are the undifferentiated commodities: fuels, mineral products, and fertilizers. In theory, other commodities, such as some grains and dairy products, could also be included in the long run—subject to national consumer preferences, industrial requirements, and the degree of homogeneity in products. Thus, the maximum short-run impact of trade diversion, excluding trade creation, would be approximately CFAF 52 million or 4 percent of GDP. A likely maximum for a single year would be far less, perhaps 1 percent of GDP, because of limitations on existing productive capacity in the other UEMOA countries.

This analysis of composition has an important ramification for the impact of UEMOA on Burkina Faso's revenues. The elasticity of substitution between the two import sources is likely to be moderately high and, thus, the probability of revenue losses because of trade diversion to UEMOA countries is negligible.

General Equilibrium Analysis

The CGE model used here is a variation of the 1-2-3 model developed by Devarajan, Go, Lewis, Robinson, and Sinko (1994). In its simplest

TABLE 6. IMPORT CATEGORIES BY SOURCE, 1996
(imports CIF in millions of CFAF)

	Ratio of UEMOA to external	External		UEMOA		Total	
	Percent	*CFAF*	*Percent*	*CFAF*	*Percent*	*CFAF*	*Percent*
Primarily UEMOA	308	11,501.4	5.27	35,466.4	54.81	11,501.5	5.27
Chemicals	267	11,443.1	5.24	30,519.0	47.17	11,443.2	5.24
Nuts & fruit	8,479	58.3	0.03	4,947.3	7.65	58.3	0.03
Shared (fuels and mineral products)	97	19,198.3	8.79	18,695.8	28.89	19,198.4	8.79
Primarily external	7	153,975.3	70.51	10,142.9	15.68	153,976.0	70.51
A. Undifferentiated	6	54,015.8	24.74	3,184.3	4.92	54,016.1	24.74
Grains	1	26,537.1	12.15	165.5	0.26	26,537.2	12.15
Fertilizers	14	21,492.5	9.84	2,983.4	4.61	21,492.6	9.84
Dairy products	1	5,986.3	2.74	35.4	0.05	5,986.3	2.74
B. Other	7	99,959.5	45.77	6,958.5	10.75	99,959.9	45.77
Vehicles	4	23,417.2	10.72	896.6	1.39	23,417.3	10.72
Manufactures	1	23,061.0	10.56	180.5	0.28	23,061.1	10.56
Electrical and electronic	3	15,829.4	7.25	480.6	0.74	15,829.5	7.25
Metal products	15	13,919.3	6.37	2,064.9	3.19	13,919.4	6.37
Medical supplies	4	13,733.1	6.29	513.9	0.79	13,733.2	6.29
Paper products	53	5,272.2	2.41	2,801.4	4.33	5,272.2	2.41
Instruments	0	4,727.2	2.16	20.7	0.03	4,727.2	2.16
Other	1	33,696.9	15.43	400.3	0.62	33,697.0	15.43
Total	30	218,371.9	100.00	64,705.3	100.00	283,077.2	100.00
Percent of total		77.1		22.9		100.0	
Percent of GDP		16.3		4.8		21.1	

Source: The Burkina Faso authorities.

form, the 1-2-3 model has one country, two sectors (producer and consumer), and three goods (export, import, and domestic). In this article, imports are divided by source: UEMOA and non-UEMOA countries.[9] There are three indirect taxes (exports, imports, and one general indirect tax applied equally to all goods) and a direct income tax. World prices are given, and there is only one endogenous price for domestic

---

9. Exports should also be differentiated by UEMOA and non-UEMOA destinations. This was not done because of the difficulty in estimating (without moving to a larger multicountry exercise) the effective premium UEMOA countries would provide to Burkina Faso through their own tariff reductions.

goods. All real flows are determined as a consequence of relative prices and the drive to maximize private sector consumption. (See appendix 4-1 for the data used in the model and appendix 4-B for a full mathematical description of the model.)

Producer and Consumer Choice

Producers choose between producing goods for export, E, or for domestic use, D, according to their relative prices. They are therefore interested in the ratio of tariff-adjusted world prices for exports $Er \cdot we/(1 + te)$ relative to the aggregate price for domestic goods pd. This is the real internal exchange rate, Rx, for producers. Consumers choose between imported goods, M, and domestic goods. They react to the ratio of tariff-adjusted world import prices $Er \cdot we \cdot (1 + tm)$ relative to the price of domestic goods. This is the real internal exchange rate, Rq, for consumers.

$$Rx = Er \cdot \frac{we/(1 + te)}{pd} \qquad\qquad Rq = Er \cdot \frac{wm \cdot (1 + tm)}{pd}$$

Elasticities

The ease with which Burkinabe consumers can substitute between internal and external sources (trade diversion) for imports is governed by an elasticity of substitution, μ. The ability to substitute between imported and domestic goods (trade creation) is controlled by a second elasticity of substitution, σ. I also used an elasticity of transformation, Ω, to control how easily Burkinabe producers could switch between making goods for export and for domestic consumption.

The elasticities can be estimated econometrically. (See appendix 4-C for more details on how this can be done.) Here I made only a rough estimate for the elasticity of substitution between imports and domestic goods, σ, based on 12 years of data. The result for the elasticity of substitution is shown below. Given the likely inaccuracies resulting from such a small data set, the data and error terms were not checked for stationarity, nor did I check for serial correlation or heteroskedasticity. The elasticity for trade diversion could not be estimated because of a lack of time-series data on UEMOA versus non-UEMOA price indices. At the time of this writing, the elasticity of transformation could not be estimated because of unresolved problems with the export data.

12 observations	Constant	σ	r-squared
Estimate	–0.85	0.87	0.77
t-statistic	3.73	3.75	

Taxes

Finally, for the purposes of this model, I used the implicit tariff rates after exonerations, as calculated in table 4-5.[10] I *assumed* that the VAT and excise receipts were neutral with regard to domestic and imported goods. These taxes were therefore grouped together with other indirect taxes on domestic goods and services.[11]

Scenario

I used the CGE model to contrast the actual outcomes in 1996 against what would have happened if the proposed UEMOA tariffs had been in place that same year. I assumed that real GDP would not change, although its composition might.[12] I assumed also that real internal exchange rates would fully adjust, via the price of domestic goods, to the new tariff regime and this would therefore affect domestic direct and indirect tax revenues, as well as trade revenues. (See appendix 4-B for more details.)

---

10. I made no changes at this point to the rate of exonerations granted against gross tariffs due.

11. In fact, this simplifying assumption was acceptable only at the aggregate level of this model. It was not accurate at the product level. For example, the bulk of the excise tax on imports came from the petroleum products excise (TUPP). Another example was the excise on cigarettes, which is highly protective of local production.

12. In the short run, real GDP is a function of prior exogenous investment and should not be expected to vary much in response to trade regime changes. Changes in the level and composition of trade, however, were assumed to respond quite rapidly. In the longer run, one would expect an impact on real growth as well.

Predictions

Before going directly to the results, it would be useful to review what theory predicts. If import tariffs are reduced, the consumer price of imports will fall, boosting real aggregate imports.[13] Import tariff collections will fall because of lower tariffs on non-UEMOA imports and switching into relatively untaxed UEMOA imports. Prices for domestic goods should also fall as the demand for domestic goods falls. This will induce producers to shift their output toward more exports.[14]

As an aside, note that, under these circumstances, the real internal exchange rate for producers, Rx, will depreciate while the real internal exchange rate for consumers, Rq, will appreciate. This dichotomy occurs because the tariff-adjusted price of imports always falls faster than the domestic price. (See appendix 4-B.) By contrast, the real *external* exchange rate, defined as a nominal exchange rate index deflated by a ratio of domestic and trading partner aggregate price indices, will always depreciate.

The tax base for the VAT will be reduced by a combination of lower consumption of domestic goods, a lower price for domestic goods, and the lower post-tariff valuation of imports. The tax base for direct income taxes will also be reduced in current price terms as the price of domestic goods falls and producers shift away from these goods. If the total revenue loss from lower tariffs and lower prices is not made up by higher domestic taxes, government spending will fall. If simulated investment is maintained at the actual level achieved in 1996, the reduction in government spending will be compensated by an increase in

---

13. The large role played by foreign donors in financing Burkina Faso's imports is probably not a constraint to real adjustment because most aid is denominated in francs or other currencies rather than physical quantities. The rail link between Burkina Faso and Côte d'Ivoire could, however, act as such a constraint if its performance continues to deteriorate as it has in the past.

14. Export expansion is biased downwards in this model because it omits the trade creation resulting from potentially higher demand from UEMOA partners for Burkinabe products. This has the secondary effect of also understating the expansion in imports that exports help finance. The revenue loss from a tariff reduction is therefore also overstated. In fact, this bias may be quite small because most Burkinabe exports are primary products that already receive regional preferential tariffs that will not improve further under the UEMOA regime.

private consumption so that aggregate domestic savings also remains unchanged.

Sensitivity Analysis

Given the uncertainty surrounding the elasticities, I performed a sensitivity analysis, centered around the estimated value of σ, designed to produce the highest and lowest revenue losses for a plausible range of estimates for Ω and μ. They formed scenarios 1 through 3 in tables 7 and 8. If UEMOA and external sources are easily substituted, revenue losses will be larger. Likewise, the easier it is for Burkinabe consumers to substitute imports for domestic goods, the higher the trade revenue losses will be. This is because lower demand for domestic goods will drive down their prices and thus reduce the nominal value of the domestic tax base for indirect taxes.

Simulated Impact

If the revenue impact of the proposed regime can be absorbed by public expenditure reductions in consumption as described above, then, based on a range of plausible elasticities (see scenarios 1 through 3 in table 7), the real internal exchange rate for consumers would appreciate by an average of 1.7 percent. Imports from UEMOA sources would increase by between 7 and 21 percent of the actual 1996 outcome (between 0.5 and 1.5 percent of GDP) whereas imports from external sources would decrease by between 0.5 and 5 percent of the actual 1996 outcome (between 0.1 and 1.2 percent of GDP). The average increase in total imports would be 1 percent over the actual 1996 outcome (0.4 percent of GDP). It therefore appears that the trade diversion effect is substantial and significantly reduces net trade creation. The real internal exchange rate faced by producers would depreciate by 4.5 percent and thus real exports would also increase by 3 percent over the actual 1996 level (or 0.4 percent of GDP). (See table 7.)

Revenue Losses

Revenue losses calculated by the general equilibrium approach were larger than what was calculated in the initial, approximate analysis above because the trade diversion effect was large relative to trade creation and because the impact of domestic price changes on other revenues were omitted.

TABLE 7. IMPACT SCENARIOS, TRADE CREATION, AND DIVERSION

Adjustment scenarios	Elasticities of substitution			Changes in real GDP shares					Percent change		
	Ω	σ	μ	E	M	Mu	Mn	D	Pd	Rx	Rq
Revenue and spending[a]											
1 Least loss	0.90	0.77	0.90	0.38	0.38	0.50	−0.12	−0.4	−3.8	+4.0	−2.1
2 Average	0.75	0.87	1.95	0.36	0.36	0.99	−0.63	−0.4	−4.3	+4.5	−1.7
3 Highest loss	0.60	0.97	3.00	0.31	0.31	1.50	−1.19	−0.4	−4.7	+4.9	−1.4
4 Income tax[a]	0.75	0.87	1.95	0.36	0.36	0.99	−0.63	−0.4	−4.3	+4.5	−1.7
5 VAT[a]	0.75	0.87	1.95	0.36	0.36	0.99	−0.63	−0.4	−4.3	+4.5	−1.7
6 External aid[b]	0.75	0.87	1.95	0.09	1.40	1.26	+0.14	−0.1	−1.0	+1.0	−5.0
7 Revenue or lower exonerations	0.75	0.87	1.95	0.22	0.22	1.31	−1.09	−0.3	−2.6	+2.7	−1.0

a. These simulations hold foreign and domestic savings constant. In other words, the increase in imports is matched by an increase in exports, and the decrease in government expenditures is matched by increased private sector expenditures so that total investment remains unchanged.

b. This simulation allows foreign savings to adjust via changes in exports and imports. Private consumption absorbs these adjustments so that domestic savings and total investment remain unchanged.

Note:
GDP Gross domestic product at factor costs.
E   Exports.
M   Imports.
Pd   Price of domestic goods.
Rx   Real internal exchange rate for producers. (Positive change is a depreciation.)
Rq   Real internal exchange rate for consumers. (Negative change is an appreciation.)
Source: Author's calculations.

TABLE 8. IMPACT SCENARIOS, REVENUES

| | Elasticities of substitution | | | Revenue losses in CFAF billions | | | | | Percent change in GDP shares | |
	Ω	σ	μ	Total revenue	Import duties	Other indirect	Income taxes		Revenue losses	Real cons.
Adjustment scenarios										
Revenue and spending										
1 Least loss	0.90	0.77	0.90	28.5	24.4	2.9	1.2		2.3	1.2
2 Average	0.75	0.87	1.95	29.2	24.7	3.2	1.4		2.4	1.2
3 Highest loss	0.60	0.97	3.00	30.0	25.1	3.4	1.5		2.5	1.2
4 Income tax	0.75	0.87	1.95	15.7	24.7	3.2	12.2		1.3	0.0
5 VAT	0.75	0.87	1.95	10.8	24.7	15.3	1.4		0.9	0.0
6 External aid	0.75	0.87	1.95	25.3	24.1	0.8	0.3		2.1	1.5
7 Revenue or lower exonerations	0.75	0.87	1.95	17.9	15.1	1.9	0.9		1.5	0.7

Source: Author's calculations.

In these simulations, it appears that the UEMOA regime, if it had been implemented in 1996, would have resulted in a revenue of loss of between CFAF 28.5 and 30.0 billion compared with the actual 1996 outcome. This would have been the equivalent of between 2.3 and 2.5 percent of GDP—considerably higher than the approximate estimate of 1.8 percent of GDP made above. (See scenarios 1 through 3 in table 8.) Of this, an average of CFAF 24.7 billion would have been lost from tariff collections, CFAF 3.2 billion from the VAT and other indirect domestic taxes, and CFAF 1.4 billion from direct taxes.

Options

Three main options exist for avoiding such large expenditure reductions. The first option is to raise indirect domestic taxes, perhaps the VAT. The second is to raise domestic income taxes. The third is to increase external aid through grants or borrowing. In the first two cases, I held foreign and domestic savings constant. In other words, government savings were maintained by increasing domestic tax revenues, private savings remained unchanged, and an increase in imports was matched by an increase in exports. In the third case, I allowed foreign savings to adjust via changes in exports and imports. Private consumption absorbed these adjustments so that domestic savings and total investment would remain unchanged. I also considered a final scenario where the government eliminated almost all tariff exonerations and exemptions. This scenario was a variation on scenarios 1 through 3 where revenues and expenditures adjusted without any changes in domestic taxes or external assistance. For each case, I used the middle range of elasticities (scenario 2) based on the econometric estimate for σ.

Income Taxes

If the impact could be absorbed by increasing domestic direct taxes, these would have to be increased by CFAF 12.2 billion or 1 percent of GDP to a total of CFAF 51.7 billion, compared with the CFAF 39.5 billion actually achieved in 1996. (See scenario 4 in table 4-8.) This increase would preserve investment in relation to the actual macroeconomic outcome, but it would leave government revenues CFAF 15.7 billion or 1.3 percent of GDP lower than what was actually achieved in 1996.

Indirect Taxes

If the impact could be absorbed by increasing domestic indirect taxes, these would have to be increased by CFAF 15.3 billion or 1.3 percent of

GDP to a total of CFAF 82.1 billion, compared with the CFAF 66.8 billion actually achieved in 1996.[15] (See scenario 5 in table 8.) As above, this would preserve investment, but it would leave government revenues CFAF 10.8 billion, or 0.9 percent of GDP, lower.

External Aid

The outcome of the third option, increasing external support, was a bit trickier. This was because the use of external grants or lending would reduce the real depreciation faced by producers and exacerbate the real appreciation faced by consumers. If the impact could be absorbed this way, external assistance would have to be increased by CFAF 16.1 billion or 1.3 percent of GDP to a total of CFAF 62.6 billion, compared with the CFAF 46.5 billion actually received in 1996. (See scenario 6 in table 8.) Real imports would rise by 1.4 percent of GDP, whereas real exports would increase by only one-tenth of a percent of GDP.

Reduced Exonerations

In this scenario, for illustrative purposes, I assumed that the government eliminated exonerations for all categories of import transactions, except for those made for diplomatic purposes—in addition to the implementation of the UEMOA tariff regime.[16] The resulting tariff calculations are summarized in table 9.

The effective tariff rate in this scenario was higher than what was used in scenarios 1 through 6 because of the elimination of exonerations. This had the effect of reducing the change in the price of domestic goods and the consequent shifts in the real internal exchange rates. In turn, the losses on tariff collections and net indirect taxes were also lower. (See scenario 7 in tables 7 and 8.) The total revenue loss was CFAF 17.9 billion or 1.5 percent of GDP. Of this, CFAF 15.1 billion came from tariff collection losses, CFAF 1.9 billion from indirect tax losses, and CFAF 0.9

---

15. This estimate included excise taxes collected on imports, the largest of these being the "TUPP" levied on petroleum products.

16. It was understood that the elimination of exonerations for imports purchased by the government would not be fiscally neutral because expenditures would be increased to cover the costs. It was also understood that a number of technical and political arguments may justify the retention of many exonerations. The scenario is merely illustrative.

Table 9. Import Duties with Lower Exonerations, 1996
(billions of CFAF)

	CFAF billions			Percent of imports	
Actual outcome	Gross tariff	Exone-rations	Net tariff	Gross tariff	Net tariff
Actual outcome					
Non-UEMOA			30.09		13.8
UEMOA			11.62		18.0
Total	80.86	39.14	41.71	28.6	14.7
Simulation					
Non-UEMOA	27.43	0.08	27.35	12.6	12.5
UEMOA	0.65	0.01	0.64	1.0	1.0
Total	28.08	0.09	27.99	9.9	9.9

Note: Tariff rates are weighted by import data supplied by the Burkinabe authorities. Details on gross tariff receipts due were available only for the categories shown in table 4 at the time of this writing.
Source: Author's calculations.

billion from direct tax losses. This scenario showed that significant gains (nearly 1 percent of GDP) can be made from the elimination of exonerations and exemptions.

Caveats

These findings must be tempered by an understanding of the limitations of the model employed and by the nature of several assumptions that should be subject to scrutiny.

- The model does not allow an exploration of the trade expansion that would arise from increased exports from Burkina Faso to other UEMOA countries.[17] This biases downward trade creation in both exports and imports and overstates the potential revenue

---

17. In addition to gains from the lower tariffs for UEMOA countries, there is additional potential for export expansion resulting from lower transportation and transaction costs. These are not discussed in this article.

losses from the implementation of the UEMOA regime. This bias may be small because most Burkinabe exports are primary products that already receive preferential tariffs that will not improve much under the UEMOA regime. The impact should also be limited because the elasticity of transformation, Ω, is likely to be less than one: producers cannot easily shift substitute domestic goods for primary commodities. Any subsequent analysis should include a deeper exploration of these issues.

- Revenue losses are also overstated by ignoring potential output expansion resulting from less expensive imports of inputs and capital and from increased UEMOA demand for exports.

- Domestic prices are assumed to adjust instantaneously. A cursory examination of the data does show a fairly rapid transmission of the 1994 devaluation to domestic prices. Further econometric investigation would be helpful to confirm or correct this impression.

- It is assumed that the composition of imports across consumption, intermediate, and capital goods will not change even though relative tariff rates do. This would affect the average weighted tariff rates.

- Burkina Faso's exports are mainly primary commodities. To the extent that there is a single world price for these commodities, this implies that the imperfect substitutes approach, upon which this model is based, is not appropriate (Goldstein and Khan 1985). There is, however, ample evidence that the law of one price does not hold for most commodities and, therefore, the model's structure is appropriate.

- It is assumed no significant nontariff barriers to trade have been imposed by Burkina Faso or by its trading partners. Cost-increasing measures, such as special standards for imports, would reduce the change in real exchange rates (Laird and Yeats 1990). Import quotas would have a similar effect. This assumption should be reviewed in any subsequent work.

The CGE model is well suited to examine "what-if" simulations in a nondynamic setting, but it cannot shed light on issues related to the links between trade and real growth, nor to any issues associated with capital flows (foreign or domestic) and interest rates. I did not examine the impact of any harmonization of investment codes or other aspects of the UEMOA proposals. I did not examine issues of protection. Moreover, the model is limited to a single country and, thus, the combined effects of the interactions between all UEMOA countries were ignored.

Conclusions

The UEMOA regime, if it had been implemented in 1996, would have succeeded in inducing more trade between countries within the UEMOA membership. It would also have resulted in a revenue loss for Burkina Faso of between CFAF 28.5 billion and CFAF 30.0 billion compared with the actual outcome in 1996. This would be the equivalent of between 2.3 and 2.5 percent of GDP. This could be partially ameliorated by a combination of increased domestic taxes, increased borrowing, or reduced tariff exonerations. These results are only preliminary in nature because the model employed cannot fully explore all the relevant issues associated with the implementation of a customs union.

Appendix A: Data for 1996

The main objective in assembling these data was to create an internally consistent set of accounts. This was accomplished by employing flow-of-funds accounting to the national accounts. Flow-of-funds principles require that flows out of one account—for example, government external interest payments—should match flows into another account, in this case the external sector's balance of payments. In achieving this, a number of data inconsistencies were discovered. The final results are shown in table A1.

TABLE A1. DATA FOR 1996

	CFAF millions
Goods	
Value added (X)[a]	1,223,600
Imports of goods and nonfactor services (M)	375,100
Exports of goods and nonfactor services (E)	150,670
Consumption, government (G)[b]	91,680
Consumption, private, (C)[c]	1,137,131
Direct taxes	39,540
Price distortions	
Indirect taxes, imports	42,149
A. Tariff[d]	41,710
B. Other[e]	439
C. Less exonerations	39,142
Indirect taxes, exports	0
Indirect taxes, domestic[c]	66,786
Subsidies	0
Net transfers: government or private (tr)	−22,831
Nontax revenue	11,429
Interest, net official to private	−2,600
Net transfers, to private from government	−31,660
Net transfers: government and external (ft)	100,00
Interest, net official to external	−8,900
Net official transfers, to government from external[f]	108,900
Net transfers: private and external (re)	77,900
Interest receipts: monetary sector	5,900
Interest payments: private	−1,800
Dividends paid by private sector	−700
Net transfers to private sector[f]	74,500
Changes in assets and liabilities	
Investment, government (Zg)	142,050
Investment, private (Zp)[c,g]	186,104
All other	0

a. Imputed bank services are treated as if they were part of GDP at factor cost.

b. Government consumption is from fiscal goods and services plus wages and salaries.

c. Domestic indirect taxes and other trade taxes (VAT and excise) are prorated across private consumption and investment. They were originally omitted from the calculation of GDP at market prices.

d. Assumed to equal fiscal number less exonerations.

e. Other trade taxes are assumed to be chamber of commerce import duties.

f. Discrepancy between BOP official transfers and fiscal estimate is accounted for by food and other aid passed on to the private sector.

g. Change in stocks is imputed to private investment.

Source: The Burkina Faso authorities.

Appendix B: Description of the Model

The model used here is a variation of the 1-2-3 model developed by Devarajan, Go, Lewis, Robinson, and Sinko (1994). In its simplest form, the model has one country, two sectors (producer and consumer), and three goods (export, import, and domestic). There are three indirect taxes (exports, imports, and one general indirect tax applied equally to all goods) and a direct income tax. World prices are given, and there is only one endogenous price for domestic goods. All real flows are determined as a consequence of relative prices and the drive to maximize private sector consumption.

Production. National output (X) is divided by means of a constant elasticity of transformation (CET) function into just two classes of goods: those that are exported (E) and those that are sold domestically (D).[18] (Note that a full list of variable names and descriptions can be found in table B1 below.) Output is held constant, whereas the allocation of production between exports and domestic goods varies. Producers will export more when the real internal exchange rate for producers (Rx) depreciates. This will occur if the world price of exports (we) rises, if the nominal exchange rate (Er) depreciates, if the export tax (te) is reduced, or if the price of domestic goods (pd) is reduced.[19] See equations 1.0 through 1.2 below. (Carets over variables denote the change in the log of a variable, an approximation of percentage changes.)

$$X = \text{CET } (E, D^S, \Omega) \text{ and } px \cdot X = pd \cdot D^S + we \cdot Er \cdot E \qquad (1.0)$$

$$\frac{E}{D^S} = x \cdot Rx^\Omega \text{ where } Rx = \frac{we \cdot Er / Te}{pd} \text{ and } Te = (1 + te)$$

$$\text{and } x \text{ is a scale factor} \qquad (1.1)$$

$$\hat{E} - \hat{D}^S = \Omega \cdot (\hat{we} + \hat{Er} - \hat{Te} - \hat{pd}) \qquad (1.2)$$

---

18. Import substitutes are included in the domestic goods category.

19. It is assumed that the country being modeled cannot influence world prices for any of its exports or imports.

Absorption. By the same token, the consumer and government sectors maximize a constant elasticity of substitution (CES) function by choosing between domestic goods and imported goods (*M*). See equations 2.0 through 2.1 below. Consumers and the government will import more if the real internal exchange rate (*Rq*) appreciates. This will occur if the world price of imports (*wm*) falls, if the nominal exchange rate (*Er*) appreciates, if the import tariff (*tm*) is reduced, or if the price of domestic goods (*pd*) is increased.

$$\text{Maximize } Q = \text{CES}(D^D, M, \sigma) \text{ subject to}$$
$$pq \cdot Q = pd \cdot D^D + wm \cdot Er \cdot M \qquad (2.0)$$

$$\frac{D^D}{M} = q \cdot Rq^\sigma \text{ where } Rq = \frac{wm \cdot Er \cdot Tm}{pd}$$

and $Tm = (1 + tm)$ and q is a scale factor   (2.1)

$$\hat{D}^D - \hat{M} = \sigma \cdot (\hat{wm} + \hat{Er} + \hat{Tm} - \hat{pd}) \qquad (2.2)$$

Note that all elements of absorption are measured *before* taxes. Thus the posttax (market price) concept utilized in the national accounts for domestic absorption would be expressed as

$$pq \cdot (1 + ts) \cdot Q^D = Er \cdot wm \cdot (1 + tm) \cdot (1 + ts) \cdot M + pd \cdot (1 + ts) \cdot D^D \qquad (2.3)$$

or

$$pq \cdot (1 + ts) \cdot Q^D = pq \cdot (1 + ts) \cdot (C + G + Z) \qquad (2.4)$$

where *ts* is an indirect tax on all domestic absorption, *C* is private consumption, *G* is government consumption, and *Z* is total investment.

The balance of payments. The difference between exports and imports, adjusted for net transfers to the government (*ft*) and the private sector (*re*), is defined as external savings, which is financed by net foreign borrowing (*B*) as shown in equation 3.0.[20] The balance of payments

---

20. Net transfers, in both cases, include interest receipts and payments, dividend receipts and payments, grants, and other forms of transfers.

can also be rewritten in ratios where λ is the ratio of exports to imports where λ increases with net borrowing or reserve drawings. See equations 3.1 through 3.2 below.

$$wm \cdot M - we \cdot E - ft - re = B \qquad (3.0)$$

$$\frac{M}{E} = \lambda \cdot \frac{we}{wm} \text{ where } \lambda = \frac{we \cdot E}{wm \cdot M} = \frac{B + ft + re}{we \cdot E} + 1 \qquad (3.1)$$

$$\hat{M} - \hat{E} = \lambda + \hat{we} - \hat{wm} \qquad (3.2)$$

Endogenous domestic price. Combining equations 1.2, 2.2, and 3.2 allows us to solve for the one endogenous price in the model, *pd*.

$$\hat{pd} = \hat{E}r + \frac{1}{\sigma + \Omega} \cdot [\hat{we} \cdot (\Omega + 1) + \hat{wm} \cdot (\sigma - 1) + \hat{Tm} \cdot \sigma - \hat{Te} \cdot \Omega + \hat{\lambda}] \qquad (4.0)$$

Note that a terms of trade improvement or increased capital inflows will increase *pd*, whereas a lower import tariff will always decrease domestic prices.

We can also calculate the real exchange rates faced by producers (*Rx*) and consumers (*Rq*) by subtracting the percent change in *pd* from the percent change in tariff adjusted world prices:

$$\hat{Rx} = (\hat{we} - \hat{wm}) \cdot \left(\frac{\sigma - 1}{\sigma + \Omega}\right) - (\hat{Te} + \hat{Tm}) \cdot \left(\frac{\sigma}{\sigma + \Omega}\right) - \hat{\lambda} \cdot \left(\frac{1}{\sigma + \Omega}\right) \qquad (5.0)$$

$$\hat{Rq} = -(\hat{we} - \hat{wm}) \cdot \left(\frac{\Omega + 1}{\sigma + \Omega}\right) + (\hat{Te} + \hat{Tm}) \cdot \left(\frac{\Omega}{\sigma + \Omega}\right) - \hat{\lambda} \cdot \left(\frac{1}{\sigma + \Omega}\right) \qquad (6.0)$$

From equations 5.0 and 6.0, it can be seen that a reduction in import tariffs, as proposed for the UEMOA countries, would result in a real internal exchange rate depreciation for producers and a real internal exchange rate appreciation for consumers. Thus, exports and imports would both rise.

Discriminatory tariffs. Imports are further divided into those coming from UEMOA sources (Mu) and those coming from external sources (Mn). The choice between the two sources is governed by the overall level of desired imports (M), the prices of the two import categories (wmu and wme), and a constant elasticity of substitution (μ).

$$\text{Maximize CES}(Mu, Mn, \mu) \text{ subject to}$$
$$wmu \cdot Mu + wmn \cdot Mn = wm \cdot M \tag{7.0}$$

$$\frac{Mu}{Mn} = m \cdot \left[\frac{wmn \cdot (1 + tmn)}{wmu \cdot (1 + tmu)} \right]^{\mu} \text{ where } m \text{ is a scale factor} \tag{7.1}$$

$$\hat{M}u - \hat{M}n = \mu \cdot (w\hat{m}n - w\hat{m}nu + T\hat{m}n - T\hat{m}u) \tag{7.2}$$

where $Tmn = (1 + tmn)$ and $Tmu = (1 + tmu)$.

As equation 7.1 makes clear, consumers will increasingly prefer UEMOA sources for their imports as long as world prices for non-UEMOA goods, adjusted for tariff rates, are higher than those for UEMOA prices for the same goods.

Government sector. Government tax revenues (T) are the sum of direct taxes, indirect taxes on domestic goods, import tariff receipts, and export tariff receipts.

$$T = ty \cdot Y + ts \cdot pq \cdot Q^D + Er \cdot (tm \cdot wm \cdot M + te \cdot we \cdot E) \tag{8.0}$$

where

$$Y = px \cdot X + tr \cdot pq + re \cdot Er \tag{9.0}$$

Expenditures consist of government consumption (G), subsidies (SUB), net external transfers (ft), net domestic transfers (tr), and investment (Zg).[21] The entire budget constraint is

---

21. Net transfers include nontax revenues, interest receipts and payments, dividend receipts and payments, grants, and other forms of transfers.

$$T - pq \cdot (1 + ts) \cdot G - pq \cdot tr - Er \cdot ft = Sg = Zg \qquad (10.0)$$

where G is real government expenditure before taxes, Sg is government savings, and Zg is government expenditures before taxes.

Private sector. The budget constraint for the private sector is set up in a similar way so that private savings equals private investment. Thus, income less direct taxes less consumption at market prices equals private savings (a fixed share of income multiplied by income) equals investment:

$$Y - ty \cdot Y - pq \cdot (1 + ts) \cdot C = s \cdot Y = Zp \qquad (11.0)$$

National accounts identities. In addition to equations 1.0 and 2.0, I also require the sum of external savings, government savings, and private savings to equal investment.

$$pq \cdot (1 + ts) \cdot (Zp + Zg) = Er \cdot B + Sg + s \cdot Y \qquad (12.0)$$

Equilibrium conditions. In addition to equations 3.0, 8.0, 11.0, and 13.0, the model solves for equilibrium in the product and consumer markets so that

$$D^D = D^S \qquad (13.0)$$

and

$$Q^D = Q^S \qquad (14.0)$$

TABLE B1. SUMMARY AND DESCRIPTION OF VARIABLES

Endogenous variables	Exogenous variables

Real flows

E:	Export goods	G:	Real government demand, at
M:	Import goods		factor costs
Mu:	Imports from UEMOA sources	tr:	Government transfers
Mn:	Imports from non-UEMOA sources		
D^s:	Supply of domestic good		
D^d:	Demand for domestic good		
Q^s:	Supply of composite good		
Q^d:	Demand for composite good		
T:	Tax revenue		
Sg:	Government savings		
Sp:	Private savings		
Zg:	Government investment, factor costs		
Zp:	Private investment, at factor costs		
X:	Aggregate output, at factor costs		
Y:	Total income		
C:	Private consumption, at factor costs		

Current price flows

ft:	External transfers to government
re:	External remittances to private sector
B:	Net external borrowing

Prices and tax rates

pd:	Producer price of domestic good	Er:	Nominal exchange rate ($/CFAF)
pq:	Price of composite good	we:	World price of export good
px:	Price of aggregate output	te:	Export tax rate
Rx:	Real internal exchange rate for producers	wm:	World price of import good
		wmu:	World price of imports from UEMOA
Rq:	Real internal exchange rate for consumers	wmn:	World price of all other imports
		tm:	Tariff rate
		tmu:	Tariff rate on UEMOA imports
		tmn:	Tariff rate on all other imports
		ts:	Sales/excise/value added tax rate
		ty:	Direct tax rate

Main parameters

s:	Average savings rate for private sector
Ω:	Producer transformation elasticity
σ:	Consumer substitution elasticity
μ:	Trade diversion elasticity

Appendix C: Estimation of Elasticities

The production and the absorption functions are both based on constant elasticity of transformation (or substitution) functions:

$$X = \alpha[\delta_x \cdot E^\rho + (1 - \delta_x) \cdot D^\rho]^{1/\rho} \text{ where } \Omega = 1/(\rho - 1) \qquad (1.0)$$

$$Q = b[\delta_q \cdot M^{-\rho} + (1 - \delta_q) \cdot D^{-\rho}]^{-1/\rho} \text{ where } \sigma = 1/(1 - \rho) \qquad (2.0)$$

When subjected to a budget constraint, the maximizing first order conditions can be written as:

$$\frac{E}{D} = \left[\left(\frac{1 - \delta_x}{\delta_x} \right) \cdot \left(\frac{we \cdot Er/(1 + te)}{pd} \right) \right]^\Omega \text{ or} \qquad (1.1)$$

$$\frac{E}{D} = x \cdot Rx^\Omega \quad \text{where } x = \left(\frac{1 - \delta_x}{\delta_x} \right)^\sigma \text{ and } Rx = \frac{we \cdot Er/(1 + te)}{pd} \qquad (1.2)$$

$$\frac{D}{M} = \left[\left(\frac{1 - \delta_q}{\delta_q} \right) \cdot \left(\frac{wm \cdot Er \cdot (1 + tm)}{pd} \right) \right]^\sigma \text{ or} \qquad (2.1)$$

$$\frac{D}{M} = q \cdot Rq^\sigma \quad \text{where } q = \left(\frac{1 - \delta_q}{\delta_q} \right)^\sigma \text{ and } Rq = \frac{wm \cdot Er \cdot (1 + tm)}{pd} \qquad (2.2)$$

Equations 1.2 and 2.2 can be log-linearized into a form that is easily estimated:

$$\ln\left(\frac{E}{D} \right) = \ln(x) + \Omega \cdot \ln(Rx) \qquad (1.3)$$

$$\ln\left(\frac{D}{M} \right) = \ln(q) + \sigma \cdot \ln(Rq) \qquad (2.3)$$

If the data are not stationary in levels, these equations can also be first-differenced.

At the time this was written, there were only 12 years of data available and only for equation 2.3. Given the likely inaccuracies resulting from such a small data set, I did not check the data and error terms for stationarity, nor did I check for serial correlation or heteroskedasticity. The results are reported in the main body of the text.

Bibliography

Baldwin, R., and A. Venables. 1995. "Regional Economic Integration." In G. Grossman and K. Rogoff, eds., *Handbook of International Economics, Vol. III.* Oxford, U.K.: Elsevier.

Centre d'Etudes et de Formations aux Technologies Economiques. 1997. *Burkina Faso: Programme d'Appui Regional a l'Integration des Pays de l'UEMOA.* Paris: CEFTE.

Devarajan, S., D. Go, J. Lewis, S. Robinson, and P. Sinko. 1994. "Policy Lessons from a Simple Open-Economy Model." Policy Research Working Paper 1375. World Bank, Policy Research Department, Washington D.C.

Devarajan, S., D. Go, S. Suthiwart-Narueput, and J. Voss. 1997. "Direct and Indirect Fiscal Effects of the Euro-Mediterranean Free Trade Agreements." World Bank, Policy Research Department, Washington D.C. Unpublished.

Goldstein, M., and M. Khan. 1984. *"Income and Price Effects in Foreign Trade."* In R. Jones and P. Kenen, *Handbook of International Economics, Vol. I.* Oxford, U.K.: Elsevier.

Laird, S., and A. Yeats. 1990. *Two Sources of Bias in Standard Partial Equilibrium Trade Models.* Working Paper Series 374. World Bank, International Economics Department, Washington D.C.

Decentralization in Russian Regional Budgets and Its Impact on Economic Performance

Lev Freinkman and Plamen Yossifov

Abstract

Fiscal decentralization in Russia has been an important dimension of reforms since 1992. The issue has received a lot of attention in academic literature and applied economic research (Lavrov 1995; Le Houerou 1995; McLure, Wallich, and Litvack 1995; Treisman 1998; Wallich 1994). As a rule, these studies have focused on three aspects of evolving Russian federalism: delegation of specific revenue and expenditure assignments to regional governments, relationships between federal and regional budgets through various types of explicit and implicit transfers, and cross-regional budget equalization. The main goal of this article is to look at one more aspect of the decentralization process, which relates to intergovernment fiscal relations within regions. The article focuses on two elements of such a process. We review both channels of fiscal allocation within regions—tax-sharing and local transfer schemes. The second element relates to the potential impact of various decentralization patterns on regional economic performance, such as economic growth and budget deficit. We use subnational fiscal data from the 89 regions of the Russian Federation for the period 1992–97 to analyze the dynamics of the decentralization process and provide regression analysis of the links between regional decentralization and economic performance.

We are grateful to Daniel Treisman for fruitful discussions of various aspects of the analysis presented here and to Alexei M. Lavrov for sharing with us the database on Russian regional budget. Comments by Martha de Melo were also quite helpful.

The next section presents an analytical framework used for developing a statistical model. In the second section, "Fiscal Decentralization in the Russian Federation, 1992–97," we suggest simple indicators of fiscal decentralization and subordination at the regional level and review the dynamics of their values during the period 1992–97. We also consider overall trends in allocation of fiscal resources within regional fiscal systems, primarily between regional and municipal levels of government. The next section, "Data," provides a brief description of the data. In the next section, "Regression Analysis," we explore the relationships between regional economic performance and fiscal decentralization using panel-data regression analysis. The last section discusses the main conclusions.

Analytical Framework

Political and fiscal decentralization has recently become a global trend that is widely considered supportive of economic growth and efficiency improvements in the provision of public services (Bahl and Linn 1992). These gains could derive from informational advantages of local governments, which are better positioned to reflect recipients' preferences in the process of service delivery, and also from competition between local governments (Oates 1972).[1] The political dimension of decentralization is also viewed positively because it facilitates the establishment and strengthening of democratic institutions (Inman and Rubinfeld 1997).

By conventional measures, fiscal decentralization in Russia has been evolving quite successfully in the 1990s. Consolidated regional budgets are now responsible for more than one-half of total budget spending, whereas their share amounted to about 15 percent in the late 1980s (Freinkman and Haney 1997). Given the relatively large size of most Russian regions, however, it is not clear that the devolution of functions from the center to regions is sufficient to enjoy all decentralization gains mentioned above. If most resources and functions are concentrated within regional governments and not delegated to the local level, there is a risk that the single centralized state would be replaced by numerous centralized entities of a smaller size that could neither exploit informational advantages nor be seriously influenced by competitive

---

1. Zhang and Zou (1997b) provide a general model for analyzing the impact of intergovernment and intersectoral allocation of budget expenditures on economic growth.

pressures. In the latter case, another stage of the decentralization process would be required to force regions to share more resources with local governments.

In reality, the Russian environment for decentralization is characterized by wide opportunities for regions to decide almost unilaterally on specific settings for power- and budget-sharing with municipalities. Federal legislation for fiscal decentralization at the regional level is weak, and regional authorities have full discretion to determine a desirable degree of centralization and redistribution of fiscal flows and can also make frequent changes in the rules of the game (Freinkman, Treisman, and Titov 1999). Analysis of various aspects of economic policy conducted by Russian regional governments suggests high cross-regional variation in both selected strategies and outcomes of economic development (Lavrov 1996a), as well as in regional governance regimes used (Mitchneck 1997). In such an environment, it seems likely to expect a substantial cross-regional variation in actual decentralization patterns. Regions may experiment with more or less centralized schemes depending on their political preferences, specifics of economic structure, and social and geographical features. Given the above predictions of the theory of fiscal federalism, one may expect that the actual degree of regional decentralization would matter: more decentralized regions, all other factors being equal, would demonstrate stronger economic growth (less decline).

Thus, recent Russian developments provide interesting statistical material—a relatively large sample of similar government entities that have been pursuing different decentralization policies—to be tested against some conventional theoretical principles. Traditionally, the impact of decentralization on economic performance has been studied based on cross-country regressions, which have their own limitations related to high heterogeneity of the sample. Decentralization is a complex multidimensional process, and its impact on economic performance is difficult to isolate from influences of various cultural, political, and historical factors. In this respect, the sample of Russian regions is much more homogeneous because, notwithstanding all existing cross-regional variation, all Russian regions have strong common roots in the modern history of the Russian or Soviet state. This common cultural and political background may provide more chances for identification and accurate statistical measuring of links and correlations in the sample.

There are also some country-specific arguments in support of a possible positive link between regional decentralization and regional growth in Russia. Recent experience of the most advanced countries in transition demonstrated that economic recovery and growth are primarily concentrated in the largest cities (urban municipalities), which derives from more favorable industrial structure and better access to infrastructure and human capital. In Russia, however, local governments in urban areas with growth potential face economic disincentives caused by excessive and discretionary centralization of fiscal gains that such growth may bring. Under current fiscal arrangements, the rules of tax sharing between local and regional governments are negotiated annually or sometimes several times a year. The shares tend to be differentiated sharply across municipalities, with a few of the largest industrial centers often contributing large shares of main taxes, while rural *rayons* (rural area administrations) keep 100 percent and also receive most of the regional budget transfers. The shares vary not just between urban and rural districts within the same region, but also between urban districts in different regions. Furthermore, research suggests that urban municipalities are punished for better revenue performance by having their tax shares lowered. One study of the budgets of 35 large cities from Russia's 29 regions in the years 1992–97 found that, for every ruble local budgets' own revenues increased in a given year, about 90 kopecks were taxed away by reductions in the transfers and tax shares that the superior regional government allowed (Zhuravskaya 1998).

Thus, any increase in the effectiveness of tax collection or any increase in local revenues caused by growth-promoting policies would leave the local government almost no better off than before. Analysis of the trends in tax-sharing rates for *rayon* (city districts and rural area administrations) budgets in Yaroslavl Oblast in 1994–98 also suggests that urban municipalities are the most affected by the existing system (Freinkman, Treisman, and Titov 1999).[2] As in most other Russian regions, all 12 rural *rayons* are recipients of transfers within the regional budget system and always have been receiving maximum possible tax shares. In contrast, all urban *rayons* are facing a gradual decline in their tax share. The rate of this decline is not monotonic, influenced by bargaining power of specific municipal leaders, and hardly could be predicted in advance by municipal authorities.

Overall, these and other examples suggest that, when decentralization of Russian regional budgets happens, large cities are its main beneficiaries. Decentralization brings them more resources and more incentives to use them more efficiently. Although we believe that in Russia, as in other countries in transition, an average rate of return of

---

2. The term *oblast* designates a region with no significant non-Russian ethnic groups.

budget spending is much higher in main urban centers, decentralization may support growth through simple reallocation of resources from less to more efficient users.[3]

There is also a growing stream of research that explores links between fiscal incentives of subnational governments and economic growth (Jin, Qian, and Weingast 1999; Blanchard and Shleifer 2000). Specifically, Jin, Qian, and Weingast (1999) found that stronger fiscal incentives of subnational governments in China, measured in terms of a higher marginal revenue retention rate, are positively correlated with regional indicators of private sector development and enterprise restructuring. In turn, Blanchard and Shleifer (2000) suggest that, in contrast to China, Russian subnational governments do not have sufficient fiscal incentives to conduct policies in support of private sector–driven growth. This article attempts to expand further this line of analysis. It argues that, while fiscal arrangements between the center and regions are important, the major incentive problem of Russian fiscal federalism derives from distorted fiscal relations within regional systems, that is, from arrangements between regional and municipal governments.

Several studies of the relation between decentralization and growth in developing countries found, contrary to theoretical predictions, a negative correlation between these two variables. These results hold for three different cases: a cross-country model estimated for 46 developing countries (Davoodi and Zou 1998), a cross-country model for developed and developing countries (Fukasaku and de Melo 1998), and a cross-provincial model for a specific country, China (Zhang and Zou 1997a).[4] Several factors are named that could be responsible for this inconsistency between the theory and the outcome of statistical analysis. They include (a) the wrong composition of expenditures made by local governments, which may in part derive from that fact that local governments in many countries are not elected and thus not responsive

---

3. By the same reason, decentralization, by reducing redistribution, may lead to increases in fiscal inequality across local governments, especially between urban and rural municipalities.

4. However, for India the same authors (Zhang and Zou 1997b) found that most measures of decentralization are positively associated with the state's economic growth. In both cases, for China and India, they consider a two-level government model with the municipal level being excluded from analysis. Also, the study by Hunter and Shah (1998) provides indirect evidence of a positive link between decentralization and growth. They develop an index of good governance and show that the index is positively related to both decentralization and economic growth.

to local preferences; (b) limited local government autonomy in expenditure decisions because of excessive interventions of the central government—in other words, simple measures of fiscal decentralization based on a share of subnational governments in consolidated budget expenditures may overestimate actual degree of decentralization—and (c) the possibility that, in some countries (for example, China), programs of the central government could be more efficient because of nationwide externalities associated with large infrastructure projects and similar types of spending.

These results, however, are still far from conclusive. Specifically, Jin, Qian, and Weingast (1999) reexamined the effect of decentralization along the lines of Zhang and Zou (1997a), and obtained different results—a positive and significant effect of decentralization on regional growth. This drastic change in conclusions happened when an additional set of independent variables, reflecting economywide cyclical effects, was added to the model.

While traditionally decentralization and growth were seen as positively correlated, the impact of decentralization on fiscal performance was usually considered potentially more problematic (Wildasin 1998). Furthermore, Wildasin (1997) argues that the ultimate impact of the decentralization on fiscal performance is highly dependent on basic characteristics of the system of intergovernmental fiscal relations, such as transparency, accountability, and predictability. These worries that decentralization may contribute to fiscal imbalance and accumulation of public debt have recently become stronger (Tanzi 1996), in part as a reflection of the subnational debt crisis in Latin America (Dillinger and Webb 1999).

In a recent paper, de Melo (2000) argues that decentralization entails greater complexity in intergovernmental fiscal relations, raises the risk of coordination failures, and thus is likely to have fiscal costs. Evidence provided in their paper for a sample of 30 countries suggests that decentralization is positively correlated with the size of the subnational budget deficit, especially for developing countries. Another paper (Fornasari, Webb, and Zou 1998), which is also based on the cross-country analysis, shows that the size of the consolidated subnational government is positively correlated with the size of the central government's budget deficit.

From this perspective, it seems interesting to explore the impact of decentralization on fiscal performance within the sample of Russian regions. Changes in the degree of decentralization lead to substantive modifications in the institutional setting for budget management. Peculiar features of budget institutions are likely to bring about changes in fiscal performance (Alesina and others 1996). Thus, it seems plausible to expect some correlation between decentralization and, for example, the size of budget deficit. Following Wildasin's model, we would argue that, given the existing nontransparency and nonpredictability in budget relations between regional and municipal governments in Russia, more decentralized regions would have less fiscal discipline and higher budget deficits.[5]

Fiscal Decentralization in the Russian Federation, 1992–97

The process of fiscal decentralization in the Russian Federation takes two main forms (Freinkman, Treisman, and Titov 1999): (a) fiscal decentralization at the federal level—referring to the transfer of spending and revenue-raising responsibilities from federal to consolidated regional governments, and (b) fiscal decentralization at the regional level—encompassing the devolution of expenditure responsibilities and revenue assignments from regional to local governments. In this section we analyze the nature and scope of the latter aspect of fiscal decentralization in the Russian Federation. To evaluate the level of fiscal decentralization within Russia's regions, we constructed two simple measures, using data from the revenue and expenditure sides of consolidated regional budgets, respectively: ·

- The ratio between local governments' total revenues and the consolidated regional budget revenues
- The ratio between local governments' total expenditures net of transfers to regions and the consolidated regional budget expenditures

Local governments' total revenues and expenditures exclude horizontal transfers, whereas consolidated regional governments' total revenues and expenditures exclude vertical transfers within their

---

5. However, one may need to make a caveat: in Russia, individual local governments have less access to capital markets than regional ones because municipalities have less control over their revenue flow and thus are considered by creditors as more risky. So far, the bulk of subnational debt and deficit in Russia is concentrated at the regional level, which to a large extent reflects restricted opportunities of municipal governments to attract deficit financing. This could be a factor that would limit deficit and debt accumulation in decentralized regional systems.

jurisdictions. The measure of fiscal decentralization on the expenditure side of consolidated regional budgets is defined in such a manner as to provide information about the share of local governments in ultimate budget outlays (that is, purchases of goods and services from the rest of the economy, excluding interbudgetary flows). Our database does not provide data on regional transfers to the federal government, and as a consequence, this type of interbudgetary transfer is not netted out of the consolidated regional budget expenditures.

Furthermore, we explored the dependence of local governments on transfers from the regions with the help of the following measure of fiscal subordination:

- The ratio between regional transfers to local governments and local governments' total expenditures

Table 1 presents the values of the above measures of regional decentralization and subordination together with comparable data on the dynamics of these processes at the federal level. Between 1992 and 1994, the shares of consolidated regional governments in general government's total revenues and total ultimate expenditures increased from 43 percent and 25 percent to 64 percent and 47 percent, respectively. Since then, the evolution of fiscal decentralization at the federal level has been marked by a major effort of the federal authorities to close the persistent gap between the shares of consolidated regional governments in overall budget revenues and final expenditures. In the period from 1994 to 1996, this was achieved by a 10 percentage point reduction in the portion of general government's revenues allocated to subnational governments, which was not accompanied by a commensurate cutback in the relative size of their budget outlays. In 1997, the push for more equitable distribution of revenue-raising and spending responsibilities among government tiers took a different form—in the course of the year the increase in consolidated regional governments' share in the overall budget expenditures outpaced their share in general government revenue pool by a two-to-one margin. As a result, at the end of 1997 the share of consolidated regional governments in the general government budget revenues (61 percent) was more commensurate with their share in the ultimate budget expenditures (55 percent) than at the outset of reforms.

Between 1992 and 1997, the shares of local governments in consolidated regional governments' total revenues and total expenditures increased from 68 percent and 65 percent to 70 percent and 66 percent, respectively. Throughout this period, the gap between local govern-

TABLE 1. FISCAL DECENTRALIZATION AND SUBORDINATION
IN THE RUSSIAN FEDERATION, 1992–97
(percent)

Measures of fiscal decentralization and subordination	1992	1993	1994	1995	1996	1997
I. Fiscal decentralization and sub-ordination on federal level						
A. Ratio between consolidated regional budget revenues and consolidated general government's budget revenues	43		64	54	55	61
B. Ratio between consolidated regional budget expenditures net of transfers to the federal government and consolidated general government's budget expenditures	25		47	48	45	55
C. Ratio between federal transfers to regions and consolidated regional budget expenditures	7		19	12	15	14
II. Fiscal decentralization and sub-ordination on regional level[a]						
A. Ratio between local governments' total revenues and consolidated regional budget revenues	68		66	70	73	70
B. Ratio between local governments' total expenditures net of transfers to regions and consolidated regional budget expenditures	65		67	68	69	66
C. Ratio between regional transfers to local governments and local governments' total expenditures.	25		32	29	31	30

Note: Data for the Russian Federation is a weighted average of regional data. Local governments' total revenues and expenditures exclude horizontal transfers. Consolidated regional and general governments' total revenues and expenditures exclude vertical transfers within their jurisdictions.

a. Excluding St. Petersburg City and Moscow City, which have a dual status of "region-municipality."

Source: Ministry of Finance of the Russian Federation and authors' calculations.

ments' shares in consolidated regional budget revenues and outlays remained modest, at around 3–4 percentage points.

Between 1992 and 1994, the ratios between transfers from the higher levels of government and the total expenditures of consolidated regional and local governments rose from 7 percent and 25 percent to 19 percent and 32 percent, respectively. The degree of subordination of local governments has remained relatively constant ever since, whereas the dependence of consolidated regional budgets on federal grants has diminished.

Overall, the processes of fiscal decentralization and subordination were much more dynamic at the federal level, while the local governments passively absorbed a steady portion of the enlarged subnational budgets.

Data

The fiscal data used in this article initially came from a study by Lavrov (1996b), for which a special database on the structure of Russian regional budgets in the period 1992–95 was collected.[6] Dr. Alexei Lavrov gave us access to this database, which is derived from the standard reporting forms filed by regions with the federal ministry of finance. He also provided the additional budget data for 1996–97. The database contains consolidated budgets for each level of subnational governments for all 89 regions: regions, cities of regional status, *rayons*, cities of *rayon* status, and rural municipalities.

The data reflect the actual outcomes of annual budget execution (that is, it is not just agreed budget allocation). According to Russian budget accounting standards, the data include both cash and noncash components of the actual budget flows. That is, they include budget revenues and expenditures occurred, for example, through barter or cancellation of mutual debts. Furthermore, according to Russian budget accounting standards, subnational budgets are separated from and do not include results of financial operations of municipal companies (other than budget subsidies to these companies). For the purposes of our analysis, we consolidated the budgets of all types of local governments (that is, governments below the regional level), netting out horizontal transfers between them. Although budget mechanisms in different types of municipalities are quite different (especially between major cities and

---

6. Some results of this report were also presented in the paper by Kuznetsova, Lavrov, and David (1997).

rural *rayons* and municipalities), these differences are less important from a decentralization perspective compared to a fundamental contrast between municipalities in general and regional administrations.

The data on social, economic, geographic and administrative variables were taken from Goskomstat Rossii (1998). In our analysis, we used the physical volume of industrial production, expressed as a percentage of its value in the preceding year, as a proxy of economic growth in Russian regions. We used this variable, instead of more traditional measures of real economic outcomes, such as real per capita growth of regional GDP or annual income, because Goskomstat—the Russian Statistical Agency—does not report separate values of the latter for 10 autonomous okrugs and one autonomous oblast (Russian regions with a special administrative status).

The analysis presented below was conducted with data on 85 of the 89 regions of the Russian Federation over the period 1994–97. The regions removed from the sample are Chechnya, Ingushetia, Moscow City, and St. Petersburg City. The first two were dropped because of the poor quality or a lack of data on most of the variables. The special status of the last two as federal cities puts the issue of fiscal decentralization out of context. Figure 1 presents a biplot chart of the pooled data set. The values of all variables are standardized by subtracting the mean and dividing by the standard deviation of the pooled sample. The axes are the first two principal components (defined as linear combinations of all variables in the data set, the values of which capture best the variability of the original data). The individual points in the chart are the linear projections, in the two-dimensional space defined by the first two principal components, of the "region–time period" observations of the values of all variables from the original multidimensional data set.[7] The rays originating from the center of the graph are the linear projections of all variables from the original data set in the space defined by the first two principal components.[8]

A close inspection of figure 1 reveals one striking feature of Russian regional data with implications on the choice of econometric techniques used in the subsequent regression analysis: despite heterogeneous economic, social, political, and geographic characteristics of Russia's

---

7. That is to say, for each Russian region in each sample year. There are 340 individual points—85 regions observed over a period of four years.

8. The center of the graph represents the average values of the first two principal components in the pooled sample, which are both equal to zero because of the standardization of the original data.

FIGURE 1.   PRINCIPAL COMPONENTS BIPLOT
(pooled standardized observations, 1994–97)

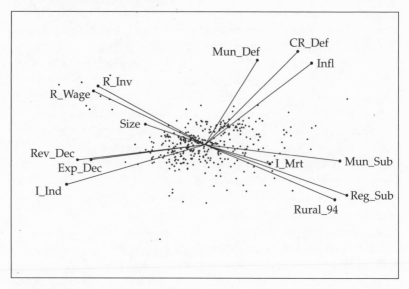

Note: The Principal Components and Biplot analysis was conducted with software developed by Ilya Lipkovich, Ph.D. student in Statistics at Virginia Polytechnic Institute and State University.

Source: Goskomstat Rossii 1998, Russian Federation Ministry of Finance, and authors' calculations.

Variables Set

CR_Def: Consolidated regional budget balance (negative sign indicates a deficit) as a percentage of the consolidated regional budget expenditures (%)

Exp_Dec: The ratio between local governments' total expenditures net of transfers to regions and the consolidated regional budget expenditures (%)

I_Ind: Index of physical volume of industrial production as a percentage of its value in the preceding year

I_Mrt: Infant mortality (number of babies per 1,000 live births who died before reaching the age of one)

Infl: Annual rate of inflation (%)

Mun_Def: Local governments' budget balance (negative sign indicates a deficit) as a percentage of local governments' total expenditures (%)

Mun_Sub: Regional transfers to local governments as a percentage of local governments' total expenditures (%)

R_Inv: Real per capita fixed investment in industry (1991 rubles)

R_Wage: Real monthly wage (1991 rubles)

Reg_Sub: Federal transfers to regions as a percentage of total regional expenditures (%)

Rev_Dec: The ratio between local governments' total revenues and the consolidated regional budget revenues (%)

Rural_94: Share of rural population in 1994 (%)

Size: Territory of region as a percentage of the total territory of the Russian Federation (%)

regions, the standardized values of the variables under examination are surprisingly homogeneous, with no apparent clusters of observations on different regions.[9] This argues against the use of fixed-effect panel-data models and in favor of a more parsimonious model with a common constant term for all regions. Furthermore, figure 5-1 demonstrates that the measures of fiscal decentralization on the revenue and expenditure sides of consolidated regional budgets are highly correlated. A separate analysis of their effects on economic outcomes is therefore not necessary. In our regression analysis, we used the measure of revenue decentralization as a proxy for the degree of fiscal decentralization within Russian regions.

In terms of the main theme of this article, the biplot chart suggests that fiscal decentralization is positively correlated with economic growth and negatively correlated with the fiscal balance of consolidated regional governments. These results are supported by conventional correlation analysis. The Pearson correlation coefficients (0.23 and –0.29, respectively) are both statistically significant at the 99 percent level of confidence. Furthermore, the partial correlation coefficients (0.29 and –0.51), obtained by controlling for region-specific "fixed effects," are also statistically significant at the 99 percent level of confidence.[10] The fact that the values of the partial correlation coefficients are higher in absolute terms than the values of the bivariate coefficients suggests the existence of interdependencies between the variables under consideration and other regional indicators that obscure the link between fiscal decentralization and economic outcomes. In this respect, the biplot chart singles

---

9. The following rules of thumb can be used in interpreting biplot charts (see Gabriel 1971). Data points located in close proximity have similar values for all variables. Data points bunched together away from the main cluster of points represent observations on regions with markedly different characteristics from that of the overall population. Variable rays representing uncorrelated variables are orthogonal. Variable rays of positively correlated variables span in the same direction—the smaller the inner angle between them, the higher the correlation between the values of the variables. Variable rays of negatively correlated variables span in opposite directions (with the inner angle between them greater than 90°)—the bigger the inner angle between them, the higher the correlation between the values of the variables.

10. The partial correlation coefficient is obtained by first transforming the observations over time for each region into differences from the respective regional mean over the period 1994–97. Then, the Pearson correlation coefficient is estimated with the pooled transformed data.

out the annual rate of inflation and the real monthly wage as potentially important control variables in the subsequent regression analysis.

Regression Analysis

Table 2 presents the results from the regression analysis of the link between fiscal decentralization and regional economic performance (real growth in industrial production and consolidated regional fiscal balance), controlling for a number of regional characteristics. The following variables have been used as control variables in the initial estimation of our regressions: administrative type of regions (republic, oblast and *krai*, or autonomous *okrug*), geographic location (regions divided into 11 zones, so-called economic regions), annual rate of inflation, real monthly wages, real level of investments per capita, territory of region as a percentage of the total territory of the Russian Federation, educational level of population, demographic characteristics (urbanization, infant mortality, life expectancy, and population density), and so forth. In the final specifications of the two regressions, we retained only those control variables with statistically significant OLS coefficients.

Because of the intrinsic endogeneity of some control variables—namely, the annual rate of inflation and real monthly wages—we estimated our regressions using two-stage least squares (TSLS).[11] OLS results are also reported for comparison purposes. As shown in Freinkman and Yossifov (1999), the measure of revenue decentralization can be broadly considered an exogenous variable, determined by the administrative types of regions, their geographic location, and poverty level at the start

---

11. In the first stage of the TSLS, we regress the annual rate of inflation and real monthly wages on the one-period lagged values of the annual rate of inflation, real monthly wages, federal transfers to regions as a percentage of total regional expenditures, the contemporaneous values of the measure of revenue decentralization, and the rate of infant mortality in 1990. In addition to this common set of exogenous variables, the first-stage regressions for the economic growth model include a common constant across regions and the one-period lagged values of the relative size of the consolidated regional budget balance, while those for the consolidated regional fiscal balance model include the one-period lagged values of the index of physical volume of industrial production. In the second stage of the TSLS, we use the predicted values of the annual rate of inflation and real monthly wages from the auxiliary regressions instead of their actual realizations together with the actual values of the exogenous variables (see Greene 1997, pp. 740–42).

TABLE 2. IMPACT OF DECENTRALIZATION ON REGIONAL
ECONOMIC PERFORMANCE

Regressors/Dependent variable	Physical volume of industrial production as a percentage of its value in the preceding year		Consolidated regional budget balance as a percentage of the consolidated regional budget expenditures	
	OLS	TSLS	OLS	TSLS
Constant	84.10 (4.63)	87.51 (4.98)	—	—
Local governments' total revenues as a percentage of the consolidated regional budget revenues	0.12 (0.06)	0.05 * (0.07)	–0.18 (0.02)	–0.15 (0.02)
Annual rate of inflation (%)	–0.05 (0.005)	–0.006 * (0.008)	0.05 (0.004)	0.05 (0.006)
Real average monthly wage (1991 rubles)	0.005 (0.001)	0.004 (0.001)	0.007 (0.002)	0.006 (0.003)
Dummy variables				
Republic	—	—	–3.76 (1.17)	–6.02 (1.27)
Autonomous Okrug	—	—	–9.41 (2.94)	–11.46 (3.74)
Northern Region	5.78 (1.81)	5.14 (1.84)	—	—
North Caucasus Region	—	—	4.51 (1.93)	3.54 (1.37)
Ural Region	—	—	3.02 (1.19)	3.85 (1.38)
Time period	*1994–97*	*1995–97*	*1994–97*	*1995–97*
Total panel observations	336	252	340	255
Adjusted R-squared	0.29	0.02	0.40	0.24
Durbin-Watson	2.29	1.96	1.91	1.96
White's heteroskedasticity test	43.40 (0.00)		40.15 (0.00)	

Note: Unless otherwise noted, regression coefficients are statistically significant at the 95 percent level of confidence.

Numbers in parentheses are White heteroskedasticity-consistent standard errors of regression coefficients.

— = not applicable.

* Statistically insignificant at the 90 percent level of confidence.

of the transition. As such, we used actual values of this decentralization variable in the second stage of the TSLS estimation. In both regressions, the White test statistic is significant at the 99 percent level of confidence, indicating the presence of general heteroskedasticity in regression residuals. Consequently, in table 2 we report the White heteroskedasticity-consistent standard errors of OLS coefficients.[12]

Fiscal Decentralization and Economic Growth

As seen from the second column of table 2, in the regression of the real growth of industrial production on select control variables and the measure of fiscal decentralization, the OLS coefficient of the latter is positive and statistically significant at the 95 percent confidence level.[13] This finding is in line with the results of the correlation and biplot analysis presented in the preceding section. When the regression is estimated with the more robust TSLS, however, the coefficient of the measure of fiscal decentralization drops by more than one half in value and becomes statistically insignificant. This suggests that the observed positive correlation between these two variables in bivariate setting is an artifact of a set of interactions between the endogenous variables in the data set. Thus, using Russian regional data, we found no evidence in support of either of the two rival hypotheses (respectively, of positive and negative relationships between fiscal decentralization at the regional level and economic growth).

We interpret this basic result as showing that the existing highly volatile decentralization environment does not provide Russian municipal governments with sufficiently strong incentives to facilitate economic growth. There is no strong evidence that Russian economic performance benefited from recent decentralization.

The fact that the coefficient of the annual rate of inflation and the adjusted R^2 of the regression drop tenfold when the latter is evaluated

---

12. The test statistics are computed using auxiliary regressions, in which the squared residuals from the regressions presented in table 2 are regressed on a constant, the explanatory variables from the original regressions and all possible (nonredundant) cross-products of the explanatory variables, with the exception of those involving dummy variables.

13. In this regression, Nenetz Autonomous Okrug was excluded from the panel, because its extremely low values on the level of fiscal decentralization and high real growth of industrial production single it out as an apparent outlier in the overall population.

by TSLS suggests that the strong negative association between inflation and real industrial output growth is driven entirely by exogenous shocks that have opposite effects on the two variables. The removal of the effect of these exogenous variables on the annual rate of inflation in the first stage of the TSLS eliminates the interdependency.

Fiscal Decentralization and Consolidated Regional Fiscal Balance

In contrast with the economic growth regression, the coefficients in the regression of the consolidated regional fiscal balance on select control variables and the measure of fiscal decentralization remain substantively the same when evaluated with OLS and TSLS. Below, we describe only the regression results obtained with the more robust TSLS technique.

As evidenced in the last column in table 2, the consolidated regional fiscal balance is negatively associated with the level of fiscal decentralization. This suggests that overall fiscal control is weaker in more decentralized regions. A 10 percentage point difference in the ratio between local governments' total revenues and consolidated regional budget revenues in two otherwise identical regions results in a consolidated regional budget balance (measured as a percentage of total expenditures) that is 1.5 percentage points smaller (less positive or more negative) in the fiscally more decentralized region. The coefficient of the measure of fiscal decentralization is statistically significant at the 95 percent confidence level. The coefficients of the control variables provide further insights on the nature of fiscal behavior of municipal and regional governments in Russian regions.

The positive and statistically significant coefficients of the annual rate of inflation and the real monthly wages could be interpreted as being driven by the indirect seignorage collected by subnational governments in a high-inflation environment. Most of the subnational budget liabilities are not fully indexed for inflation, while the real revenues from personal income tax automatically rise as the growth in nominal wages moves household incomes into higher tax brackets. Thus persistently high inflation, in combination with infrequently indexed budget expenditures and rarely revised thresholds of personal income tax brackets, helps reduce the relative size of consolidated regional budget deficit.

Furthermore, the strongly negative coefficients of the dummy variables "autonomous okrug" and "republic" imply that regions of these administrative types are far less fiscally responsible than oblasts and *krais* with similar economic and decentralization characteristics. Finally, regions situated in the North Caucasus and Ural "economic regions" tend to enjoy more favorable fiscal positions.

We checked the robustness of all regression coefficients discussed above by evaluating their dependence on the particular set of cross-sectional units used in the panel-data analysis. To achieve this, we reestimated the regression with all possible subsamples of 84 out of 85 regions and plotted the resulting OLS coefficients and their 95 percent confidence intervals (results not shown here). If the full-sample estimates of regression coefficients hinge on the extreme realizations of the dependent or explanatory variables in a given region, the elimination of this outlier from the sample will have a profound impact on the magnitude or sign of the corresponding OLS coefficients. This test proves the robustness of the results presented above: in all subsamples, the above coefficients remained statistically significant at the 95 percent level of confidence and close to their full-sample estimates.

Conclusions

The analysis of the dynamics of the process of fiscal decentralization on federal and regional levels over the period 1992–97 suggests that, although quite substantial, the relative share of local governments in the Russian consolidated budget has not expanded since 1994, and local governments remain in control of about 40 percent of total budget expenditures. At the subnational level, however, the relative size of the local budgets increased at the expense of some compression in regional budgets.

The panel-data regression and correlation analysis provided robust and statistically significant estimates of the impact of decentralization on fiscal performance. In particular, controlling for various social and economic variables, we found that regions with more decentralized finances tend to experience larger budget deficits. This suggests that overall fiscal control is weaker in more decentralized regions. Instability and nontransparency of intergovernmental fiscal relations at the regional level in Russia do not provide subnational governments with sufficient incentives for responsible fiscal policy. Under existing fiscal arrangements, there is a risk that further decentralization could be accompanied by additional growth in public deficit and debt.

We did not find any significant impact of fiscal decentralization on regional industrial growth. In contrast to conventional predictions of the decentralization theory, on average Russian regions did not benefit much from decentralization. The existing highly volatile decentralization environment does not provide Russian municipal governments with sufficiently strong incentives to facilitate economic growth. Overall, Russia seems to incur fiscal costs of decentralization without enjoying its growth benefits.

Given the current impact of decentralization in Russia on economic performance, the federal government should be more decisive in protecting local self-governance and budget autonomy. It should develop and enforce some universal models of interactions between regional and municipal governments that would provide for more stability and predictability in formation of municipal budgets and expand minimum requirements on municipal shares in primary taxes. To address potential negative fiscal impacts of decentralization, the federal government has to impose stricter limits on the size of subnational governments' current budget deficit, as well as on the overall stock of their debts.

References

Alesina, Alberto, Ricardo Hausmann, Rudolf Hommes, and Ernesto Stein. 1996. "Budget Institutions and Fiscal Performance in Latin America." NBER Working Paper Series 5586, May. Boston, Mass.

Bahl, Roy B., and Johannes J. Linn. 1992. *Urban Public Finance in Developing Countries.* New York: Oxford University Press.

Bird, Richard M., Robert D. Ebel, and Christine I. Wallich. 1995. "Fiscal Decentralization: From Command to Market." In Richard M. Bird, Robert D. Ebel, and Christine I. Wallich, eds., *Decentralization of the Socialist State: Intergovernmental Finance in Transition Economies.* Washington, D.C.: World Bank.

Blanchard, Olivier, and Andrei Shleifer. 2000. "Federalism with and without Political Centralization: China versus Russia." NBER Working Paper Series No. 7616, March. Boston, Mass.

de Melo, Luiz R., Jr. 2000. "Fiscal Decentralization and Intergovernmental Fiscal Relations: A Cross-Country Analysis." *World Development* 28(2):365–80.

Davoodi, Hamid, and Heng-Fu Zou. 1998. "Fiscal Decentralization and Economic Growth." *Journal of Urban Economics* 43:244–57.

Dillinger, William, and Steven B. Webb. 1999. "Fiscal Management in Federal Democracies: Argentina and Brazil." Policy Research Working Paper 1818. World Bank, Washington, D.C.

Fornasari, Francesca, Steven B. Webb, and Heng-Fu Zou. 1998. "Decentralized Spending and Central Government Deficit: International Evidence." World Bank, Development Economics Department, Washington, D.C. September 23.

Freinkman, Lev, and Michael Haney. 1997. "What Affects the Propensity to Subsidize: Determinants of Budget Subsidies and Transfers Financed by the Russian Regional Governments in 1992–1995?" Policy Research Working Paper 1818, World Bank, Washington, D.C.

Freinkman, Lev, and Stepan Titov. 1994. "Decentralization of the Russian Fiscal System: The Case of Yaroslavl." World Bank Discussion Paper IDP-143, Washington, D.C.

Freinkman, Lev, Daniel Treisman, and Stepan Titov. 1999. "Subnational Budgeting in Russia: Preempting a Potential Debt Crisis." World Bank Technical Paper 452. Washington, D.C.

Freinkman, Lev, and Plamen Yossifov. 1999. "Decentralization in Regional Fiscal Systems in Russia: Trends and Links to Economic Performance." Policy Research Working Paper 2100. World Bank, Washington, D.C.

Fukasaku, Kiichiro, and Luis R. de Melo, Jr. 1998. "Fiscal Decentralization and Macroeconomic Stability: The Experience of Large Developing and Transition Economies." In K. Fukasaku and R. Hausmann, eds., *Democracy, Decentralization and Deficit in Latin America*. Paris: IDB-OECD.

Gabriel, K. R. 1971. "The Biplot Graphical Display of Matrices with Application to Principal Component Analysis." *Biometrika* 58(3):453–67.

Goskomstat Rossii. 1998. *Regiony Rossii (Regions of Russia), Vol. 2*. Moscow: Goskomstat Rossii.

Greene, William H. 1997. *Econometric Analysis*. Third Edition. New York: Prentice-Hall.

Hunter, Jeff, and Anwar Shah. 1998. "Applying a Simple Measure of Good Governance to the Debate of Fiscal Decentralization." Policy Research Working Paper 1894, World Bank, Washington, D.C.

Inman, Robert P., and Daniel L. Rubinfeld. 1997. "Rethinking Federalism." *Journal of Economic Perspective* 11(4):43–64.

Jin, Hehui, Yingyi Qian, and Barry R.Weingast. 1999. "Regional Decentralization and Fiscal Incentives: Federalism, Chinese Style." Manuscript, March.

Kuznetsova O., Lavrov A., and Y. David. 1997. "Interbudgetary Relations in Subjects of the Russian Federation." In *Budgetnoye Ustroistvo v Rossiskoi Federatsii*. Moscow: Moskovskii Pbshetsvenyi Nauchnyi Fond.

Lavrov, Aleksei. 1995. *Problemy Stanovleniya i Razvitiya Byudzhetnogo Federalizma v Rossii*. Analytical Department of the Presidential Administration. Moscow, September.

Lavrov, Aleksei (ed.). 1996a. *Economic Policies of Subjects of the Russian Federation* Report prepared for World Bank, November.

——— (ed.). 1996b. *Budget System of Subjects of the Russian Federation*. Report prepared for World Bank, November.

Le Houerou, Philippe. 1995. *Fiscal Management in the Russian Federation*. World Bank Report 14862-RU, Washington, D.C.

McLure, Charles, Christine Wallich, and Jennie Litvack. 1995. "Special Issues in Russian Federal Finance: Ethnic Separatism and Natural Resources." In Richard M. Bird, Robert D. Ebel, and Christine I. Wallich, eds., *Decentralization of the Socialist State: Intergovernmental Finance in Transition Economies*. Washington, D.C.: World Bank.

Mitchneck, Beth. 1997. "Regional Governance in Russia: The Role of Accumulated Alliances." Discussion Paper 97-4. University of Arizona, Department of Geography. Tucson.

Oates, Wallace. 1972. *Fiscal Federalism*. New York: Harcourt Brace Jovanovich.

Savin, N. E., and K. J. White. 1977. "The Durbin-Watson Test for Serial Correlation with Extreme Sample Sizes of Many Regressors." *Econometrica* 45(8):1992–95.

Tanzi, Vito. 1996. "Fiscal Federalism and Decentralization: A Review of Some Efficiency and Macroeconomic Aspects." *Annual World Bank Conference on Development Economics, 1995*. Washington, D.C.: World Bank.

Treisman, Daniel. 1998. Deciphering Russia's Federal Finance: Transfers to the Regions in 1995–6. *Europe-Asia Studies* 50(5):893–906.

Wallich, Christine.1994. *Russia and the Challenge of Fiscal Federalism*. Washington, D.C.: World Bank.

Wildasin, David E. 1997. "Externalities and Bailouts: Hard and Soft Budget Constraints in Intergovernmental Fiscal Relations." Policy Research Working Paper 1843. World Bank, Washington, D.C.

———. 1998. "Fiscal Aspects of Evolving Federations." Policy Research Working Paper 1884. World Bank, Washington, D.C.

Zhang, Tao, and Heng-Fu Zou. 1997a. "Fiscal Decentralization, Public Spending, and Economic Growth in China." *Journal of Public Economics* 67(February):221–40.

———. 1997b. "The Growth Impact of Intersectoral and Intergovernmental Allocation of Public Expenditures: With Applications to China and India." World Bank, Development Research Group, Washington, D.C. December.

Zhuravskaya, Ekaterina V. 1998. "Incentives to Provide Local Public Goods: Fiscal Federalism Russian Style." Harvard University, Department of Economics, Cambridge, Mass.

Part III

Understanding and Managing Unemployment

Self-Employment and Labor Turnover in Developing Countries: Cross-Country Evidence

William F. Maloney

Abstract

This article argues that neither the share of the workforce in self-employment nor the labor turnover rate are useful measures of labor market distortion or rigidity unless adjusted for country-specific economic and demographic variables. A growth model that incorporates efficiency wage effects and offers an alternative to traditional models of informal self-employment is developed and is used to generate predictions about the determinants of both measures. These predictions are supported by cross-country data from Latin America and the Caribbean (LAC) and the Organisation for Economic Co-operation and Development (OECD) countries. Though somewhat speculative, the data further suggest that Latin American labor markets may be neither especially rigid nor distorted.

This article develops and tests an integrated approach to understanding two outstanding questions central to the analysis of labor markets in developing countries and the impact of labor legislation. Though the article focuses primarily on Latin America, the issues and analysis are germane both to other developing countries and to industrial countries.

My thanks to Wendy Cunningham, Norman Hicks, Tom Krebs, Guillermo Perry, and Martín Rama for helpful comments. Special thanks to Kihoon Lee for able research assistance.

The first issue is the role of the large informal sector in the region (see table 1). A traditional view argues that the sector testifies to government or union-induced rigidities that force formal remuneration above market clearing and that ration workers into informality.[1] This article argues that this view is probably incorrect and that it is difficult to draw any conclusions about labor market efficiency from sector size alone.

The second question centers on what recent findings of high turnover, a common measure of rigidities (see, for example, Nickell 1997), imply about the flexibility of labor markets in the region.[2] It is often asserted that high firing costs and excessive benefits in the formal sector prevent the efficient allocation of workers among jobs.[3] However, as table 1 suggests, average tenure is shorter, and a larger fraction of the workforce has been employed in their current position for less than two years in Latin America than in the Organisation for Economic Co-operation and Development (OECD). This article argues that this probably cannot be interpreted a priori as evidence of greater flexibility.

The first section, "Motivation and Theoretical Overview," heuristically develops a model that moves beyond the standard segmentation-based view of the relationship of formal and informal sectors, and incorporates the increasing evidence that a large fraction of the employment in the informal sector is voluntary. It is developed in an efficiency wage context both because recent evidence suggests that much observed segmentation may arise endogenously rather than being imposed by labor unions or minimum wages, and because it permits explicit modeling of the determinants of turnover. Predictions can be made about how the size of the self-employed sector, the degree of segmentation in the market, and turnover should move with the development process and policy innovations.

The next section, "Cross-Sectional Regressions," examines cross-country data from Asia, Europe, and Latin America with three objectives. The first two are straightforward: to test the predictions of the model about the size of the informal sector and rates of turnover with respect to several key labor market, productivity, and demographic variables suggested by the theoretical framework; and to suggest the

---

1. See Harris and Todaro (1970) for an early presentation of this view.

2. See Maloney (1999) for Mexico; Gonzaga (1996) for Brazil; Anderson Shaffner (1997) for Colombia; and Márquez and Pagés (1998) more generally.

3. See for example Burki and Perry (1997).

TABLE 1. SIZE OF INFORMAL SELF-EMPLOYMENT AND TURNOVER RATES

Measure	LAC	OECD
% workforce in informal self-employment	31.5	12.9
% < 2 years' seniority (manufactures)	38.1	24.5
Average tenure (manufactures)	7.61	10.5

direction of possible influence of variables that are theoretically ambiguous. Somewhat speculatively, however, the article also attempts to provide more informed estimates of the incidence of immeasurable distortions that ration more workers into the informal sector, or rigidities that decrease turnover. Since our theoretical framework abstracts from such exogenous phenomena, we tentatively measure their impact by the deviations from the model's predicted values. Although it is trivial to raise objections to this approach on either theoretical or empirical grounds, the results at once strongly coincide with the stylized facts about industrial countries, and challenge what is commonly thought about Latin America: with some predictable exceptions, regional labor markets do not appear unusually distorted or inflexible.

Motivation and Theoretical Overview

The empirical work here is motivated by a macroeconomic model based on microbehavior of workers described in detail in Krebs and Maloney (1998). It is built in a growth context so that secular movements in labor productivity can be incorporated, and it makes predictions about movements in formal and informal sector employment, the degree of market segmentation, and labor turnover rates across the course of the development process. It also attempts to incorporate two emerging stylized facts about labor markets in developing countries.

1. *The informal sector is extremely heterogeneous and contains both voluntary and involuntary members.* The informal sector is frequently considered the disadvantaged sector of a labor market segmented by government or union intervention in the formal sector wage-setting process.[4] During downturns, the sector is thought to expand as it absorbs displaced workers and then to contract again with recovery.

---

4. See the classic statement of this view in Harris and Todaro (1970).

While some fraction of the sector corresponds to this view, recent studies have found that many of the informal self-employed are voluntarily so and should probably be viewed as unregulated entrepreneurs. Comparisons of formal and informal wage differentials traditionally used to show segmentation are unreliable, and there appears to be a high degree of mobility among sectors.[5] The Mexican microenterprise survey suggests that 70 percent of workers enter the sector voluntarily for reasons of independence or higher income, and recent time-series data from Chile and Mexico suggest that both the size of and transitions into the self-employed sector behave procyclically.[6] There is increasing evidence both in the sociology and economics literature that suggests a life cycle view of the trajectory between formal and informal self-employment: in the absence of well-functioning credit markets and effective education systems, workers may take formal sector jobs to accumulate human and financial capital and then quit to open their own businesses.[7] In sum, ample evidence suggests that informal self-employment is a desirable destination for many workers who voluntarily leave formal employment.

2. *In the absence of government or union-induced rigidities, there is still strong evidence of "segmentation."* Recent work on Mexico has challenged the customary view of the sources of labor market segmentation. Minimum wages are not binding (see Bell 1997), and the evidence suggests that union power is directed largely to the maintenance of employment and suggests no significant effect on wages.[8] As Márquez and

---

5. In the absence of any distortions, we should find a wedge between formal and informal incomes that incorporates the value of benefits forgone, the value of taxes evaded, the value of lifestyle differences between wage and self-employment, capital costs, implicit training costs, and payments in kind. Without this information, wage comparisons tell us nothing about segmentation or relative welfare between sectors. See MacIsaac and Rama (1997) and Maloney (1999).

6. See Fiess, Maloney, and Shankar (2000); Maloney (1997); and Marquez and Pagés (1998).

7. Aroca and Maloney (1998) model the transitions into informality as a destination of entrepreneurs and find evidence using logit techniques adapted to panel logit context.

8. See Maloney and Ribeiro (1998). As Maloney (2000) finds, Latin America generally has fairly low minimum wages and, for countries like Honduras with very high legislated minimum wages, they appear not to be enforced. Gindling and Terrell (1995) find similar nonenforcement in Costa Rica.

Ros (1990), noted, and as has been confirmed by later studies for Peru (Schaffner 1998) and Guatemala (Funkhouser 1998), wages of similar workers rise with firm size, much as they do in industrial countries. Further, Márquez (1990), and Abuhadba and Romaguera (1993) find evidence consistent with efficiency wage effects in the high correlation of wage differentials among Brazil, Chile, the United States, and the República Bolivariana de Venezuela. This evidence suggests that the conditional wage dispersion (wages adjusted for human capital) may be emerging endogenously and is not caused by either government or union intervention.

Both stylized facts suggest an interpretation of the interaction of formal and informal markets rooted in the extensive literature on efficiency wages where firms *voluntarily* pay wages above the market clearing level.[9] One common variant of these models arises from the difficulty of monitoring individual workers and the lack of any penalty from being caught "shirking"—any activity, or lack thereof, that might be detrimental to the firm. If wages are at market clearing, a worker fired for shirking can simply get another job at the same wage. If all firms pay higher than market clearing wages, however, unemployment will be created in the economy that creates a disincentive to being laid off, and hence a disincentive to shirking.

Since in many Latin American countries workers can be fired only with difficulty, the "turnover" variant of efficiency wage models seems more appropriate: firms make an investment in workers when they are hired, perhaps in training or recruitment, that will be lost if the worker leaves.[10] Hence, it is worthwhile for firms to pay higher wages and raise the opportunity cost of leaving to other firms or jobs. This argument may be particularly compelling in developing countries, given the life cycle model of self-employment suggested above. *In an inversion of the commonly held view that higher-than-market clearing wages create informality, it may be that the attractiveness of self-employment causes firms to pay above-market clearing wages.* This, in fact, does create a subset of the informal sector that is involuntarily self-employed and that is unable to easily move back into the formal sector. Thus, the potentially self-

---

9. For discussions of the theory of efficiency wages, see Stiglitz (1974) and Krueger and Summers (1988).

10. In 1990, only the Bahamas, Chile, and Jamaica permitted firing for economic reasons and El Salvador and Guatemala somewhat. In 1995, Argentina (temporarily) and Peru joined. See Burki and Perry (1997), pp. 40–41.

employed, aware of the high rates of failure of small businesses, will think twice about leaving formal employment if the probability of being rehired is reduced.[11]

The efficiency wage approach has the advantage of dealing explicitly with the issue of turnover, the second of our central issues to be examined. However, it also complicates our view of the informal sector and what its existence reveals about inequality, poverty, or labor market distortions. A large fraction of workers may treat the sector as a very desirable destination either to attempt to run a business, or as a place where workers quitting an undesirable formal sector job may search for another. For these entrepreneurs, the traditional conflation of informality with disadvantage or relative poverty is inappropriate. It is also clear, however, that some fraction is trapped there involuntarily— that is the expected by-product of efficiency wages.

This approach is useful for understanding labor markets in LAC. First, for many countries in the region, the nonbinding minimum wages and curbed power of labor unions are unconvincing as the principal sources of segmentation.[12] Second, efficiency wage phenomena are likely to exist as an important underlying determinant of wage structure, however overlaid by other local institutions, and they have long-term implications for labor, education, and poverty-alleviation policies. Third, careful modeling of these effects aids in identifying abnormalities in informal sector size or turnover that may be interpretable as more reliable evidence of distortions that are not explicitly introduced through the model.

Though the model is general equilibrium in design, the intuition can be distilled to two equations. These can be broadly represented as an upward-sloping "incentive curve," and as a downward-sloping labor demand curve, as shown in figure 1. The curves are plotted with the probability of being hired in the formal sector (P) on the x-axis and formal wages *relative to the average in the self-employed sector* (W) on the y-axis. The incentive curve II captures the essence of the efficiency wage story.

---

11. For the worker's decision to enter self-employment, we have in mind a model something like the "noisy selection" model of Jovanovic (1982). Here, workers have only a very diffuse idea of their ability as entrepreneurs and whether they will be able to stay in business. Only by actually opening a business can they learn about their true underlying abilities. The ability to be rehired is therefore an important consideration in risking self-employment.

12. See Maloney (2000). For Argentina, Bolivia, Brazil, Chile, Mexico, Peru, and Uruguay, the ratio of the minimum wage to mean wages is very low by OECD standards, and kernel density plots suggest that they are not binding.

Figure 1. Equilibrium in the Formal Sector

Normal wage

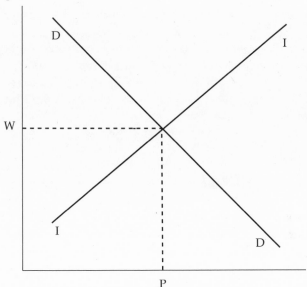

P

Probability of being hired

It represents the constraint that firms face in trying to prevent workers from leaving with their training and opening a business in the informal sector. The higher the probability that a worker will be rehired in the formal sector if the business turns out to be less successful than expected, the greater the likelihood that he will quit his current formal sector job, and hence the higher the formal sector wage must be to persuade him not to try his luck. Although it is not a traditional labor supply curve, it incorporates the usual depressing effects on labor supply to the formal sector of increased attractiveness of the informal sector, or a rise in taxation of formal sector wages. The second curve DD is similar to the traditional labor demand curve. It can be argued that, as wages rise, formal firms hire fewer workers, and the probability of being hired falls.

More formally, we can write these equations as

(1)   II: $W = I(P, \tau, h)$ DD: $W = D(P, Z, \tau, h)$

where the position and slopes of the II and DD curves may be affected, as discussed below, by increases in labor productivity or firm profitability (Z), a rise in the benefit to being self-employed (τ), and changes in hiring costs (h).

Comparative Statics

These two curves allow analysis of the impact of several important variables on the size of the informal sector (S) and rates of turnover (T). From equation (1), it can be shown that both these measures of turnover are functions of the policy interventions or economic innovations encompassed in Z, τ, and h:

(2) $S = s(Z, τ, h)$ $T = t(Z, τ, h)$

The impacts of these variables are analyzed in the next sections.

Increases in labor productivity or firm profitability (Z). This includes technological progress, a fall in labor taxes, or a reduction in any regulation that adversely affects productivity. Any of these changes has the effect of shifting the DD curve to the right along the II curve (figure 2). As productivity increases, firms are willing to hire more workers, and hence to increase the probability of being hired. The movement along the incentive curve implies that a higher wage *relative to that in the self-employment sector* must be paid to retain workers, but this also necessarily implies that a larger fraction of informal workers is involuntary and would experience welfare enhancements upon finding a job in the formal sector. The impact on turnover is ambiguous. Both wages and the probability of being hired rise over time with opposing effects on turnover, and it is not clear, ex ante, what the net effect should be. Although the implied shifts of curves are the same for the following cases, it is worth highlighting certain aspects:

- *Technological progress:* A secular rise in formal sector productivity caused by technological progress has the effect of raising both the level of employment in the formal sector and the wages paid there. The model has the prediction, then, that as countries grow, a larger and larger fraction of self-employment is involuntary, and segmentation increases among the sectors. The indeterminacy of turnover suggests that it is not obvious that developing countries should have higher or lower rates of turnover.
- *Regulations and taxes:* Any regulation that can be reinterpreted as a tax on firms—nonwage benefits, firing costs—or any economy-

Figure 2. Formal Sector Productivity Gain (Z)

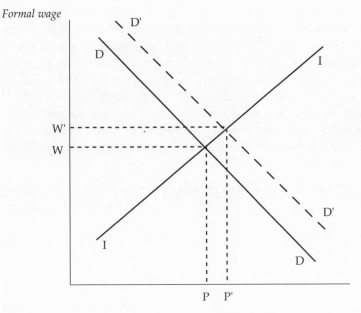

Probability of being hired

wide regulation that leads to lowering the marginal product of labor reduces the size of the formal sector and lowers the formal sector wage. It is important, however, to bear in mind that this effect is most compelling if workers do not value these benefits. To the degree that they do, this is simply payment in a different form.

This even applies in some measure to restrictions on firings, which can be seen as a tax equal to the option value of the ability to divest of an underperforming asset. To the degree that the worker sees these costs as an insurance premium against termination, they are passed along to workers as lower wages with no impact. It is easy, however, to generate scenarios where this might not be the case, and the net result is to reduce employment and turnover.[13]

_____

13. See Bentolila and Bertola (1990) for a discussion of the impact of firing costs and labor demand.

Rise in the benefit to being self-employed, or a reduction in worker taxes (τ).
Anything that raises the benefit of being self-employed relative to being formally employed increases the rate of turnover and causes a shift in both the incentive curve and the demand curve (figure 3). In the former, for any probability of being hired, the formal wage must rise to offset the increased desirability of the informal sector. In the latter, the increased cost of retaining workers also shifts the labor demand curve to the left. What is clear is that employment in the formal sector falls.[14] The impact on relative wages, however, is ambiguous since both curves shift left and this indeterminacy prevents any ex ante statement about turnover, despite the increased difficulty of finding a formal job. Examples may be:

- *Income or other taxes:* Any tax that finances a public good or whose benefits are perceived as below its cost in terms of taxation renders the informal sector more attractive.
- *Internal mobility restrictions:* Where internal reallocation in the formal firm is highly regulated, talented workers may choose to work on their own.

Changes in hiring costs (h). Any policy that serves to lower the fixed costs of hiring (for example, recruitment and training) reduces the loss involved with a quit and hence the magnitude of efficiency wage effects. Showing the effect graphically is difficult, since it involves both shifting and changing the slopes of both curves. What is clear, however, is that in the limit where training and recruitment costs fall to zero, there is no longer any need to pay efficiency wages, there is no segmentation, and formal sector employment rises. The impact on turnover is positive because there is no reason for firms to prevent identical work-

---

14. This coincides with existing literature on unemployment in the OECD countries that increasingly focuses on the level and duration of benefits as the key determinant of unemployment. Nickell (1997) finds the duration to be the key determinant of long-run unemployment levels while Blanchard and Jimeno (1995) attribute the relatively high Spanish unemployment to the fact that Spaniards get access to benefits of indefinite duration if employed only six months of the previous four years, while Portuguese workers must have been working one and a half of the previous two years. Benefits of indefinite duration are similar in principle to self-employment as an alternative to formal work. The absence of unemployment benefits in developing countries has the effect of collapsing both the self-employed and the unemployed into one sector.

FIGURE 3. RISE IN INFORMAL ATTRACTIVENESS (J)

Formal wage

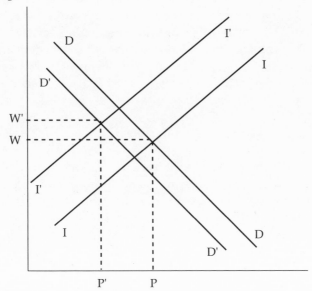

Probability of being hired

ers from leaving and to replace them with new workers. The cost of hiring may be lowered by the following:

- *Public education:* Public education has long been justified on the grounds that it addresses the externality implicit in the efficiency wage story. The private sector will underinvest because the basic skills they pay to impart can easily be transferred elsewhere. To the degree that poor education systems in developing countries force both training and socialization costs on individual firms, the wage gap between self-employed and formally salaried workers will be larger, segmentation greater, and a larger fraction of the self-employed involuntarily employed. This offers another channel through which improving education may equalize the distribution of income in the economy.
- *Reduced interest rates:* Reduced interest rates lower the cost of investment in human capital and thus lower hiring costs.
- *Better job matching and signaling:* If the recruitment and selection process constitutes a sizeable fixed cost, any improvement in

mechanisms that promotes good matching, or that reliably signals workers' skills, such as the education certification schemes
in Mexico, causes all the same desirable outcomes.

*   *Trade reforms:* To the degree to which other reforms, such as liber-
    alization of the current account, increase the demand for skilled
    labor and raise implicit training costs, segmentation and wage
    dispersion may increase. This may offer one explanation for the
    increasing wage dispersion observed with trade liberalization in
    Chile and Mexico.

Cross-Sectional Regressions

These hypotheses are then tested using a cross-section of countries for
which a consistent set of productivity and distortion variables are available. The first set of regressions examines the determinants of self-
employment as a share of the total workforce. The second set focuses
on two measures of turnover. Using deviations from the predicted values of these regressions it is possible to construct somewhat speculative
measures of the magnitude of distortions and of rigidities.

Variables

The data sources and more detailed descriptions are listed in appendix A. All correspond to 1995, unless otherwise stated in the appendix.

Dependent Variables

Share of workforce in self-employment. The OECD tabulates the share of
nonagricultural workers in self-employment or as owners of firms. To
the degree possible, the same variable was created from the employment and household surveys from Latin America. The focus is on self-
employment rather than informality more generally for two reasons.
First, it is the act of opening a business that is the central issue: informality, while important and often highly correlated, is secondary.[15] Second, data on informality in the OECD are largely unavailable, and the
data sets from Latin America and the Caribbean differ in the variables
available to use as proxies. Third, data on those employed in micro-
enterprises are not available for the OECD. We assume that the total

---

15. See Levenson and Maloney (1998) for a development of this view.

population employed in the self-employed sector, both as owners and workers, is proportional to the share declaring themselves self-employed.

Mean tenure in the manufacturing sector and share of the manufacturing workforce with under two years of tenure. These are two alternative variables available from the OECD and generated from the LAC household and labor market surveys. The focus is on manufacturing turnover because this is the best available proxy for formal sector turnover.

Formal Sector Labor Productivity and Profitability (Z)

Industrial value added (Indust. VA): The log of industrial value added per industrial worker is the proxy for formal sector labor productivity.

Social security tax—employers (SSEmp): These are social security (broadly defined) taxes as a share of the wage.

Employment protection (Protection): This is an index of employment protection constructed by Gustavo Márquez (1998) that captures both the difficulty of laying off workers and the cost in terms of severance pay. Unfortunately, this leads to roughly a halving of the available observations, so a separate set of regressions was run using this reduced sample.

Rise in the Benefits to Being Self-Employed, or a Reduction in Worker Taxes (τ)

Social security tax—workers (SSWorker). These are social security (broadly defined) taxes as a share of the wage by worker. The contributions by employers and workers are broken out for two reasons. First, the calculation of the employers' contributions is straightforward, but for workers the schedules are more involved and there is substantially more measurement error: in roughly 25 percent of the cases, the social security law dictates a progressive tax that varies greatly across the range of incomes. The midpoint of this range was chosen, but there is no way of knowing if, in fact, this represents the average tax on labor. Combining the components of the social security tax would unnecessarily bias downward the coefficient on the employers' contributions as well. Second, in the presence of wage rigidities, the incidence of the two components may differ: transferring part from the employer to the employee would reduce costs to the employer and the attractiveness of formal sector employment to the worker.

Ideally, we would have a measure of labor productivity in the self-employed sector. Unfortunately, this is not feasible as even in the OECD possible proxies, such as data on wages in the commerce or other services, are not consistent across countries. Social security tax incidence on workers, however, does capture an important element of the relative attractiveness of each sector.

Hiring Costs

Education (Education). This is the share of the relevant age group with secondary education. No cross-country direct measures of hiring costs are available. However, public education is a public good that addresses exactly the externality identified in the efficiency wage model. The more firms have to invest in training, the more they have to lose by workers moving to other firms or to self-employment. We interpret any effect of this variable as working through training costs.

Real interest rate (Real interest). The real interest rate affects the cost of training workers to raise future productivity as it would in the case of any other investment. We use the average of the 30- to 90-day borrowing rate deflated by changes in the CPI in most cases. Although this is not generally the rate at which larger corporations borrow, it is nonetheless a rough indicator of the cost of investing in workers in the economy.[16]

Other Variables

Duration of unemployment benefits (U benefits). Some share of the self-employed in Latin America would be found unemployed in the industrial countries where unemployment benefits exist and are often generous. Its exclusion as an alternative to self-employment may bias results. For OECD countries with traditional unemployment benefits, the variable takes the value of the duration of unemployment benefits that Nickell (1997) found to be the most important variable for explaining levels of unemployment. For Latin America and other countries,

---

16. Clearly, this may also capture deviations of output from full employment and hence cyclical movements in the residual component of the informal sector in the more dualistic view. From the point of view of using the residual to measure the incidence of labor codes, this is not necessarily bad, because we would like to abstract from cyclical movements in sector size.

the standard severance pay package was calculated, given the mean tenure (or predicted if unavailable).

Youth (Youth). The share of the working population between the ages of 16 and 20 is included as the only demographic variable. The model implicitly assumes homogeneous workforces across countries. This is clearly not true since the share of young workers is much higher in Latin America than in the OECD countries. This variable is most relevant to the turnover regressions where young workers traditionally have higher rates of turnover as they shop around for careers. It may also, however, have a similar interpretation in the self-employment regressions.

Latin America dummy (LA dummy). A dummy is included for countries in the Latin American region. In theory, the dummy may capture any difference between OECD economies and the region, including labor legislation.[17] Ideally, we would like to eliminate the significance of this variable by including the labor market variables for which it may be acting as proxy.

Results

The results must be interpreted with caution. First, the sample has at best 40 observations and, in the most restricted case, only 17. This, in some cases, can make the results sensitive to the countries included. Second, the data are not uniform. Most of the OECD variables were gleaned from presumably consistent publications of that organization, whereas the variables for Latin America were individually extracted from survey data that are not necessarily consistent. The Latin America dummy may pick up some of these data discrepancies.

Despite these potential pitfalls, the regressions prove surprisingly robust and consistent with the model. The three formerly socialist countries in the sample—the Czech Republic, Hungary, and Poland—have extraordinarily small self-employed sectors, given their income level, which affected the results. Since it seems likely that the repression of entrepreneurial freedom under communism is related to this result, these observations were dropped. The addition or subtraction of most of the other countries, however, might change the parameter values some, but the overall story remains the same.

---

17. We included a squared income term as well, but it was never significant. This does not, however, preclude more exotic nonlinear functions.

Self-employment results. The results are broadly consistent across the regressions. Column 1-a in table 2 presents the complete regression of self-employment on all variables, except the employment protection measure. As is clear, the employers' social security tax, the real interest rate, the level of education, and the share of young people enter significantly and of predicted sign. Progressive parsing out of the less significant variables in column 1-b makes the labor productivity and educational variables significant. In no case was the worker's share of social security remotely significant. Part of this poor performance may

TABLE 2. DETERMINANTS OF SELF-EMPLOYMENT

	Self-employed as share of workforce				
Variables	1-a	1-b	1-c	1-d	1-e
C	0.26	0.36	0.11	0.25	0.50
	(1.33)	(2.46)	(.36)	(1.46)	(3.29)
Indust. VA	–0.02	–0.03	0.00	–0.01	–0.05
	(1.26)	(2.24)	(.02)	(.25)	(3.19)
SSWorker	–0.09	–	0.02	–	–
	(.89)	–	(.14)	–	–
SSEmp	0.16	0.16	0.09	0.00	0.15
	(2.81)	(2.81)	(.95)	(3.69)	(1.63)
Protection	–	–	3.90E-03	4.50E-03	4.00E-03
	–	–	(2.58)	(3.69)	(2.93)
U benefits	4.00E-04	–	–1.20E-04	–	–
	(.72)	–	(.01)	–	–
Real interest	0.22	0.23	0.23	0.24	0.21
	(3.91)	(4.71)	(3.29)	(4.13)	(3.21)
Education	–1.00E-03	–1.00E-03	–1.50E-03	–1.60E-03	–
	(1.91)	(2.37)	(1.53)	(2.4)	–
Youth	3.86	4.14	1.79	–	–
	(2.33)	(2.8)	(.63)	–	–
LA dummy	0.04	–	0.02	–	–
	(1.14)	–	(.32)	–	–
NOBS	36	40	19	20	20
R^2	0.92	0.90	0.94	0.93	0.90

Note: t-statistics below coefficients. Indust. VA = industrial value added per worker; SSWorker = social security tax—workers; SSEmp = social security tax—employers; Protection = employment protection; U benefits = duration of unemployment benefits; Real interest = real interest rate; Education = percentage of relevant cohort completing secondary school; Youth = share of working population between ages of 16 and 20; LA dummy = dummy for Latin country; NOBS = number of observations.

be caused by measurement error discussed earlier. Similarly, the unemployment benefits variable is never significant, nor, in this case, is the LA dummy.

The significant variables enter the regressions with the signs predicted by theory. Most important in terms of magnitude is formal sector labor productivity. Taking the extreme values of this variable would account for 9.6 points of the variance in the share of self-employments detailed in the first column of table 3. Figure 4 suggests the same, but important, conclusion: a large self-employed sector is not ipso facto evidence of distortions, but it may reflect a lower opportunity cost of self-employment in poorer countries.

The relative youth of Latin America's population also explains much of the variance with the spread across the sample accounting for 8.8 percent of the higher share in self-employment. The education variable that measures the degree to which firms must bear the burden of financing overall education would account for roughly a 7.5 percentage point difference. Real interest rates are also surprisingly important. Peru's very high self-employed sector (46 percent) and high real interest rates (67 percent) clearly dominate the relationship, although even dropping this outlier yields a significant coefficient. The difference between real interest rates of under 5 percent in the OECD countries compared to those often above 30 percent in Latin America accounts for more than 6 percent. Once again, the importance of ensuring macroeconomic stability and reducing risk to bring down interest rates seems clear.

In general, these effects dwarf the impact of any of the three labor market variables. Across the range observed, social security taxes on employers explain relatively little of the size of the sector—3.2 percentage points in the share of self-employment.

The same exercise was repeated with the smaller sample arising from using the Márquez protection index, 1c–1e. With fewer observations, the apparent collinearity of the productivity variable and education variables makes identifying the "correct" parsimonious form difficult (1d–1e). In all cases, however, the employment protection index has the impact of increasing the size of the self-employed sector, although the magnitude is small: the difference between the highly protective Bolivia, Honduras, Mexico, Peru, or Spain compared to the unprotective United Kingdom or United States is worth only about 1.35 percentage points in the share of self-employment. The results are similar to those of Márquez (1998), who also found a positive impact of his protection index, as well as a negative sign on GDP per capita, which may be seen as a proxy for formal-sector productivity.

FIGURE 4.   SELF-EMPLOYMENT VERSUS INDUSTRIAL PRODUCTIVITY

Share of labor force in self-employment

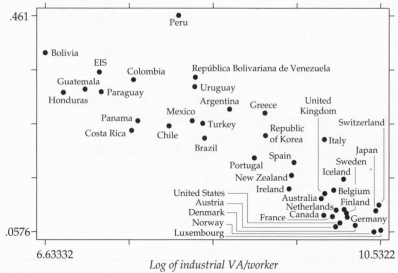

Log of industrial VA/worker

In sum, the three labor distortion variables, the taxes on salaries and on payroll, and the restrictions on hiring and firing have relatively small impacts compared with those of the productivity, real interest rate, education variables and, in the larger sample, the relative youth measure. Thus, given the level of productivity in a country, which again may be affected by labor legislation, it is hard to argue that these distortions are responsible for the size of the sector.

The adjusted size of the informal sector: a measure of unobserved distortions? Can we say anything about distortions on which we have little reliable information, such as union- or government-induced wage rigidities from these regressions? Perhaps. In theory, the residuals of the regression capture the impact of all variables not explicitly included in the regression, including other labor market distortions. It is absolutely correct to argue that they also include any country-specific variables and that any error in measuring sector size would cast doubt on using the residuals for this purpose. This critique, however, applies to the use of the raw sector sizes as well, and if sector size is thought to contain information, the adjusted values obtained from the residuals are probably more appropriate.

Table 3 tabulates three sets of residuals from regressions on subsets of the significant explanatory variables. The results tell a reasonable story with a few exceptions. The first set of residuals are those from regressing only on formal sector labor productivity only (Resid 1). The complete reranking of size shows immediately the importance of compensating for productivity, or more generally, the level of development when drawing inferences from the size of the sector. Among the OECD countries, they tell a story that is broadly consistent with the literature and suggest that the approach is not entirely misguided. Canada and the United States show up as relatively clean, while Greece, Italy, and Spain appear heavily burdened. Among the Latin American countries, Brazil, Chile, Costa Rica, Guatemala, Honduras, Paraguay, are all below trend in their share of the workforce in self-employment and hence, arguably, with less onerous legislation than the mean, while Argentina, Colombia, Peru, Uruguay, and the República Bolivariana de Venezuela are far above.

The second set of residuals add the structural variables measuring the share of young people in the workforce and the level of education, as well as the level of interest rates (Resid 2). The high variance of this last variable and the difficulty of measuring it may distort the results somewhat. Mexico is now firmly below trend and Chile, with relatively moderate interest rates, is actually above, although not by a significant amount. Peru now emerges as far less pathological than previously, but it still is joined by Argentina and the República Bolivariana de Venezuela as appearing to have a high level of unobserved distortions.

The third set of residuals adds to the regressors the burden of taxation for social security (Resid 3). Consistent with the previous findings, this does little to change the overall ranking, although Mexico's sector share is now even more below trend, and Colombia approaches the trend.

The final set of residuals attempts to incorporate the Márquez index. To take advantage of the more precise parameter estimates from the large sample, they are constructed by taking Resid 3 and regressing it on the measure of employment protection for the countries for which it was available. In general, Latin America shifts up in the rankings because of their overall higher firing costs. Now Bolivia, Costa Rica, El Salvador, Honduras, Mexico, and Paraguay appear to have fewer residual distortions than the United States or most OECD countries. The Latin American countries that still appear with residual distortions are Argentina, Peru, and the República Bolivariana de Venezuela and, to a lesser degree, Chile and Colombia.

TABLE 3. RESIDUALS OF SELF-EMPLOYMENT REGRESSIONS
(ranked by deviation from predicted share)

Country	Percent self-employed	Resid 1	Country	Resid 2	Country	Resid 3	Country	Resid 4
Costa Rica	24.4	-7.6	Costa Rica	-7.9	Brazil	-8.9	Brazil	-7.2
Honduras	31.8	-6.8	France	-7.5	France	-5.5	Costa Rica	-6.4
Austria	6.6	-5.9	Austria	-7.2	Costa Rica	-5.5	Bolivia	-5.2
Panama	26.2	-5.1	Honduras	-4.7	Austria	-3.9	Mexico	-4.8
United States	7.3	-4.8	Sweden	-4.5	Sweden	-3.5	France	-3.3
Canada	8.9	-4.6	United States	-3.6	Mexico	-3.3	Honduras	-3.1
Guatemala	32.3	-4.1	Brazil	-3.0	Norway	-2.9	Portugal	-2.3
France	8.6	-4.1	Guatemala	-2.7	United States	-2.9	Guatemala	-1.1
Denmark	6.9	-3.6	Germany	-2.5	Ireland	-2.8	El Salvador	-0.4
Ireland	13.5	-3.3	Portugal	-2.5	Bolivia	-2.6	Ireland	-0.4
Chile	25.2	-3.2	Finland	-2.5	Canada	-2.2	Paraguay	-0.2
Paraguay	31.7	-3.2	Canada	-2.4	Portugal	-2.1	Denmark	0.7
Germany	8.5	-2.8	Paraguay	-2.3	Netherlands	-1.2	Spain	0.9
Netherlands	9.6	-2.7	Panama	-1.9	Japan	-1.1	United States	1.0
Norway	5.9	-2.7	Ireland	-1.9	Guatemala	-1.0	Germany	1.0
Luxembourg	5.8	-2.3	Norway	-1.6	Honduras	-1.0	Chile	1.1
Sweden	9.3	-1.9	Bolivia	-1.4	Panama	-1.0	Netherlands	1.5
Brazil	23.2	-1.8	Mexico	-1.3	Germany	-0.5	Colombia	1.7
Finland	9.7	-1.8	Belgium	-1.1	Paraguay	-0.3	Peru	2.4
Australia	12.3	-1.4	Chile	-1.1	Denmark	0.0	Italy	2.6

Bolivia	39.2	−1.2	Netherlands	−1.0	Republic of Korea	0.3	Argentina	2.7
United Kingdom	12.6	−0.7	Luxembourg	−0.9	Australia	0.3	United Kingdom	2.7
Portugal	19.5	−0.7	Spain	−0.5	Uruguay	0.4	Belgium	3.5
New Zealand	16.2	−0.5	Republic of Korea	−0.2	Luxembourg	0.7	República Bolivariana de Venezuela	6.1
Mexico	26.5	0.2	Turkey	0.4	El Salvador	0.8	Greece	6.6
El Salvador	35.2	0.2	Colombia	0.4	Belgium	1.5		
Turkey	26.0	0.7	Denmark	0.5	Turkey	1.5		
Belgium	13.3	0.8	United Kingdom	1.1	Chile	1.8		
Japan	9.9	1.7	El Salvador	1.9	Spain	2.2		
Colombia	34.2	2.3	Australia	2.7	Italy	2.2		
Spain	18.6	2.4	Japan	2.8	Finland	2.2		
Switzerland	10.6	2.5	Argentina	2.9	Iceland	2.3		
Iceland	15.5	4.0	New Zealand	3.1	United Kingdom	2.3		
Republic of Korea	23.6	4.3	Italy	3.2	New Zealand	2.9		
Argentina	28.5	5.9	Iceland	4.7	Argentina	3.1		
Uruguay	32.8	6.8	Switzerland	5.0	Switzerland	3.1		
República Bolivariana de Venezuela	34.4	8.4	Uruguay	5.3	Colombia	3.9		
Greece	27.7	8.4	Greece	7.2	Peru	4.3		
Italy	22.8	9.4	República Bolivariana de Venezuela	8.2	Greece	7.3		
Peru	46.1	18.6	Peru	17.2	República Bolivariana de Venezuela	8.9		

Note: Resid 1 is from regression on formal productivity. Resid 2 is from regression that also includes employers' social security contributions. Resid 3 also includes education, youth, and real interest rates. Resid 4 includes residuals of Resid 3 on job protection.

Again, this entire exercise is distorted to the degree that sector size is poorly measured, or that included variables are correlated with those excluded. Still, as a measure of segmentation, it is probably better than conventional comparisons of wages among sectors and suggests a fairly robust story. Numerous countries in the region do not appear to be unduly saddled by labor legislation compared with those in OECD countries.

These results may be at odds with some previous work. Loayza (1996) built a model of informality that focuses largely on issues of taxes and regulation of business. He also generates standardized estimates of the size of the informal sector as a share of production, based on the VAT evasion rate. Argentina, Chile, and Costa Rica have the lowest adjusted size and Bolivia, Panama, and Peru have the largest. Given the possible divergence of VAT evasion rates from the relative share of employment in self-employment, these differences are, perhaps, not surprising. The results are also not entirely consistent with the indexes of distortion calculated in *The Long March* (Burki and Perry 1997), a regional reform perspective published by the World Bank, which showed Chile, Colombia, and Peru among the most liberalized countries and Bolivia, Mexico, and perhaps Brazil among the least. This divergence, again, may be caused by data problems. Chile may count its self-employed more conscientiously, but the divergence also may be caused by differences in enforcement that render nominally distorted economies to be de facto relatively undistorted.

Turnover Results

The turnover results are more difficult to interpret: first, because of the fewer degrees of freedom available and second, because the theory is far less clear about what the signs should be. Nonetheless, the results are provocative.[18]

Mean tenure. Columns 1-a to 1-c in table 4 present various specifications of average tenure in manufacturing employment. Column 1-a includes all variables in the specification, again excluding the protection variable. The LA dummy, Youth, and Unemployment Benefits do not enter significantly. Labor productivity enters both in levels and with its

---

18. See Márquez and Pagés (1998) for a graphic treatment of these issues. The econometric results here are broadly consistent with their findings.

TABLE 4. DETERMINANTS OF TURNOVER

| | Manufacturing | | | | | |
| | Mean tenure | | | Percent < 2 years | | |
Variable	1-a	1-b	1-c	2-a	2-b	2-c
C	60.58	74.35	43.30	−288.38	−288.67	−272.71
	(3.09)	(4.23)	(6.03)	(3.82)	(4.78)	(2.23)
Indust. VA	−11.95	−16.21	−3.19	84.40	77.61	73.37
	(2.35)	(3.99)	(4.88)	(4.17)	(4.02)	(2.47)
IVA sq.	0.64	0.92	–	−4.84	−4.31	−3.98
	(2.07)	(3.99)	–	(3.84)	(3.89)	(2.12)
SSWorker	8.13	8.68	–	−2.51	–	–
	(3.29)	(3.62)	–	(.16)	–	–
SSEmp	7.00	6.23	11.65	−46.92	−44.45	−41.84
	(1.79)	(1.79)	(5.86)	−(4.63)	(3.92)	(2.54)
Protection	–	–	0.09	–	–	−0.05
	–	–	(2.99)	–	–	(.21)
U benefits	−0.03	–	–	−0.13	–	–
	−(1.13)	–	–	−(1.42)	–	–
Real interest	−7.41	−7.10	–	14.45	21.44	24.14
	(1.92)	(1.89)	–	(1.65)	(2.22)	(1.98)
Education	0.05	0.04	–	−0.07	−0.24	−0.31
	(2.15)	(2.23)	–	(.69)	(2.57)	(2.11)
Youth	−39.23	–	–	−754.73	–	–
	(.48)	–	–	(2.38)	–	–
LA dummy	−0.70	–	–	10.13	–	–
	(.41)	–	–	(1.33)	–	–
NOBS	25	26	17	23	24	16
R^2	0.63	0.68	0.81	0.50	0.65	0.54

Note: t–statistics below coefficients. Indust. VA = industrial value added per worker; IVA sq. = indust. VA square; SSWorker = social security tax—workers; SSEmp = social security tax—employers; Protection = employment protection; U benefits = duration of unemployment benefits; Real interest = real interest rate; Education = percentage of relevant cohort completing secondary school; Youth = share of working population between ages of 16 and 20; LA dummy = dummy for Latin country; NOBS = number of observations.

square suggesting a nonlinear relationship. Taken at the mean, labor productivity appears to have a *negative* impact on tenure. This can be reversed with the exclusion of all other variables, but the inclusion of the share of the population with secondary schooling reverses its sign. Thus, although the OECD countries have more stable workforces, it appears that their education rather than their wealth drives the result. Both taxes on social security appear to increase tenure and real interest rates to decrease it. Again, these results are consistent with the theoretical framework.

The reduction of the sample to 17 observations with the inclusion of the employment protection variable leaves only the productivity, social security tax on employers, and protection variables significant. The latter enters with predicted sign, suggesting that it does negatively affect turnover, and importantly so. The difference across the range from the United States (1) to the República Bolivariana de Venezuela (37) accounts for 3.24 years on a mean of about 9.

Table 5 presents a set of residuals for the average job tenure regression analogous to those previous. With the usual caveats about small sample size and the possible correlation of omitted variables with those included, Bolivia, Brazil, and the República Bolivariana de Venezuela appear with greater than average turnover when adjusted for productivity, whereas Argentina, Honduras, Panama, and Paraguay are below average. When adjusted for education levels and interest rates, Brazil shows turnover closer to the mean and Panama above the mean. Adding employers' social security contributions has the effects of bringing Honduras above mean turnover and moving Panama below.

The share of the manufacturing workforce with under two years of seniority. The results for the second measure of turnover, and the share of the manufacturing workforce with less than two years of tenure, are broadly consistent, but suggest the sensitivity of the results when sample sizes are so small. Labor productivity, the real interest rate, the employers' contributions to social security, and education variables enter significantly and with signs consistent with the previous results. As column 2-a in table 4 suggests, the education variable proved very unstable with the youth variable included. However, because the youth variable entered with the sign opposite to that expected, the preferred regression was that presented in 2-b. Regression 2-c suggests that, in these regressions, the Márquez protection variable does not enter significantly. The residuals are not presented in tabular form for this regression.

The Overall Picture

Figures 5a and 5b plot the residuals from the second set of residuals (productivity, education, real interest rate, and youth) from the self-employment regression and from the turnover regression to see if the combination of the two can reveal anything about the functioning of a given labor market. Though speculative, we will interpret these residu-

TABLE 5. RESIDUALS OF AVERAGE JOB TENURE IN MANUFACTURING REGRESSIONS

(ranked by deviations from predicted tenure)

Country	Average tenure	Resid 1	Country	Resid 2	Country	Resid 3
Denmark	7.80	-3.35	Denmark	-3.76	Bolivia	-1.84
Australia	7.00	-3.08	Australia	-2.69	República Bolivariana de Venezuela	-1.56
República Bolivariana de Venezuela	5.77	-1.87	Ireland	-1.78	Austria	-1.49
Bolivia	6.22	-1.84	Bolivia	-1.69	Denmark	-1.47
Brazil	6.25	-1.50	United States	-1.38	Netherlands	-0.95
Switzerland	10.60	-1.43	United Kingdom	-1.11	United States	-0.81
United States	9.20	-1.40	República Bolivariana de Venezuela	-1.10	Ireland	-0.79
Canada	8.90	-1.25	Canada	-0.98	Italy	-0.54
United Kingdom	9.00	-1.20	Switzerland	-0.65	Australia	-0.46
Ireland	8.30	-0.93	Austria	-0.36	United Kingdom	-0.45
Netherlands	10.30	-0.21	Panama	-0.29	France	-0.43
Germany	10.80	-0.09	Brazil	-0.24	Germany	-0.27
Austria	10.60	0.14	Germany	-0.03	Spain	-0.26
Greece	9.00	0.34	Netherlands	0.03	Honduras	-0.16
Panama	7.84	0.45	Honduras	0.21	Switzerland	0.16
Honduras	8.39	0.56	Greece	0.39	Sweden	0.17
Sweden	11.50	0.60	Spain	0.40	Canada	0.29
Argentina	8.89	0.83	Finland	0.75	Argentina	0.30
Italy	11.20	1.03	Sweden	0.75	Brazil	0.36
Japan	13.10	1.09	Argentina	0.97	Belgium	0.39
Belgium	11.80	1.34	Belgium	1.15	Greece	0.47
Finland	12.30	1.53	France	1.32	Finland	0.69
Spain	10.90	1.53	Japan	1.63	Panama	1.00
France	12.10	1.71	Italy	1.68	Japan	1.45
Portugal	10.40	1.92	Portugal	1.80	Portugal	1.55
Paraguay	9.93	2.44	Luxembourg	2.43	Luxembourg	2.22
Luxembourg	14.70	2.63	Paraguay	2.54	Paraguay	2.44

Note: Resid 1 is from regression on formal sector productivity. Resid 2 is from regression that also includes real interest rate, and education. Resid 3 also includes employers' social security contributions.

FIGURE 5A.   DISTORTION AND RIGIDITY?

Adjusted share in self-employment

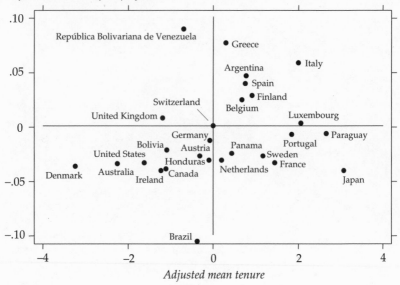

Adjusted mean tenure

FIGURE 5B.   DISTORTION AND RIGIDITY?

Adjusted share in self-employment

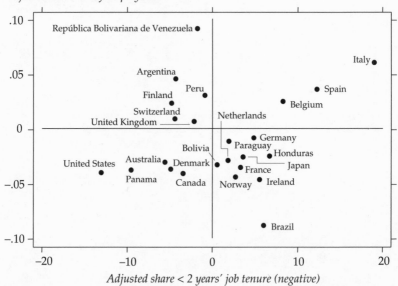

Adjusted share < 2 years' job tenure (negative)

als as measuring labor market distortion (self-employment above the conditional mean) and rigidity (average tenure above the conditional mean).

In the northeast quadrant of figure 5a—rigid and distorted economies—we find Greece, Italy, and Spain, all European countries renowned for repressive labor codes. It is, however, interesting to note that only one Latin American country appears in this quadrant: Argentina. Honduras and Paraguay also appear somewhat rigid, although less distorted than average. Among the most flexible and undistorted, in the southwest quadrant, we find, unsurprisingly, Canada and the United States, accompanied by Bolivia, Brazil, Panama, Peru, and the República Bolivariana de Venezuela. The results show some sensitivity to the measure of turnover employed. Using the share of workers with less than two years of tenure, figure 5b suggests that Argentina now has above-average flexibility, and Brazil below-average flexibility.

The graphs were redone replacing industrial value added per worker with purchasing power parity–adjusted per capita GNP. The placement of countries changed little, which suggests that the results are not very sensitive to the exact measure of labor productivity used. In sum, with some exceptions and with strong caveats about the reliability of the results, Latin American labor markets do not appear exceptionally distorted or inflexible.

Conclusion

This article has presented the results of cross-country regressions motivated by an efficiency wage model of the economy in developing countries. The model takes as its point of departure the assumption that, for many workers, informal self-employment is a desirable destination for salaried workers rather than the disadvantaged sector of a market made dual by union- or government-induced wage rigidities. Nonetheless, segmentation will always be present in all labor markets, even in the absence of unions or minimum wages, as long as firms seek to retain workers in whom they have invested. Firms will pay above-market-clearing "efficiency wages" to lower turnover, and in the process, create unemployment or segmentation that may cut across lines of formality. The predictions about the size of the self-employed sector and turnover were tested using cross-sectional OECD and Latin American data and were generally supported.

The size of the informal sector and the rate of turnover can tell something about the impact of labor legislation on rigidity or flexibility, but only if adjusted for demographic and other variables that, theory suggests, are important. Though highly speculative, the adjusted measures do not suggest that, overall, Latin American labor markets are especially distorted or rigid.

Barriers to firing workers and social security taxes on firms appear to reduce the size of the formal sector. Anticipation of costly firing may lead to a reluctance to employ new workers, whereas high nonwage benefits raise labor costs. That said, empirically, the level of formal sector productivity, real interest rates, and education levels in general have a larger impact on the size of the informal sector than do labor market taxes or barriers to firing.

Appendix A: Data Sources

1. Tenure variables of the OECD countries are from the following sources:

- Nickell 1995—table 2: "Measures of the Sluggishness of Employment and of Adjustment Costs," p. 11.
- OECD 1997b—table 5.5: "Distribution of Employment by Employer Tenure, 1995," p. 138.
- OECD 1997b—table 5.6: "Average Employer Tenure by Gender, Age, Industry, Occupation, 1995," p. 139.

2. The self-employment rate of the OECD countries is from OECD 1997a.

3. The self-employment rate and tenure variables of countries in Latin America are from various CEPAL surveys of the following countries and years: Argentina 1992, Bolivia 1995, Chile 1995, Colombia 1995, Costa Rica 1995, El Salvador 1995, Guatemala 1989, Honduras 1995, Mexico 1994, Panama 1995, Paraguay 1995, Peru 1996, Uruguay 1995, the República Bolivariana de Venezuela 1995.

4. Per capita GNP and wages of industrial workers are from World Bank 1997—table 1: "Basic Indicators," pp. 214–15, and table 12, "Structure of the Economy: Production."

5. Employment protection variables were provided by Gustavo Márquez, Office of the Chief Economist, Inter-American Development Bank.

6. Social security variables are from U.S. Social Security Administration 1997, table 3, "Contribution Rates for Social Security Programs—OECD Countries (1997)," and table 5.8, "Social Security and Non-Wage Labour Costs."

References

Abuhadba, Mario, and Pilar Romaguera. 1993. "Interindustrial Wage Differentials: Evidence from Latin American Countries." *Journal of Development Studies* 30 (1): 190–206.

Aroca, P., and W. F. Maloney. 1998. "Logit Analysis in a Rotating Panel Context and an Application to Self-Employment Decisions." World Bank Poverty Reduction and Economic Management, Washington, D.C., and Universidad Católica del Norte, Chile.

Begin, James P. 1995. "Singapore's Industrial Relations System." In Stephen Frenkel and Jeffrey Harrod, eds., *Industrialization and Labor Relations: Contemporary Research in Seven Countries*. Ithaca, N.Y.: ILR Press.

Bell, L. 1997. "The Impact of Minimum Wages in Mexico and Colombia." *Journal of Labor Economics* 15: 3 (part 2): s44–72.

Blanchard, Olivier, and Juan F. Jimeno. 1985. "Structural Unemployment: Spain vs. Portugal." *American Economic Review* 85: 212–17.

Boyer, 1994. "Do Labour Institutions Matter for Economic Development?" In Gerry Rodgers, ed., *Workers, Institutions, and Economic Growth in Asia*. Geneva: International Labour Organization.

Burki, Javed, and Guillermo Perry. 1997. *The Long March: A Reform Agenda for Latin America and the Caribbean in the Next Decade*. Washington, D.C.: World Bank.

Comisión Económica para America Latina. 1989. *CEPAL Review*. Santiago, Chile.

———. 1992. *CEPAL Review*. Santiago, Chile.

———. 1994. *CEPAL Review*. Santiago, Chile.

———. 1996. *CEPAL Review*. Santiago, Chile.

Cox-Edwards, Alejandra. 1993. "Labor Market Legislation in Latin America and the Caribbean." Report 31, Latin America and the Caribbean Technical Department, World Bank, Washington, D.C.

Cunningham, Wendy, and William F. Maloney. Forthcoming. "Heterogeneity among Mexico's Micro-Enterprises: An Application of Factor and Cluster Analysis." *Economic Development and Cultural Change*.

Fiess, Norbert, William F. Maloney, and Rashmi Shankar. 2000. "The Informal Sector, Wage Rigidities, and Real Exchange Rates." World Bank, Poverty Reduction and Economic Management Department, Washington, D.C.

Funkhouser, E. 1998. "The Importance of Firm Wage Differentials in Explaining Hourly Earnings Variation in the Large Scale Sector of Guatemala." *Journal of Development Economics* 55 (1): 115–31.

Gindling, T. H., and Katherine Terrell. 1995. "The Nature of Minimum Wages and Their Effectiveness as a Wage Floor in Costa Rica, 1976–91." *World Development* 23 (14): 39–58.

Gonzaga, Gustavo. 1996. "The Effects of Openness on Industrial Employment in Brazil." Discussion paper 362 Brazil. Pontificia Universidade Católica do Rio de Jaineiro, Departamento de Economia, Brazil.

Harris, J. R., and M. P. Todaro. 1970. "Migration, Unemployment and Development: A Two Sector Analysis." *American Economic Review* 60 (1): 126–42.

Krebs, T., and W. F. Maloney. 1998. "Quitting and Labor Turnover: Microeconomic Evidence and Macroeconomic Consequences." IBRD Working Paper 2068, Poverty Reduction and Economic Management Department, Washington, D.C.

Krueger, Anne O., and L. H. Summers. 1988. " Efficiency Wages and the Inter-Industry Wage Structure." *Econometrica* 56 (2): 259–93.

Levenson, Alec, and William F. Maloney. 1997. "The Informal Sector, Firm Dynamics and Institutional Participation." IBRD Working Paper 1988. Poverty Reduction and Economic Management Department, Washington, D.C.

Loayza, N. 1996. "The Economics of the Informal Sector: A Simple Model and Some Empirical Evidence from Latin America." *Carnegie-Rochester Conference Series on Public Policy* 45: 129–62, North Holland.

MacIsaac, Donna, and Martín Rama. 1997. "Determinants of Hourly Earnings in Ecuador: The Role of Labor Market Regulations." *Journal of Labor Economics* 15(3) (part 2) (July): S136–65.

Maloney, William F. 1997. "Labor Market Structure in LDC's: Time Series Evidence on Competing Views." IBRD Working Paper 1940, World Bank, Washington, D.C.

———. 1999. "Does Informality Imply Segmentation in Urban Labor Markets? Evidence from Sectoral Transitions in Mexico." *World Bank Economic Review* 13: 275–302.

———. 2000. "Minimum Wages in Latin America, A Note." Poverty Reduction and Economic Management Department, World Bank, Washington, D.C.

Maloney, William F., and Eduardo Ribeiro. 1998. "Efficiency Wage and Union Effects in Labor Demand and Wage Structure in Mexico." IBRD Working Paper 2131, Poverty Reduction and Economic Management Department, World Bank, Washington, D.C.

Márquez, Gustavo. 1990. "Wage Differentials and Labor market Equilibrium in Venezuela." Ph.D. dissertation. Boston University, Department of Economics, Boston.

———. 1998. "Protección al empleo y funcionamiento del mercado de trabajo: una aproximación comparativa." Uncitable paper, Office of the Chief Economist. Inter-American Development Bank, Washington, D.C.

Márquez, Gustavo, and Carmen Pagés. 1998. "Ties That Bind: Employment Protection and Labor Market Outcomes in Latin America." Office of the Chief Economist, Inter-American Development Bank, Washington, D.C.

Nickell, Stephen. 1995. "Labour Market Dynamics in OECD Countries." Discussion Paper 255. The London School of Economics and Political Science, Centre for Economic Performance, London.

———. 1997. "Unemployment and Market Rigidities: Europe versus North America." *Journal of Economic Perspectives* 11 (3): 5–74.

OECD (Organisation for Economic Co-operation and Development). 1997a. "Labour Force Statistics *(Statistiques de main-d'oeuvre)* 1976/96." Paris.

———. 1997b. "OECD Employment Outlook." July. Paris.

Revenga, Ana, and William F. Maloney. 1994. "Mexico Labor Market Strategy Paper." Mexico Country Management Unit, World Bank, Washington, D.C.

Schaffner, J. A. 1998. "Premiums to Employment in Larger Establishments: Evidence from Peru." *Journal of Development Economics* 55 (1): 81–113.

Shapiro, Carl, and Joseph Stiglitz. 1984. Equilibrium Unemployment as a Worker Discipline Device." *American Economic Review* 74 (3): 431–44.

Stiglitz, Joseph E. 1974. "Alternative Theories of Wage Determination and Unemployment in LDC's: The Labor Turnover Model." *Quarterly Journal of Economics* 88: 194–227.

U.S. Social Security Administration. 1997. "Social Security Programs throughout the World." Office of Policy, Office of Research and Statistics, U.S. Department of Health and Human Services, Washington, D.C.

World Bank. 1990, 1995, 1997. *World Development Report.* New York: Oxford University Press.

———. 1995. *World Development Report.* New York: Oxford University Press.

———. 1997. *World Development Report.* New York: Oxford University Press.

You, Jong Il. 1994. "Labour Institution and Economic Development in the Republic of Korea." In Gerry Rodgers, ed., *Workers, Institutions, Economic Growth in Asia.* Geneva: ILO.

Do Separation Packages Need to Be That Generous? Simulations for Government Employees in Guinea-Bissau

Alberto Chong and Martín Rama

Abstract

Separation packages may be needed to overcome resistance to public sector downsizing, and they can be justified on fairness grounds. But what is the "right" amount of compensation? This article offers a practical answer to this question, using the case of Guinea-Bissau as an illustration. Building on previous work by Ariel Fiszbein and Ragui Assaad, the article assumes that a "just right" package has to offset the loss in earnings and benefits from job separation. Two approaches are used to quantify the loss in benefits. The direct approach explicitly measures the present value of old-age pensions, for those workers who end up in the informal sector of the economy. The indirect approach infers the value of benefits from the situation of public sector workers who could apparently earn more out of the public sector than in it, but do not voluntarily leave. The two approaches yield remarkably similar distributions of predicted losses. These distributions are used to compare the performance of four separation packages: three based on usual rules of thumb and one "tai-

This article was first produced as a paper for the Sub-Saharan Africa Region of the World Bank with support from the research project on "Efficient Public Sector Downsizing." Comments and suggestions by Marcelo Andrade, Paulo Gomes, William Maloney, Zafiris Tzannatos, and an anonymous referee are gratefully acknowledged.

lored" to individual characteristics, such as gender, education, and region of residence. If the goal is to satisfy a majority of the workers, the tailored package outperforms all others.

Public sector downsizing should not be a final objective of economic policy. Downsizing may, however, be needed to make the public sector more efficient and to facilitate the development of a more vibrant private sector. It is increasingly accepted that governments should focus their efforts on the core public activities that are crucial to development, such as delivering sound economic policies and providing basic health and education. Conversely, they should not waste scarce resources in activities the private sector can perform better, such as producing goods and services, including among the latter the cleaning, maintenance and surveillance of its own facilities. Restructuring the public sector may therefore require expanding some activities, but also shrinking or privatizing others.

Separation packages are a way to overcome labor resistance to downsizing, restructuring, or privatization. If no compensation were provided, many public sector workers would suffer as a result of job separation. They would experience a decline in earnings and benefits, possibly including some or all of their old-age pensions. They could also have to work harder, or be exposed to sharper fluctuations in their income. On the other hand, if very generous separation packages were offered, and workers had a choice, they could all feel compelled to leave of their own will. In between these two extremes, the compensation package would be "just right" if the amount of money offered made each public sector worker roughly indifferent between staying in his or her current job and leaving.

Compensation packages for separated public sector workers are not new. They have been used by governments all around the world, often with support from donor countries and multilateral organizations (Kikeri 1997). Workers have sometimes, however, been compensated better than "just right"—actually, far better than "just right." In a survey of the cross-country experience with public sector retrenchment in developing countries and transition economies, Haltiwanger and Singh (1999) estimated the average spending per job separation at $2,400. But the figure was as high as $13,000 in the civil service of Senegal, $16,000 in the mining sector of Bolivia, and $17,000 in the public enterprises of India, despite the fact that all three countries had a per capita income of less than $1,000 per year. When practical tools to design compensation packages are lacking, past mistakes translate into present overspending, as the excessive figures or formulas of previous downsizing episodes become a reference for new public sector restructuring endeavors.

The reasons for overspending on separation packages are somewhat understandable. One of them is policy credibility. If the compensation offered was too low, workers would not be compelled to leave, and the political costs of such a failure could be high. Given that the package that elicits indifference on the worker (that is, the "just right" amount) is not directly observable, policymakers may prefer to err in the direction of overcompensation. Another reason why governments may pay more than the "just right" amount is that they usually face tight constraints on their current expenditures, but may all of a sudden have access to abundant resources for public sector restructuring from donor countries and multilateral organizations. This combination of a hard-budget constraint for salaries and a soft-budget constraint for separation packages creates an incentive to compensate better than "just right."[1]

Overspending in compensation packages is questionable, both on economic and on fairness grounds. From an economic point of view, every transfer entails a cost. Sooner or later, taxes will have to be raised, or other government expenditures will have to be cut, to make up for the compensation of separated public sector workers. The larger this compensation, the heavier the burden on the rest of society. In regard to fairness, it is important to keep in mind that public sector workers are usually not poor, at least compared to their fellow citizens working in the informal sector or living in rural areas. A government committed to poverty alleviation could therefore find better uses for its resources than offering far better than "just right" compensation to public sector workers.

The aim of this article is to discuss the design of a "just right" compensation package from a practical perspective, using the case of Guinea-Bissau as an illustration. In the preparation for its third structural adjustment program, the government of Guinea-Bissau had considered suppressing all positions in occupational categories "O" to "Z", which correspond to unskilled personnel working on services like cleaning, maintenance, and surveillance. The objective was to subcontract these

---

1. Cases where workers are undercompensated abound as well. Even when the average compensation package is overly generous, some workers may get much less than needed to offset the impact of job separation. Bankrupt state-owned enterprises in Tanzania provide a clear example of undercompensation (Chong and Radwan 1999).

activities to private firms, to be selected through competitive bidding. The bidding mechanism was to be designed so as to favor those firms that would hire the largest number of separated government employees. It was estimated that roughly one-fifth of the separated employees could be hired by the new private contractors. The implementation of this program had to be postponed due to the rebellion of part of the military against the government, in 1998. This rebellion was not prompted by, or related to, the structural adjustment program in preparation. Therefore, as the political situation stabilizes, the retrenchment of government employees in categories "O" to "Z" will probably regain prominence in the economic policy agenda. The article thus focuses on the appropriate level of compensation for those employees.

The choice of Guinea-Bissau as an illustration is deliberate, as this is one of the poorest countries on earth. A credible assessment of the losses in earnings and benefits that government employees can expect as a result of separation has to be based on careful data analysis. Simplifying a bit, it is necessary to evaluate the loss in earnings and benefits of a representative sample of government employees in the event of job separation. For this evaluation to be feasible, detailed databases of government employees and labor force participants at-large are needed. If these data requirements can be satisfied in Guinea-Bissau, they can probably be met in most other developing countries.

Methodology

The methodology used in this article is not entirely novel, although it differs from previous applications in several important respects. The basic approach was proposed by Fiszbein (1994). It was subsequently refined by Assaad (1999) in the context of a broader research project on public sector downsizing.[2] Fiszbein's contribution was to use a forward-looking formula to assess the "just right" package for each worker. If public sector jobs are seen as an entitlement for life, this package has to compensate for the resulting decline in earnings during all the years of denied service. In an application for Sri Lanka, Fiszbein took into account not only the average earnings separated workers could expect in their new jobs, but also the probability that they would not find any job. The present value of the resulting loss served to estimate the "just right" package for workers of different ages.

---

2. For an overview of the findings of this project, see Rama (1999).

Fiszbein did not take into account the potential loss in benefits, both tangible and intangible, from separation. This omission is problematic in countries where the earnings alternatives of separated public sector workers are mainly in the informal sector of the economy. In Ghana, for instance, a large number of separated public sector workers went back to their villages, to work in agriculture (Alderman, Canagarajah, and Younger 1996). Even in a richer country, like Ecuador, half of the separated government employees ended up in the informal sector of the economy (Rama and MacIsaac 1999). Public sector jobs are characterized by better working conditions, lower effort levels, and better old-age benefits than informal sector jobs. If these tangible and intangible benefits are not taken into account, the loss resulting from job separation may be seriously underestimated.

Assaad refined the forward-looking approach by combining it with detailed labor market data analysis, using Egypt as an example. Individual records from household surveys can indeed be used to predict the alternative earnings of public sector employees. When this is done, it appears that many among them could earn more if they left the public sector. The fact that they do not do it suggests that they value the other benefits associated with their jobs at least as much as the earnings they forgo. Assaad's main contribution was to use this information to infer the loss in benefits that public sector workers would experience in the event of separation. In Egypt, the group whose earnings would increase by more in the event of separation is made of female employees of state-owned enterprises who have university education. Over their working lives the members of this group could earn more than double out of the public sector. Based on this result, Assaad concluded that the value of total compensation in the Egyptian public sector, including tangible and intangible benefits, was twice the value of monetary earnings. This kind of upward adjustment to monetary earnings leads to a higher present value of the loss from job separation.

This article builds on the work of Fiszbein and Assaad by computing the loss in benefits in two different ways. One of them (called "direct" in what follows) extends the time horizon of the present value calculation proposed by Fiszbein. Now, the loss in earnings is computed not only over the years until retirement, but also over the years from retirement to death. The direct approach thus takes into consideration the possible loss of old-age pensions resulting from separation. Old-age security is arguably the most important benefit associated with public sector jobs. In the case of Guinea-Bissau, it had been decided that separated employees would lose their entitlement to old-age pensions. But

Guinea-Bissau is no exception, as old-age pensions are usually not portable and separated public sector workers can expect at best a lump-sum "refund" for their past contributions. The direct approach calculates the level of the old-age pension for each employee if he or she was to remain in the public sector until reaching retirement age. The present value of this pension (over all the years from retirement to death) is then added to the present value of the loss in earnings (over all the years from present to retirement). The result of this calculation depends, of course, on the assumed life expectancy of government employees, but the sensitivity to the death age is small for plausible values of the discount rate.

The second approach (called "indirect") uses a variant of the methodology proposed by Assaad to compute the loss in benefits. Instead of focusing on the group of public sector workers whose earnings would increase most in the event of separation, as Assaad did, the indirect approach considered the entire distribution of the predicted change in earnings. For a majority of public sector workers, this predicted change was negative, although the right "tail" of this distribution was long, as some workers could apparently earn much more out of the public sector than in it. Such a long tail could reflect the fact that some workers attach a remarkably high value to the benefits associated with their jobs. They could, however, also be due to measurement error. Databases are incomplete and inaccurate. Some figures can be truncated or mistyped, whereas information on individual characteristics that are key to predicting alternative earnings may just be missing. The indirect approach gets rid of the upper tail of the distribution of the predicted change in earnings, as it assumes that its highest values simply reflect measurement error. The highest predicted change in earnings, once the tail has been removed, is then used as an indicator of the value of the benefits associated with public sector jobs. The result depends of course on the "size" of the tail that is removed from the distribution. Sensitivity analysis, however, shows that the variation is not substantial for plausible sizes of the tail.

Using both the direct and indirect approaches to estimate the losses from separation is a simple way to assess the robustness of the results, because the two approaches are based on different assumptions. The estimation is carried out using the downsizing options simulation exercise (DOSE), an Excel-based application that incorporates the lessons from the broader research project on public sector downsizing. The DOSE also generates summary statistics on the characteristics of the public sector workers who would be satisfied by the compensation received, and estimates the financial and economic returns to downsizing. The results on summary statistics and returns to downsizing are not reported here, because the focus of this article is on the design of a "just right" compensation package, not on the merits or demerits of the public sector downsizing operation considered by the government of Guinea-Bissau.

Data

Two main data sets are needed to predict the losses from separation. First, a national household survey is required to get information on the earnings and individual characteristics of labor force participants. This information allows an estimation of how earnings vary with age, education, gender, region of residence, and other observable individual characteristics. The resulting relationship between earnings and individual characteristics is known as an earnings function, or a Mincerian equation. Second, a public sector data base is needed to get information on the individual characteristics of the workers who might be separated from their jobs. Combining this information with the earnings function, it is possible to predict the earnings of each worker in the public sector data base in the event of separation.

In the case of Guinea-Bissau, information on the earnings and individual characteristics of labor force participants was collected by the 1991 national household survey. This survey is somewhat dated, and there actually is a more recent one that has not been processed yet. In spite of its age, however, the 1991 survey serves well the purposes of this article, to the extent that the structure of earnings did not change much during the 1990s. The list of individual characteristics reported by the survey is quite large. Most of these characteristics have a relatively straightforward interpretation, but some variables need to be constructed out of the responses to the survey. One of them is the dummy variable for the private formal sector. Labor earnings may differ substantially between the formal and the informal sector, so that the loss from separation crucially depends on the nature of the job taken subsequently. In this article, the formal private sector variable is set at equal to one for individuals who are either affiliated with social security or entitled to annual leave. It is set at equal to zero otherwise.

Another variable that needs to be constructed out of the responses to the survey is the one measuring individual earnings. For the purpose of this article, earnings were evaluated taking into account both the primary and secondary occupations of the workers (when applicable) over a one-year period. The resulting figures were adjusted by the consumer price index to express them in 1997 prices. Focusing on annual earnings—rather than, say, daily or weekly earnings—is important in developing countries, because many jobs out of the public sector are casual or seasonal. Annual earnings can be low despite occasionally high daily or weekly earnings. The chosen earnings variable thus captures the fact that workers separated from the public sector may spend long periods out of a job. Unfortunately, data on the labor earnings of many farmers and self-employed workers were missing in the national household survey. Discarding the corresponding observations led to an over-representation of the public sector and the private formal sector in the sample.

Data on public sector workers came from two different sources. A public sector census provided information on the individual characteristics of those workers as of 1996, whereas the data base of the ministry of finance provided information on public sector wages as of 1997. The individual records from these two sources were matched after adding one year of age and one year of service to the public sector census, to have all the data reflect the situation as of 1997. Only workers in the occupational categories "O" to "Z", which were the ones targeted by the downsizing program, were retained in the matching process. The earnings data included bonuses and other allowances.

Summary statistics on earnings and individual characteristics in the two data sets are reported in table 1. The first two columns in this table correspond to the national household survey, whereas the third column is from the public sector database.

Predicted Losses

A key step toward predicting the losses from separation is to estimate earnings functions for people who do not work in the public sector. Earnings functions are among the best-established empirical regularities in economics. These functions quantify the relationship between individual characteristics, such as those listed in table 1, and labor earnings. Let annual earnings be denoted as E_i, and characteristics such as gender, education, age or region of residence as "X_1", "X_2", ..., "X_k". For reasons that will become clear below, the dummy variable that indicates whether the person works in the private formal sector is highlighted by notating it differently, as F_i. An earnings function can be written as follows:

$$\text{Log } E_i = \beta_0 + \beta_1 X_{1i} + \beta_2 X_{2i} + \ldots + \beta_k X_{ki} + \beta_F F_i + \varepsilon_i \tag{1}$$

Table 1. Summary Statistics

Individual characteristics	Household survey		Public sector database
	All workers	Private sector	
Male (yes = 1)	0.73	0.71	0.61
Schooling (years)	6.57	6.38	5.89
Age (years)	31.95	32.27	38.94
Seniority in the job (years)	—	—	11.67
Married (yes = 1)	0.92	0.91	0.76
Number of dependents	5.78	5.65	3.59
Bissau (yes = 1)	0.71	0.68	0.65
Public sector (yes = 1)	0.22	0.00	1.00
Formal private sector (yes = 1)	0.11	0.12	0.00
Earnings (thousands of CFAF per year)	372.0	354.5	169.9
Number of observations	488	344	3,048

— Not available.

Note: Earnings figures are measured as of 1997. In the household survey data, they include earnings in main and secondary occupations. In the public sector data, they include bonuses and allowances. The public sector data base includes employees in categories "O" to "Z" only.

In this expression, ε_i is an individual-specific disturbance, on average equal to zero.

Data from the 1991 national household survey are used to estimate equation (1). The results can be found in table 2. Several regularities emerge from these results. First, it appears that labor earnings increase significantly with the level of education. The premium for an additional year of schooling is roughly 12 percent. Second, earnings are higher for those who are married, and they are marginally higher for those with more dependents as well. Third, there are wide regional disparities. Earnings for individuals with the same characteristics could be about 30 percent higher in Bissau than elsewhere. And fourth, individuals with the same characteristics earn 30 to 40 percent more in the formal private sector than in the informal sector.[3]

Predicted earnings after separation are given by the following equation:

$$\hat{E}_i = \exp\left(\hat{\beta}_0 + \hat{\beta}_1 X_{1i} + \hat{\beta}_2 X_{2i} + \ldots + \hat{\beta}_k X_{ki} + \hat{\beta}_F F^*_i\right) \qquad (2)$$

3. The coefficient multiplying a dummy variable can be interpreted as a percentage only if it is small, in absolute terms. For relatively large coefficients, like β_F, the percentage effect is given by $[\exp(1 + \beta_F) - 1] \times 100$.

TABLE 2. EARNINGS OUTSIDE THE PUBLIC SECTOR
CFAF, 1997 prices

Individual characteristics	Dependent variable: Log of annual earnings in main and secondary occupations		
Male (yes = 1)	0.0963	0.0551	0.0897
	(0.813)	(0.464)	(0.759)
Schooling (years)	0.1198***	0.1204***	0.1224***
	(7.832)	(7.929)	(8.130)
Experience (years)	−0.0046	−0.0061	−0.0065
	(−0.705)	(−0.939)	(−1.008)
Married (yes = 1)	0.4987***	0.4501**	0.4068
	(2.777)	(2.510)	(0.023)
Number of dependents	0.0224*	0.0244*	0.0191
	(1.677)	(1.836)	(1.438)
Bissau (yes = 1)			0.3115***
			(2.774)
Formal sector (yes = 1)		0.3854**	0.3387**
		(2.448)	(2.160)
Constant	10.633***	10.692***	10.529***
	(32.636)	(32.967)	(32.253)
F-statistic	16.90	15.29	14.46
Adjusted R^2	0.200	0.200	0.216
Observations	344	344	344

Note: All regressions were estimated by ordinary least squares; t-statistics are reported in parentheses. Significant coefficients at the 10, 5, and 1 percent levels are indicated by one, two, and three asterisks, respectively.

where estimated coefficients are indicated by a caret, and F^*_i is a dummy variable for the sector in which the separated worker is expected to end up. This variable is equal to one if the worker gets a job in the formal private sector, and equal to zero if he or she gets a job in the informal sector. Equation (2) makes use of the all the individual characteristics for which data are available, despite the fact that some of them do not appear to play a substantial role in explaining earnings outside the public sector. For instance, according to the earnings functions in table 2, men earn 5 to 10 percent more than women, other things being equal, but the coefficient multiplying the gender variable is not statistically significant (the corresponding t-statistic is low).[4] The aim of the exercise, however, is not to identify the determinants of earnings outside the

4. Note that the hypothesis that all the coefficients are statistically insignificant is rejected by the data (the F-statistic is high).

FIGURE 1. ANNUAL LOSS IN EARNINGS FROM SEPARATION

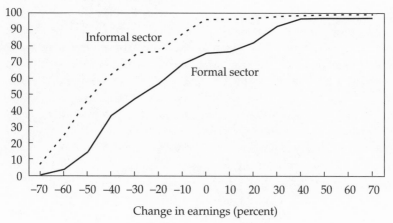

Accumulated employees (percent)

Change in earnings (percent)

Note: The solid line is constructed under the assumption that all separated workers get jobs in the private formal sector of the economy, whereas the dotted line assumes that they all end up working in the informal sector.

public sector, but rather to predict them in the most accurate way. Consequently, the regression that yields the highest coefficient of determination is used in the exercise. This is the regression reported in the last column of table 2.

Equation (2) can be used to estimate the predicted change in earnings from separation, η_i, as follows:

$$\eta_i = \frac{\hat{E}_i - W_i}{W_i} \tag{3}$$

Figure 1 displays the distribution of η_i for the 3,048 employees in categories "O" to "Z", using two different assumptions. The solid line is drawn under the hypothesis that no separated workers get a formal sector job ($F^*_i = 0$ for all "i"). In this case, almost all employees can be expected to experience a loss in earnings. At the other end, the dotted line assumes that all separated workers end up in the formal private sector of the economy ($F^*_i = 1$). In this case, roughly a quarter of the separated employees would earn more after separation than in the public sector. Some could even expect to make roughly 300 percent more.

It would be unrealistic, however, to assume that all separated workers will get formal sector jobs. In the case of Guinea-Bissau, roughly one-fifth of the separated workers could be hired by the new private contractors in charge of the cleaning, surveillance, and maintenance of government facilities. These contractors will be under close scrutiny to comply with labor market regulations. The rest of the separated workers, on the other hand, will most likely end up in the informal sector, and get no perquisites or benefits attached to their jobs. The indicator F^*_i is therefore generated randomly, assuming that the probability of getting a formal sector job after separation is one-fifth for all workers. Several random draws were produced, but the earnings distribution only changed marginally, because the public sector database contains a very large number of employees in the categories "O" to "Z".

The direct approach measures the loss L^D_i that the separated public sector worker "i" would experience based on the following expression:

$$L^D_i = \sum_{t=1}^{A_i} \frac{W_i - \hat{E}_i}{(1+r)^t} + \sum_{t=A_i+1}^{N_i} \frac{(1-F^*_i)\,P_i}{(1+r)^t} \tag{4}$$

The first sum of terms in the right-hand side of equation (4) is the earnings loss the worker would experience in all the years since displacement until retirement, measured in present value. In this sum, W_i represents salaries and tangible benefits in the public sector, A_i is the number of years before the worker reaches the legal retirement age, and r is a subjective discount rate. The second sum of terms is the income loss over all the years between retirement and death. In this sum, P_i is the old-age pension the worker would be entitled to if he or she stayed in the public sector until retirement age, and N_i is the expected number of years before death. Equation (4) assumes no loss in old-age income if the worker gets a formal sector job after separation.

To calculate L^D_i, information on the retirement program for civil servants is needed. In the case of Guinea-Bissau, the legal retirement age is 55 years for both men and women ($A_i = 55$ for all i). In fact, 300 employees in the public sector database exceed that age. Losses were not computed for those employees, as a sensible downsizing program would not have to compensate them, but just require them to retire. The pension P_i was calculated by applying the regulations in force as of 1998, under the assumption of continued service until retirement age, without any change in real remuneration. It was also assumed that the life

FIGURE 2.   Total Loss in Earnings and Benefits from Separation

Accumulated employees (percent)

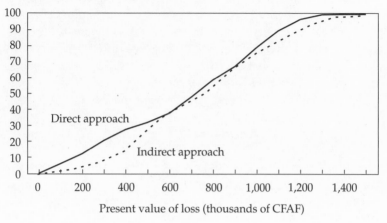

Present value of loss (thousands of CFAF)

Note: The solid line is constructed using the direct approach to estimate the value of benefits, whereas the dotted line is based on the indirect approach.

expectancy is 70 years for male civil servants, and 75 years for females. Finally, the discount rate was set at 10 percent, which is a commonly used value of the time preference in the social assessment of investment projects.

The indirect approach, in turn, measures the loss L_i^I as follows:

$$L_i^I = \sum_{t=1}^{A_i} \frac{W_i(1 + \eta_{max}) - \hat{E}_i}{(1 + r)^t} \qquad (5)$$

In this expression, η_{max} is the highest "credible" value of the predicted change in earnings. To implement this approach, it was assumed that the highest 5 percent of the estimated η_i reflect measurement error, rather than potential gains in earnings from separation. Under this assumption, η_{max} is slightly higher than 20 percent. Put differently, public sector employees would value the benefits associated with their jobs, including old-age income security, at roughly one-fifth of their cash earnings. As for the direct approach, the loss from separation was not estimated for employees who had already reached retirement age.

Figure 2 summarizes the predicted losses from separation. The solid line corresponds to the direct approach, and the dotted line to the indirect approach. It is quite remarkable how close the two estimates are. The average loss is CFAF 672,000 per worker based on the direct approach, and CFAF 745,000 based on the indirect approach. These figures amount to roughly $1,300 per worker.[5] The two approaches also yielded consistent results at the individual level, as shown by the correlation coefficient between L_i^D and L_i^I, which was 0.765. This similarity of the results suggests that the estimated loss provides a reliable benchmark to assess alternative compensation offers.

Separation Packages

The compensation offered to redundant workers can be a lump sum, or it can be based on a formula involving several observable characteristics of those workers. A frequently used formula makes compensation a multiple of the salary in government. For instance, workers can be offered two years of salary. Another popular formula also takes seniority into account, as compensation is set at a specific number of months of salary per year of service in government. This is the formula that the government of Guinea-Bissau was planning to use for its public sector downsizing operation, as a December 1999 *Despacho* from the Ministry of Civil Service and Labor had set up severance pay for workers in the occupational categories "O" to "Z" at 10 months of salary per year of service.

The choice of the arguments considered in these formulas is to some extent arbitrary. There are other potentially observable individual characteristics of the worker, in addition to salary and seniority. Some of them could help predict the loss in earnings and benefits separated workers would experience. For instance, the analysis in the previous section made it clear that alternative earnings outside the public sector increase with educational attainment. The "just right" compensation may thus need to be higher for a public sector worker with primary education only than for an otherwise identical worker, with an identical public sector salary, who completed a few years of secondary or

---

5. The main difference is at the low end of the distribution. The direct approach suggests that some government employees would experience a very small loss in the event of separation. According to the indirect approach, however, roughly 85 percent of the employees would face a total loss in excess of CFAF 400,000.

technical education. Similarly, potential earnings are higher in Bissau than outside the city. The "just right" compensation could then be higher in remote areas, where job alternatives might be limited, than in the capital city.

A second problem with the usual rules of thumb is that they implicitly assume a relationship between losses from separation and the few individual characteristics they consider, which may be wrong. For instance, offering two years of salary as compensation may sound reasonable, but one or three years of salary could be reasonable as well. Similarly, putting a premium on seniority leads to higher compensation for workers who are close to retirement age than for workers at the beginning of their public sector careers. It is not clear, however, that the former lose more from displacement than the latter. If the earnings gap between jobs in and out of the public sector is large, young public sector workers may actually experience a larger loss, in present value, because they are denied decades of relatively high earnings. Thus, the relationship between tenure and losses from displacement could well be negative, or change signs, whereas usual rules of thumb assume that it is always positive.

Three of the four packages considered in this article—identified with the letters A, B, and C—are based on the usual rules of thumb. Package A is a lump sum. The amount of compensation S_i^A received by employee "i" is given by

$$S_i^A = \theta^A \tag{6}$$

Parameter θ^A is allowed to vary to make compensation more attractive. Package B, in turn, is a multiple of the employee's salary in government. The amount of compensation S_i^B thus verifies the following:

$$S_i^B = \theta^B W_i \tag{7}$$

As before, parameter θ^B can be adjusted to make the package more attractive. In package C, the amount of compensation S_i^C is set in months of salary per year of service, Y_i, as follows:

$$S_i^C = \theta^C W_i Y_i \tag{8}$$

Variable Y_i could be one of the individual characteristics X_i considered when estimating potential earnings out of the public sector in equation (1).

Package D, on the other hand, is based on an analysis of the distribution of predicted losses in benefits in earnings from separation. These losses, as defined by equations (4) and (5), are nonlinear relationships involving the individual characteristics of the employees, as well as the characteristics of their government jobs. The meaning of these equations might be too difficult to explain to public sector employees with limited education. Lack of transparency, in turn, may jeopardize the whole downsizing process. It is therefore important to devise a simple, linear formula that yields a good approximation to the present value of the earnings. For instance, the following formula could be considered:

$$S_i^D = \theta^D + \lambda_0 W_i Y_i + \lambda_1 X_{1i} + \lambda_2 X_{2i} + \ldots + \lambda_h X_{hi} \qquad (9)$$

The number of variables "h" in equation (9) is smaller than their number "k" in equation (1), because only those individual characteristics that account for a large proportion of the variation in the predicted loss should be retained. Variables that could be subject to fraud or manipulation by the displaced workers would need to be excluded as well.[6] For instance, information on marital status and the number of dependents is not reliable in countries where out-of-wedlock births and extended families are common. In the case of Guinea-Bissau, equation (9) could also include the formal sector dummy F^*_i, because workers who are hired by the new private sector contractors are likely to experience a smaller loss and, hence, need less compensation. To keep the discussion general, however, package D is designed as if the government had no information on the sector in which displaced workers will end up.

A simple statistical analysis can be used to assign values to parameters λ_0 to λ_h. In tables 3 and 4, the present value of the losses from separation (L_i^D and L_i^I, respectively) is regressed on W_i, Y_i and a series of individual characteristics. When using the direct approach to measure losses from separation, the regressions were carried out for all government employees who have not reached retirement age. When using the indirect approach, employees who could apparently earn much more out of the public sector than they earn in it were also dropped from the

---

6. In some countries, legal considerations also matter. In particular, a different level of compensation for men and women could be seen as a form of discrimination.

TABLE 3. PREDICTORS OF TOTAL LOSS—DIRECT APPROACH (thousands of CFAF)

Individual characteristics	Dependent variable: Total loss in earnings and benefits from separation					
	Lowest 1/3	Lowest 2/3	All	Lowest 1/3	Lowest 2/3	All
Earnings (thousands of CFAF)	3.054** (2.507)	1.053 (0.781)	4.625*** (3.951)			
Earnings (thousands of CFAF) × years of service				0.0194*** (4.119)	0.0091* (1.874)	0.0535*** (13.858)
Male (yes = 1)	−54.16*** (−5.520)	−81.45*** (−7.902)	−46.25*** (−5.146)	−60.47*** (−6.110)	−85.21*** (−8.096)	−76.74*** (−8.516)
Schooling (years)	−9.01*** (−3.977)	−45.50*** (−20.159)	−88.58*** (−52.699)	−9.00*** (−3.995)	−45.68*** (−20.249)	−87.61*** (−53.847)
Age (years)	3.03*** (4.579)	4.76*** (7.210)	0.50 (0.906)	1.62* (2.206)	4.23*** (5.926)	−3.39*** (−5.605)
Bissau (yes = 1)	11.53 (0.818)	−167.86*** (−14.753)	−217.74*** (−23.567)	18.27 (1.304)	−167.48*** (−14.754)	−212.37*** (−23.743)
Independent term	−283.07 (−1.342)	614.48*** (2.654)	564.36*** (2.825)	252.06*** (6.362)	801.06*** (21.308)	544.50*** (46.694)
F-Statistic	20.02	199.44	738.63	22.37	200.33	821.04
Adjusted R^2	0.094	0.352	0.574	0.105	0.353	0.599
Observations	916	1,830	2,744	916	1,830	2,744

Note: All regressions were estimated by ordinary least squares. t-statistics are reported in parentheses. Significant coefficients at the 10, 5, and 1 percent levels are indicated by one, two, and three asterisks, respectively.

TABLE 4. PREDICTORS OF TOTAL LOSS—INDIRECT APPROACH
(thousands of CFAF)

Individual characteristics	Dependent variable: Total loss in earnings and benefits from separation					
	Lowest 1/3	Lowest 2/3	All	Lowest 1/3	Lowest 2/3	All
Earnings (thousands of CFAF)	−0.2655	1.650	5.815***	n.a.	n.a.	n.a.
	(−0.235)	(1.447)	(6.376)			
Earnings (thousands of CFAF) × years of service	n.a.	n.a.	n.a.	0.0056	0.0130***	0.0123***
				(1.551)	(3.567)	(3.968)
Male (yes = 1)	−2.70	−50.68***	−56.82***	−5.81	−57.56***	−60.99***
	(−0.305)	(−5.814)	(−8.129)	(−0.649)	(−6.438)	(−8.402)
Schooling (years)	−11.83***	−57.35***	−95.04***	−12.36***	−57.01***	−94.21***
	(−4.232)	(−23.637)	(−66.406)	(−4.399)	(−23.642)	(−65.322)
Age (years)	−6.89***	−14.97***	−22.39***	−7.29**	−15.83***	−23.30***
	(−11.273)	(−23.023)	(−51.848)	(−10.989)	(−22.877)	(−47.962)
Bissau (yes = 1)	−10.95	−183.93***	−220.99***	−9.48	−181.77***	−217.61***
	(−0.943)	(−19.570)	(−30.994)	(−0.815)	(−19.433)	(−30.407)
Independent term	794.66***	1,415.06***	1,322.78***	759.24***	1,703.49***	2,317.16***
	(4.306)	(7.231)	(8.506)	(16.777)	(41.711)	(106.063)
F-statistic	32.83	180.2	1305.3	33.39	183.5	1,288.0
Adjusted R^2	0.156	0.341	0.715	0.158	0.347	0.713
Observations	864	1,730	2,595	864	1,730	2,595

n.a. Not applicable.

Note: All regressions were estimated by ordinary least squares. t-statistics are reported in parentheses. Significant coefficients at the 10, 5, and 1 percent levels are indicated by one, two, and three asterisks, respectively.

sample. In more technical terms, only those government employees for whom $\eta_i < \eta_{max}$ were considered. Also, all regressions were carried out for three groups of workers: the entire sample, the third with the smallest losses, and the two-thirds with the smallest losses. Splitting the sample in this way allowed identification of the variables for which the linear approximation assumed in equation (9) is valid.

The regressions in tables 3 and 4 do not aim to "explain" the losses from separation. The "right" model is not the linear expression in equation (9), but rather the nonlinear expressions in equations (4) and (5). The purpose of these regressions is only to find a linear relationship that could "mimic" a substantial portion of the variance in the predicted losses from separation. Moreover, the left-hand-side variables in the regressions in tables 3 and 4 were constructed using the right-hand-side variables in those same regressions, which accounts for the apparently high statistical significance (t-statistic) of some of the estimated coefficients. Not all coefficients were highly significant for all subsamples, however, which suggests that the linear approximation only holds for selected individual characteristics.

Based on the results in tables 3 and 4, three individual characteristics are good predictors of the loss from separation, regardless of the loss indicator used: gender, education, and region of residence. The sign of the corresponding coefficients was the same across all specifications. Also, their absolute size was similar across subsamples, except for the third with the smallest losses. At the other extreme, age appears to be a poor predictor, because the sign of the corresponding coefficient changed with the subsample considered. As for the arguments used in standard separation packages (earnings in government and earnings multiplied by years of service), they fell in between these two extremes. The corresponding coefficients were positive most of the times, as the usual rules of thumb assume, but their absolute size varied substantially with the subsample considered.

In what follows, the value of parameter λ_0 was set at $1/24$, which corresponds to half a month of salary per year of service. A bonus of CFAF 60,000 was given to female workers, and a bonus of CFAF 150,000 was given to those who live and work out of Bissau. Also, the resulting package was reduced by CFAF 50,000 for each additional year of education. All the other λ coefficients in equation (9) were set equal to zero, so that the only "free" parameter was θ^D. It is important to emphasize that this is not a proposed compensation package for Guinea-Bissau, but rather a reference to assess the performance of the usual rules of thumb.

Cost and Fairness

The performance of the four separation packages can be evaluated on two grounds: cost and fairness. For each government employee, the separation package can be compared to the expected loss in earnings and benefits. If the package exceeds the expected loss, it is assumed that the employee would be satisfied. It follows that each separation package is associated with a satisfaction rate, ranging from 0 to 100 percent. The cost and fairness indicators were calculated for a prespecified satisfaction rate, for instance, 60 percent. Cost was measured as the average package of those employees who would be satisfied by the amount of compensation received. Fairness was measured as the correlation coefficient between the compensation and the loss in earnings and benefits, for those employees who would be satisfied. Implicitly, both indicators used voluntary separations as a benchmark, because the fraction of employees satisfied should be the same as the fraction of employees who would take the package and leave the public sector, if they had a choice.

In practice, every "reasonable" package will overcompensate some employees and undercompensate others. Only exceptionally will compensation match exactly the predicted loss in earnings and benefits. Therefore, the employees who are satisfied with the package are most likely overcompensated. It follows that the average cost of a package is higher than the average loss in earnings and benefits of those employees who are satisfied with it. In terms of the voluntary separation benchmark, mistakes in the direction of overcompensation materialize, whereas mistakes in the direction of undercompensation have no practical implication. Overcompensation also implies that the fairness of a separation package can be low. If the package received by all satisfied employees was equal to their predicted loss (or a multiple of it), the fairness coefficient would be equal to one. In practice, however, some employees get a windfall whereas others are compensated "just right," so that the fairness coefficient can be close to zero, or even negative.

Tables 5 and 6 report the cost and fairness of each of the four packages, for nine satisfaction rates ranging from 10 to 90 percent. The zero satisfaction rate is uninteresting, because it would require no compensation. At the other end, the 100 percent satisfaction rate can only be reached at unreasonably high separation costs, because the package has to be generous enough to match the highest loss in earnings and benefits throughout the sample, and this is often an outlier. The only difference between tables 5 and 6 concerns the loss indicator used. In table 5

TABLE 5. PERFORMANCE OF ALTERNATIVE PACKAGES—DIRECT APPROACH

Percent of employees satisfied	Average compensation per separated employee (thousands of CFAF)				Correlation coefficient between compensation and loss			
	A	B	C	D	A	B	C	D
10	176.0	138.8	227.1	232.7	0.000	-0.193	0.650	0.854
20	300.5	300.4	451.5	397.8	0.000	0.015	0.656	0.743
30	468.8	464.3	660.6	465.2	0.000	0.072	0.765	0.658
40	632.5	633.9	818.8	567.2	0.000	-0.013	0.735	0.649
50	722.0	724.3	964.3	667.0	0.000	-0.040	0.686	0.644
60	818.0	816.2	1,157.3	736.7	0.000	-0.035	0.621	0.643
70	939.5	944.2	1,464.0	809.1	0.000	-0.035	0.528	0.668
80	1,007.4	1,014.4	2,143.6	871.8	0.000	-0.064	0.442	0.713
90	1,106.3	1,107.2	3,642.0	927.3	0.000	-0.038	0.351	0.749

Note: Package A is a variable lump sum; package B is a variable multiple of the salary in government; package C is a variable multiple of the salary multiplied by the number of years of service; package D is a variable lump sum, plus half a month of salary per year of service, minus CFAF 50,000 per year of completed education, plus CFAF 60,000 for female employees, plus CFAF 150,000 for employees who work out of Bissau. The variable component of each package is increased until the percentage of satisfied employees indicated in the first column of the table is reached. The figures in italics indicate the cheapest and fairest package for each satisfaction rate.

TABLE 6. PERFORMANCE OF ALTERNATIVE PACKAGES—INDIRECT APPROACH

Percent of employees satisfied	Average compensation per separated employee (thousands of CFAF)				Correlation coefficient between compensation and loss			
	A	B	C	D	A	B	C	D
10	358.0	361.0	441.0	412.7	0.000	-0.191	0.596	0.553
20	437.6	437.6	636.0	556.7	0.000	-0.059	0.629	0.524
30	513.0	514.0	813.5	620.6	0.000	-0.053	0.615	0.562
40	624.2	618.7	989.7	650.4	0.000	-0.029	0.591	0.594
50	760.0	762.4	1,188.3	705.5	0.000	-0.036	0.553	0.617
60	843.0	841.6	1,446.7	783.0	0.000	-0.027	0.496	0.633
70	932.0	930.6	1,862.8	861.0	0.000	-0.013	0.455	0.651
80	1,065.5	1,064.9	2,759.8	940.1	0.000	-0.010	0.391	0.671
90	1,193.0	1,194.8	4,806.3	1,052.8	0.000	-0.020	0.326	0.704

Note: Package *A* is a variable lump sum; package *B* is a variable multiple of the salary in government; package *C* is a variable multiple of the salary multiplied by the number of years of service; package *D* is a variable lump sum, plus half a month of salary per year of service, minus CFAF 50,000 per year of completed education, plus CFAF 60,000 for female employees, plus CFAF 150,000 for employees who work out of Bissau. The variable component of each package is increased until the percentage of satisfied employees indicated in the first column of the table is reached. The figures in italics indicate the cheapest and fairest package for each satisfaction rate.

the total loss in earnings and benefits is the one obtained using the direct approach, whereas table 6 is based on the indirect approach. The figures in italics in these two tables indicate the cheapest package, and the fairest package, for each satisfaction rate.

In the case of Guinea-Bissau, packages A and B are quite similar. This is because of the very small variation in earnings across employees in categories "O" to "Z". If all workers have roughly the same salary in government, a package defined as a multiple of this salary is not too different from a lump-sum payment. Whereas salaries in government are roughly the same for all employees in categories "O" to "Z", losses from separation are not. As the correlation coefficient between a constant and a variable is zero, packages A and B perform very poorly in terms of fairness. They are cost-effective at low satisfaction rates, however. If downsizing can be carried out without fully compensating more than one-third of government employees, "flat" packages of this sort could keep downsizing expenditures under control.

At the other end, "tailored" compensation, as in package D, is the most cost-effective alternative if satisfaction rates need to be high. Packages C and D have a similar performance at low satisfaction rates. The average cost per separated worker is slightly higher for package C, but the fairness coefficient can be higher as well. In order to attain high satisfaction rates, however, the number of months of salary per year of service required by package C becomes too high. At a 70 percent satisfaction rate, package C costs roughly twice as much as package D, but the latter does much better in terms of fairness. The gap between the two packages becomes dramatic at very high satisfaction rates. In fact, "tailored" compensation dominates all the alternatives, both on grounds of cost and fairness, if a majority of the workers need to be "bought off."

The compensation formula that the government of Guinea-Bissau was planning to use for its public sector downsizing operation, which is a special case of package C, turns out to be quite onerous. This formula would lead to a satisfaction rate of 78 percent, based on the direct approach, or 73 percent, based on the indirect approach. The average cost per satisfied worker would be roughly CFAF 2 million, and the fairness coefficient would be around 45 percent. Better outcomes could be attained spending less than half. A lump sum of less than CFAF 1 million would achieve the same satisfaction rate of the formula considered in Guinea-Bissau. A similar result, at a similar cost, would be obtained offering less than seven years of salary as compensation. Package D would be even less expensive, as it would cost roughly CFAF 880,000 per satisfied worker. The fairness coefficient would, in this case, be close to 70 percent.

Conclusion

The approach to compensation discussed in this article follows some basic economic principles, so that its validity should be quite general. The simulations presented, however, should be interpreted with caution, because they are clearly specific. This is because countries often differ in their labor market characteristics, and in the criteria underlying pay and benefits in the public sector. As a result, the distribution of the predicted losses in earnings and benefits from job separation may vary substantially from country to country. Moreover, this article has focused on a narrowly defined group of public sector workers, namely relatively unskilled individuals performing cleaning, surveillance, and maintenance tasks. Even in the specific case of Guinea-Bissau, the distribution of predicted losses could be quite different for other groups, such as clerical workers or teachers. Therefore, the "ranking" of packages resulting from the cost and fairness comparisons proposed may not have general validity.

Since the aim of this exercise was to contribute to actual policymaking, the simulations in this article were deliberately simple and may be subject to criticism on methodological grounds. Important labor market issues, including self-selection into public sector jobs, were not addressed. Earnings outside the public sector were predicted here as if government employees were not systematically different from other labor force participants. It could well be, however, that only the smartest workers make it to public sector jobs, or only the least ambitious stick to them. The earnings of a worker who is smarter than the average should be higher than those predicted by a standard earnings function, which does not include talent among its arguments. Conversely, the earnings of a worker who is less ambitious than the average could be lower. More rigorous simulations would need to be based on a deeper analysis of the labor market dealing, among others, with the self-selection problem.

It is also worth emphasizing that this article was deliberately narrow in its approach. A separation package could be cheaper and fairer than others, but still be inadvisable. When separations are voluntary, low cost is achieved by implicitly targeting those workers who have the least to lose in the event of separation, either because they earn very little in the public sector, or because they have a relatively high earnings potential outside of it. Typically, the most educated workers are those who have the least to lose. From a public sector reform perspective, however, it is not clear that separating these workers represents an improvement. The acceptability of a package is clearly not an issue when separations are involuntary, in which case the targeting of redundant workers and their compensation can be dissociated. And it is not an issue in Guinea-Bissau, where all workers in categories "O" to "Z" are redundant, because cleaning, surveillance, and maintenance functions should be performed by the private sector. In general, though, the implications of different separation packages on the characteristics of those who would be satisfied by them should not be ignored.

Even in the absence of adverse selection, a cheap and fair separation package would not be advisable if its economic returns were negative. Most compensation alternatives seem financially sound, because they trade the equivalent of a few years in salary for a lifetime of payments, in the form of salaries, benefits, and old-age pensions. However, a comprehensive economic analysis should also take into account the effects of downsizing on the allocation of labor across sectors. Many government employees have a very low productivity, but it is not at all obvious that they would be more productive out of the public sector. Moving from government employment to unemployment, or to the informal sector, could actually reduce total output. Although there is clearly no reason to overspend in compensation, even a "just right" package could be a bad idea in this case.

Finally, there is an important political caveat. If appropriate compensation is needed to make the workers accept the prospect of downsizing, it is very likely that the package will have to be negotiated with public sector trade unions. In that case, the final compensation formula may not be the cheapest one, or the fairest one, but rather a compromise shaped by the bargaining power of all the players involved. From this perspective, the simulation approach proposed in this article should not be seen as an example of "mindless social engineering," but rather as a tool to introduce some economic rationality in delicate political negotiations. Although the approach could certainly be refined, it represents an improvement compared to the ad hoc way in which these negotiations are usually carried out.

References

Alderman, Harold, Sudharshan Canagarajah, and Stephen Younger. 1996. "A Comparison of Ghanaian Civil Servants' Earnings before and after Retrenchment." *Journal of African Economies* 4(2):259–88.

Assaad, Ragui. 1999. "Matching Severance Payments with Worker Losses in the Egyptian Public Sector." *World Bank Economic Review* 13(1):117–54.

Chong, Alberto, and Ismail Radwan. 1999. "An Application of Alternative Retrenchment Schemes to State-Owned Enterprises in Tanzania." World Bank, Development Research Group, Washington, D.C.

Fiszbein, Ariel. 1994. "An Opportunity Cost Approach to Redundancy Compensation: An Application to Sri Lanka." *Estudios de Economía*, Special Issue on Labor Economics in Less Developed Countries, pp. 115–26.

Haltiwanger, John, and Manisha Singh. 1999. "Cross-Country Evidence on Public Sector Retrenchment." *World Bank Economic Review* 13(1):23–66.

Kikeri, Sunita. 1997. "Privatization and Labor: What Happens to Workers When Governments Divest." World Bank Technical Paper 396. World Bank, Washington, D.C.

Rama, Martín. 1999. "Public Sector Downsizing: An Introduction." *World Bank Economic Review* 13(1):1–22.

Rama, Martín, and Donna MacIsaac. 1999. "Earnings and Welfare after Separation: Central Bank Employees in Ecuador." *World Bank Economic Review* 13(1):89–116.

Part IV

Public Services and Development

Training for the Urban Unemployed: A Reevaluation of Mexico's Training Program, Probecat

Quentin Wodon and Mari Minowa

Abstract

For many years the government of Mexico has implemented a large training program for the unemployed. The program has been evaluated twice before with similar methodologies. These two evaluations yielded encouraging results in that the program apparently reduces unemployment and increases earnings. This article suggests that both evaluations may suffer from inappropriate controls for the endogeneity of program participation. Using the availability of the program at the state level as a determinant of individual participation, the article uses the data of the second evaluation to indicate that Probecat does not decrease unemployment, nor does it increase wages.

In 1984, the government of Mexico implemented a training program, Probecat (*Programa de Becas de Capacitación para Desempleados*), for the unemployed who live mostly in urban areas. The program has been evaluated twice, first by the World Bank using data from 1992 (Revenga, Riboud, and Tan 1994), and next by the Mexican Ministry of Labor using data from 1994 (STPS 1995).[1] Both evaluations used longitudinal data, comparing a sample of Probecat participants (the treatment group)

---

1. An earlier evaluation was attempted by Carlson (1991), but this evaluation did not consider the problem of endogeneity of program placement or selection bias, which is crucial for good evaluations.

with a sample of unemployed individuals from Mexico's urban employment survey (the control group). The second evaluation closely followed the method used in the first evaluation. The two evaluations yielded positive results. Controlling for other characteristics, such as education, family situation, and professional experience, program participants find employment faster than nonparticipants and they earn higher wages. These encouraging results have been used to support the extension of the program, which now serves about 550,000 beneficiaries per year (as of 1996–98), as compared with only 50,000 in the first decade of the program (1984–93).

This article reassesses the results of past evaluations of Probecat. We suggest that past evaluations suffered from inappropriate controls for the endogeneity of program participation. For example, past evaluations concluded from Cox regressions that the time necessary to find employment after the training was reduced for program participants, but this might have been due to sample selection because program participants may also be those most eager to work. We argue that the matching techniques used in past evaluations of Probecat were not sufficient to handle this type of problem. Following Ravallion and Wodon (1998), we use an alternative econometric method for evaluating the impact of Probecat. Specifically, the availability of Probecat at the state level is used as an instrumental variable to control for the endogeneity of program placement. We then find that Probecat has no impact on unemployment and wages.

The disappointing results of Probecat in terms of raising wages and employment should not be surprising. Most retraining programs in Organisation for Economic Co-operation and Development (OECD) countries have been found to have limited impacts, and when programs have been found to have some impact, this impact tends to vanish after a few years (Dar and Gill 1998). The fact that Probecat may not be beneficial in the medium to long run for participants does not mean that it should be suppressed. The program could be considered a temporary safety net (through the minimum wage stipend) rather than a training program. Alternatively, it could be improved to provide training with longer-lasting effects. To motivate an inquiry into how to improve the program, however, it must first be recognized that contrary to the results of earlier evaluations, the program may not be satisfactory.

The structure of the article is as follows. After a description of the program and the changes made over the years, we review the results of past evaluations. We then present our own new results. A conclusion with policy implications follows.

Program Description

Probecat, the Mexican Job Training Program for Unemployed Workers, was established in 1984 in response to rising unemployment and deteriorating living standards in the aftermath of the 1982 economic crisis. Despite a comparatively low open unemployment rate (6 percent in four major cities in 1984), Mexico suffered (then as now) from chronic underemployment. (For a discussion of unemployment and underemployment data in Mexico at that time, see, for example, Fleck and Sorrentino 1994.) Moreover, there was a recognition of the shortages of adequately trained labor in selected growing sectors of the economy. Thus, the stated objectives of the program was to improve the productivity of unemployed workers to help them find employment. The program has become massive in recent years. In the first decade of its existence (1984–93), Probecat provided training to roughly 50,000 people per year, but this rose to 199,000 people in 1994, 412,000 people in 1995, and about 550,000 people per year between 1996 and 1998.

Probecat is administered by the Mexican Ministry of Labor. The program provides publicly funded job training and a subsistence allowance during the training period to participating unemployed workers. Initially in 1986 Probecat provided training in high schools and other training centers. This first module of the program is referred to as school-based training (*Cursos Escolarizados*). Later, to strengthen the link between the training provided under the program and the actual needs of the productive sector in the economy, a new module of so-called in-service training was added (*Cursos Mixtos*). Under this module, local employers provide training, whereas the workers' stipend is paid by the government. Upon completion of the training, the employers are required to hire at least 70 percent of the trainees. A third module of the program consisting of training for the self-employed, PILEOT (*Programa de Iniciativas Locales de Empleo y Ocupación Temporal*), was created in 1995 in response to rapidly increasing unemployment after the 1994 financial crisis.

For the school-based and in-service modules, program beneficiaries are selected from the unemployed workers who register in the State Employment Service offices. The applicants' job skills and interests are evaluated against the needs of the local market. Apart from basic requirements for all, the selection procedure gives variable weights to different criteria. Only individuals with a total composite score exceeding a threshold level are eligible to participate. Participants can obtain training only once. The training lasts for two to three months on average, and participants receive stipends equivalent to the value of the minimum wage, plus transportation costs to the training site and basic health insurance coverage while on training. More details on the eligibility and features of each of the three modules are provided in table 1. It is worth mentioning that the share of in-service training within the Probecat beneficiaries increased from about 5 percent in 1987–92 to 20 percent in 1993, but dropped to 13 percent in 1996 as a result of the rapid expansion of the new PILEOT module created in 1995.

Past Evaluations

As mentioned in the introduction, two primary evaluations of Probecat have been conducted so far. The first evaluation was prepared by the World Bank (Revenga, Riboud, and Tan 1994), and used data from a survey administered in 1992 to Probecat trainees from the 1990 cohort. Data were gathered on unemployed individuals in the 1990–91 National Urban Employment Survey (*Encuesta Nacional de Empleo Urbano, or ENEU*) to construct the control group. The second evaluation was conducted in 1995 by the Ministry of Labor with a similar methodology (STPS 1995) and data for employment in 1993–94. Both studies sought to evaluate the impact of Probecat according to two main indicators: (a) the time to find a first job after the training and (b) monthly earnings. The studies also contain information on hours worked and hourly wages, as well as cost-benefit simulations, which will not be discussed here. Whereas Probecat participants were drawn only from the school-based module for the 1992 study, the 1995 study evaluated the impact of both the school-based and in-service modules.

Both studies used the posttraining labor market experiences of randomly selected program participants who graduated in the previous year, and they compared these experiences to those of a control group. For this control group, the studies used panel data on unemployed individuals drawn from the quarterly ENEU covering the main urban areas of Mexico. (Probecat is now available in rural areas, especially through the PILEOT module, but this was not the case before.) The ENEU used a quarterly rotation system so that each rotation group of individuals remained in the survey for five consecutive quarters. The choice of the quarterly data in the ENEU matched that of the survey of the Probecat participants. The ENEU included detailed information on employment status, monthly earnings, and hours worked per week. The Probecat survey administered to program participants was designed to match the questions in the ENEU, so that the information for the two

TABLE 1. MODULES OF PROBECAT'S MAIN TRAINING MODULES

	School-based training	In-service training	PILEOT
Eligibility rules	Unemployed, registered with SES, aged 16 to 55, having completed primary school and having at least 3 months of experience.	Unemployed, registered with SES, aged 18 to 55, having completed primary school (this can be waived by firm). No prior experience required.	Unemployed aiming at self-employment, aged 16 to 55, literate, no upper secondary schooling. Special module for community activities.
Training provider	Training schools or centers.	Participating firms.	Training centers or instructors.
Training duration	1 to 6 months.	1 to 3 months.	1 to 3 months.
Benefits received	Training, minimum wage, transportation costs, and health insurance.	Training, minimum wage, transportation costs, and health insurance.	Same, plus a set of tools for self employment module.
Training costs	Probecat program.	Firm (cost of instructors, equipment, and materials).	Probecat program.
Training content	Set by training provider with little customization.	Set by firm. Mostly hands-on training.	Set by the training provider with customization.
Placement	Required to register with SES. No placement.	Firms required to employ 70 percent of the trainees.	No particular follow-up.

Source: Created by the authors from information provided by the Ministry of Labor (STPS).

groups would, to a large extent, be comparable. That is, in addition to standard sociodemographic characteristics, the Probecat survey elicited information on the current or last job since completing Probecat, the first job after the training, the second job after the training, and the last job prior to participating in the program.

The two studies acknowledged that there may be unobservable characteristics influencing program participation and outcomes, and that these characteristics may be different between the treatment group (Probecat participants) and the control group (ENEU unemployed workers). To control for selection bias, the studies used two different approaches. The first approach was used for analyzing the length of the employment search, and the second for monthly earnings.

For the analysis of the length of the employment search, the studies relied on probit regressions for the probability of participating in Probecat to construct the control group. In the 1992 study, the individuals below a certain probability (0.6) of participating were eliminated from the sample. It is less clear what exactly was done in the 1995 evaluation, but the principle was the same. Next, using the (slightly) reduced sample of pooled treatment and control group members, Cox proportional hazards models were estimated to assess the impact of training on the time necessary to find employment. In 1995, for example, the regressors included dummy variables for the individual's age, the level of education, marital status, household structure, work experience, and characteristics of employment before being unemployed. The dependent variable was the number of months needed for finding employment, counted from the first month when the individual entered the control group (ENEU) or completed the training for participants.

For the analysis of earnings, both studies used Heckman's (1979) sample selection model. In the 1992 study, the first equation referred to the logarithm of monthly earnings, and the second equation to the probability of participating in the Probecat training. In the 1995 study, while the participation equation was the same, the first equation measured the difference in the logarithms of earnings before and after program participation with the logarithm set to zero in case of unemployment (neither of the studies actually provided the participation equations).

Overall, the results obtained in the two studies were encouraging for the program. In 1992, Probecat was found to reduce the length of unemployment for men, but not for women. In the 1995 study, both the school-based and in-service modules reduced the time needed to find employment for both men and women. As for monthly earnings, the 1992 study found positive impacts for men, but again not for women.

The 1995 study found positive impacts for men and negative impacts for women. Both studies also conducted cost-benefit analyses. The program costs were calculated using administrative data from the state and national program offices. Direct costs included the remuneration for instructors, the costs of training materials and facilities, and administrative costs for program operation. The training stipends paid to the program participants during the training were not included in the costs because they were considered safety net transfers. The treatment of indirect opportunity costs for participating in the program differed, but overall the two studies concluded that the program was cost effective and performing relatively well.

Although both studies were carefully implemented, several critiques can be made about the methodology used. Manski (1996) mentioned a few. First, in using the unemployed individuals in the ENEU to form the control group, it is assumed that none of the ENEU individuals have benefited from the program. This is not the case because every individual in the ENEU has some probability of having participated in Probecat. Fortunately, given that the program was small until 1993, only a very small minority of the individuals in the control group are likely to have participated in the program (this would not be true for future evaluations). Next, Manski pointed out that the combination of two random samples (Probecat trainees and ENEU unemployed individuals) was not actually a random sample, so that in the absence of the standard properties for the residuals, the results of regressions might not yield consistent parameter estimates, especially because the models used were sensitive to the assumption of bivariate normality (Goldberger 1983). In the absence of better data, not much could be done about this using standard techniques. Third, Manski argued that no theoretical proof exists that matching methods do indeed provide for a solution to the sample selection problem, although this could be debated. Finally, Manski noted that in the estimation of earnings, while participation in Probecat was controlled for, the sample selection bias resulting from the decision to work (which originally motivated the Heckman model) was not accounted for, which was recognized by the authors of the 1992 study.

In our own evaluation of Probecat to be presented in the next section, we do not solve all the above problems, but we try to solve some. Consider first the analysis of the duration of unemployment. The method used to control for endogeneity in past evaluations was rough because the matching was imprecise. Typically, when using matching procedures, one matches every participant with one, or perhaps a few, nonparticipants by minimizing the distance between the probability of participation of each participant and that of his match among the nonparticipants (Rosenbaum and Rubin 1983, 1985). Here the procedure had to be reversed because there were more participants than nonparticipants in the pooled sample, but the logic was the same: every nonparticipant should be matched on an individual basis with one, or very few, participants. This is apparently not what was done in past evaluations of Probecat. The matching was apparently not done on an individual basis. Instead, individuals with low probabilities of participating were excluded from the pooled sample. There is in fact evidence in both the 1992 and 1995 studies that there remains a problem of sample selection after the frequency matching because the coefficients of the inverse Mill's ratios in the Heckman regressions used for earnings tend to be statistically significant. This problem is not recognized in presenting the Cox regressions.

Consider next the earnings regressions. As noted by Manski, although the Heckman procedure allows in principle to control for the endogeneity of program placement, there is no control for the endogeneity of the decision to work. The procedure proposed in the next section provides a way to control for both types of endogeneity in the estimation.

Alternative Evaluation

This section provides our alternative evaluation results. After discussing the model for participation in Probecat, we analyze the impact of the program on the length of the employment search and on the earnings.

Participation Equations

To evaluate the impact of Probecat, we used the same data as that used in the 1995 study, but with an alternative methodology. Following Ravallion and Wodon (1998, 2000), we used the program availability in a geographic area as a determinant of program participation at the individual level, assuming that program availability does not influence outcomes (unemployment duration and earnings) that are conditional on individual participation. To measure geographical availability, we use 1,000 times the number of Probecat participants in a given state (Mexico is a federal entity with 32 states) as a proportion of the urban population in that state. (Up to recently, the program was targeted mainly to urban areas, and this holds for the 1994 data.) We used the same measure of program availability at the state level for the two modules (school-based and in-service) because we did not have data on the availability of each module separately.

As noted by Ravallion and Wodon (1998, 2000), if the program availability at the state level is to be used as an instrumental variable for determining program participation, apart from individual-level variables, it is important to include in the regressions state-level variables that may affect program participation, as well as outcomes. A full set of state dummies could not be included because in this case the program availability at the state level would be collinear with the state dummies. State variables, however, could be included. We used 13 such variables as controls, which are not shown in the regression tables. They include primary and secondary schooling and spending indicators, population density, shares of the urban and indigenous populations, state-level income, and variables related to wealth and consumption (cars, water, and electricity).

To tackle the problem of sample selection for the participation in the program, we first ran probit regressions for men and women separately to analyze the determinants of participation in the two modules of Probecat available at the time of the survey (school-based and in-service). The probability of participating in the school-based module is denoted by $P1_{ij}$, and the probability for individual i living in state j to participate in the in-service module is denoted by $P2_{ij}$. X_{ij} is a vector of individual level variables, and Z_j is a vector of state-level variables for state j. The relative availability of Probecat in state j is denoted by AP_j. We estimated the following:

$$P1^*_{ij} = \gamma_{P1}'X_{ij} + \delta_{P1}'Z_j + \mu_{P1}AP_j + \mu_{P1}AP_j^2 + \varepsilon_{P1ij}$$
$$\text{with } P1_{ij} = 1 \text{ if } P1^*_{ij} > 0 \text{ and } 0 \text{ if } P1^*_{ij} \leq 0 \tag{1}$$

$$P2^*_{ij} = \gamma_{P2}'X_{ij} + \delta_{P2}'Z_j + \mu_{P2}AP_j + \mu_{P2}AP_j^2 + \varepsilon_{P2ij}$$
$$\text{with } P2_{ij} = 1 \text{ if } P2^*_{ij} > 0 \text{ and } 0 \text{ if } P2^*_{ij} \leq 0 \tag{2}$$

The results of these probits are given in table 2. Individuals between 15 and 55 are more likely to participate in the program than younger and older individuals, which corresponds to the eligibility rules. Individuals with at least the primary level of education completed also tend to participate more (in comparison with the excluded category in the survey, which corresponds to the illiterate and those not having completed primary school), again because having completed primary school

TABLE 2. PARTICIPATION REGRESSIONS (PROBITS) FOR PROBECAT BY MODULE

| | School-based | | | | In-service | | | |
| | Men | | Women | | Men | | Women | |
	dF/dx	P > |z|	dF/dx	P > |z|	dF/dx	P > |z|	dF/dx	P > |z|
Aged between 15 and 25	0.183	0.004	0.288	0.243	0.283	0.997	0.973	0.000
Aged between 16 and 55	0.229	0.000	0.419	0.084	0.378	0.997	0.984	0.000
Primary education completed	0.158	0.000	0.174	0.058	0.902	0.997	0.068	0.146
Secondary or postprimary training	0.321	0.000	0.317	0.000	0.325	0.997	0.021	0.593
Higher level	0.248	0.000	0.318	0.001	0.627	0.997	-0.075	0.030
Household head	0.080	0.010	0.153	0.033	0.000	0.606	-0.008	0.796
Married individual	0.024	0.404	0.104	0.043	0.001	0.092	0.012	0.564
Household with 2 workers	0.050	0.022	0.029	0.505	0.000	0.416	0.053	0.009
Household with 3+ workers	0.042	0.078	0.027	0.601	0.000	0.915	0.042	0.078
Previous professional experience	-0.068	0.103	-0.067	0.366	-0.004	0.035	-0.217	0.000
Working experience in past year	0.108	0.006	0.115	0.061	0.000	0.891	0.021	0.434
Past year in firm 1–15 workers	0.103	0.002	0.243	0.000	0.001	0.309	0.026	0.433
Past year in firm 16–100 workers	0.035	0.355	0.156	0.055	0.003	0.041	0.094	0.048
Past year in firm 101–250 workers	0.121	0.006	0.056	0.609	0.001	0.301	0.123	0.072
Past year in firm 251+ workers	0.005	0.897	-0.048	0.535	0.001	0.303	0.159	0.002
Worked 35–48 hours in past year	0.087	0.000	0.084	0.075	0.000	0.451	0.006	0.763
Worked 48+ hours in past year	0.075	0.000	0.091	0.046	0.000	0.550	0.037	0.076
Income past year	0.000	0.000	0.000	0.001	0.000	0.664	0.000	0.911
Income squared past year	0.000	0.019	0.000	0.114	0.000	0.394	0.000	0.752
Program availability	0.107	0.000	0.092	0.014	0.003	0.005	0.155	0.015
Program availability squared	-0.004	0.001	-0.004	0.233	0.000	0.004	-0.018	0.020
Number of children	n.a.	n.a.	0.025	0.463	n.a.	n.a.	0.017	0.229
Number of children squared	n.a.	n.a.	-0.002	0.617	n.a.	n.a.	-0.003	0.198
Number of observations	2,160	n.a.	947	n.a.	2,160	n.a.	947	n.a.
Pseudo R^2	0.297	n.a.	0.233	n.a.	0.351	n.a.	0.331	n.a.

n.a. Not applicable.
Source: Authors' estimation from pooled Probecat and ENEU panel surveys (1993–94). Thirteen state-level control variables are included in the regression but not shown in the table. See text for more details.

is a requirement. Being married has an impact on participation only for women in the school-based module. There is also evidence that individuals with several workers in their household (apart from the individual considered in the sample) have higher participation rates. Having previous work experience is negatively correlated with participation (maybe because these individuals need less training), but having worked in the previous year is positively correlated (maybe because these individuals remain actively seeking employment). Having worked in firms with other workers (instead of having been self-employed) facilitates participation, as does the fact of having worked a large number of hours in the previous year. Higher incomes in the last year also influence positively the probability of participating. Finally, individual participation is positively correlated with the program availability at the state level. This is important because it confirms that state-level availability of the program is a valid instrumental variable. There is no need to discuss here the impact of the other 13 state-level variables that were included in the regressions, but not shown in the tables.

Impact of Probecat on the Length of Employment Search

We now consider the impact of Probecat on the length of the employment search. In the terminology of survival analysis, the survivor function $S(t)$ represents the length of unemployment after training (t is measured in months). Given $S(t)$, the hazard function $\lambda(t)$ denoting the chance of becoming employed (or the risk of remaining unemployed) at time t among the individuals who were not yet employed at that time is $\lambda(t) = -d(logS(t))/dt$. The survivor curve can be specified as a function of program participation, individual characteristics, and state characteristics, so that $\lambda = \lambda(t; X, Z, P1, P2)$. In Cox's proportional hazard model, we have:

$$\lambda(t; X, Z, P1, P2) = \lambda_0(t) \exp(\gamma' X_{ij} + \delta' Z_j + \mu_1 P1_{ij} + \mu_2 P2_{ij}) \qquad (3)$$

Cox proposed a partial maximum likelihood estimation of this model in which the baseline function $\lambda_0(t)$ does not need to be specified. The relative chance of two individuals being employed (or the risk of remaining unemployed) could then be compared. Consider two identical individuals, except for their participation in the school-based and in-service Probecat modules. At any given time t, the ratio of the hazard rates for the two individuals, also referred to as the relative risk ratio, is $exp(\mu_1/\mu_2)$. If μ_2 is larger than μ_1, all other things being equal, the individual having received the in-service training has a higher probability of finding employment than the individual having received the school-based training. If both μ_1 and μ_2 are positive, the individuals receiving any one of the two forms of training are likely to find employment before the individuals who received no training.

The results of the Cox regressions are given in table 3. The first columns under the "naïve" heading were obtained by using the hazard function $\lambda_0(t) \exp(\gamma'X_{ij} + \delta'Z_j + \mu_1 P1_{ij} + \mu_2 P2_{ij})$ where $P1_{ij}$ and $P2_{ij}$ denote the actual participation in the two programs. The columns under the heading "control" were obtained by using instead $\lambda_0(t) \exp(\gamma'X_{ij} + \delta'Z_j + \mu_1 IP1_{ij} + \mu_2 IP2_{ij})$, where $IP1_{ij}$ and $IP2_{ij}$ denote the index values obtained from the estimation of the probits. The index values are the right-hand sides of the probit equations less the residuals (not the expected probabilities of participation, which can be computed using the normal distribution).

If Probecat participants are among the more dynamic individuals who are willing to make sacrifices in order to be trained and to find employment, we would expect that in comparison with naïve estimates, the impact of Probecat would be smaller when suitable controls are introduced for the endogeneity of program participation. This is exactly what we observed. In the naïve estimates, because we used a model that was very similar to that used in the 1995 study, we got coefficient estimates that were fairly close to those obtained in that study (see table 3). These naïve estimates indicate that training reduces the length of unemployment for both men and women. The impacts are apparently statistically significant at the 10 percent level for the school-based module, and at the 5 percent level for the in-service module. Yet, once we use the index values from the probits instead of the actual program participation indicators, these positive impacts vanish. We even observe negative impacts in the case of men for the school-based training, although these are not statistically significant at the 5 percent level.

The results obtained for the school-based module may not sound too surprising given the short period during which individuals received training. How then can it be that despite the requirement for employers to hire 70 percent of the trainees in the in-service module, we observe no positive impact on employment after controlling for the endogeneity of program placement? It must be that without the stipend (wage subsidy) provided by the government, firms participating in the in-service module would have hired the same workers anyway. This is referred to as a deadweight loss in the literature. In OECD countries, the impact of such deadweight losses has been shown to represent from 40 to 90 percent of all hires (Foley 1992).

Impact of Probecat on Earnings

Consider now the impact of Probecat on monthly earnings. For this, we used a standard Heckman sample selection model, but in a different way than in past evaluations of Probecat. Denote by log w the logarithm of the expected wage for an individual. This wage is not zero if and only if it is larger than the individual's reservation wage (otherwise, the individual would choose not to work). Denote the unobserved difference between the individual's expected wage and his reservation wage by Δ^*. The individual's expected wage is determined by a number of individual (essentially the individual's education and experience) and state variables. The difference between the individual's expected wage and his reservation wage is determined by the same variables, plus the number of children, the fact of being a household head, and the fact of being married. If we split the individual level variables into those that influence both expected earnings and the reservation wage (vector E) and the demographic variables that influence the reservation wage only (vector D), the standard Heckman model is

$$\Delta_{ij}^* = \phi_\Delta' E_{ij} + \pi_\Delta' D_{ij} + \eta_\Delta' Z_j + \alpha_\Delta P1_{ij} + \chi_\Delta P2_{ij} + \nu_{ij}$$
$$\text{with } \Delta_{ij} = 1 \text{ if } \Delta_{ij}^* > 0, \text{ and } 0 \text{ if } \Delta_{ij}^* < 0 \tag{4}$$

$$\text{Log } w_{ij}^* = \phi_w' E_{ij} + \eta_w' Z_j + \alpha_w P1_{ij} + \chi_w P2_{ij} + \kappa_{ij}$$
$$\text{with Log } w = \log w^* \text{ if } \Delta = 1 \text{ and } 0 \text{ if } \Delta = 0 \tag{5}$$

The above model controls for the endogeneity of labor force participation. We estimated this model first with the actual values of the participation dummies $P1_{ij}$ and $P2_{ij}$ (this is the naïve estimation in table 4), and next with the index values $P1_{ij}$ and $P2_{ij}$ from the probit regressions (this is the control estimation in table 4). By estimating the program participation equations first, and then using the standard Heckman model, we were able to control for both sources of bias at once (note that all the coefficients of the inverse Mills' ratios are statistically significant in table 4, which highlights the importance of controlling for endogenous participation in the labor force). Our parameter estimates are in principle consistent, although they may not be efficient because the first probit equation is estimated separately rather than with the Heckman model. How do the results of the naïve and control estimates compare? There are fewer differences than with the Cox model. In both the naïve and control estimations, the impacts of Probecat are negative

TABLE 3. COX REGRESSIONS FOR NUMBER OF MONTHS UNEMPLOYED

| | Naïve | | | | Control | | | |
| | Men | | Women | | Men | | Women | |
	Coef.	P > |z|	Coef.	P > |z|	Coef.	P > |z|	Coef.	P > |z|
Program impact in 1995 study								
Probecat—School-based	0.107	0.115	0.361	0.002				
Probecat—In-service	0.476	0.000	0.776	0.002				
New estimates of impact								
Probecat—School-based	0.121	0.094	0.221	0.055	-0.156	0.063	0.360	0.074
Probecat—In-service	0.436	0.000	0.742	0.000	-0.023	0.091	0.045	0.284
Other variables in estimation								
Aged between 15 and 25	1.031	0.000	0.664	0.203	1.363	0.000	0.388	0.546
Aged between 16 and 55	1.032	0.000	0.705	0.179	1.376	0.000	0.264	0.693
Primary education completed	0.054	0.672	0.726	0.001	0.362	0.031	0.569	0.016
Secondary or postprimary training	0.096	0.427	0.403	0.059	0.510	0.007	0.113	0.679
Higher level	0.000	0.997	0.434	0.049	0.370	0.045	0.045	0.868
Household head	0.221	0.004	0.204	0.170	0.285	0.001	0.082	0.630

	(1)		(2)		(3)		(4)	
Married individual	0.073	0.323	−0.292	0.012	0.126	0.090	−0.350	0.007
Household with 2 workers	0.035	0.540	0.506	0.000	0.059	0.323	0.511	0.000
Household with 3+ workers	0.132	0.037	0.505	0.000	0.170	0.009	0.511	0.000
Previous professional experience	0.041	0.769	−0.186	0.273	−0.096	0.502	−0.208	0.260
Working experience in past year	0.436	0.000	0.124	0.354	0.523	0.000	0.029	0.850
Past year in firm 1–15 workers	−0.028	0.748	0.024	0.871	0.094	0.339	−0.169	0.417
Past year in firm 16–100 workers	−0.099	0.327	0.172	0.334	−0.008	0.935	0.099	0.629
Past year in firm 101–250 workers	−0.159	0.262	0.060	0.814	−0.006	0.967	0.037	0.890
Past year in firm 251+ workers	−0.140	0.131	0.017	0.922	−0.097	0.303	0.111	0.524
Worked 35–48 hours in past year	0.078	0.131	0.154	0.135	0.135	0.022	0.088	0.425
Worked 48+ hours in past year	0.045	0.375	0.112	0.252	0.091	0.097	0.057	0.601
Income past year	0.000	0.066	0.000	0.196	0.000	0.653	0.001	0.046
Income squared past year	0.000	0.234	0.000	0.532	0.000	0.300	0.000	0.225
Number of children			0.043	0.587			0.013	0.872
Number of children squared			−0.014	0.268			−0.010	0.419
Number of observations	2,160		947		2,160		947	
Log likelihood	−13,407		−4,200		−13,412		−4,217	

Source: Authors' estimation from pooled Probecat and ENEU panel surveys (1993–94). Thirteen state-level control variables are included in the regression, but not shown in the table. See text for more details.

TABLE 4. HECKMAN REGRESSIONS FOR WAGES AND EMPLOYMENT

| | Naïve | | | | Control | | | |
| | Men | | Women | | Men | | Women | |
	Coef.	P>|z|	Coef.	P>|z|	Coef.	P>|z|	Coef.	P>|z|
Logarithm of wage								
Probecat—School-based	-0.020	0.763	-0.083	0.460	-0.204	0.000	-0.080	0.421
Probecat—In-service	-0.115	0.269	-0.300	0.021	-0.021	0.082	-0.032	0.432
Aged between 15 and 25	-0.070	0.698	-0.237	0.619	0.224	0.259	0.006	0.992
Aged between 16 and 55	0.159	0.376	-0.074	0.876	0.507	0.012	0.224	0.699
Primary education completed	0.049	0.684	-0.026	0.899	0.337	0.017	0.010	0.961
Secondary or postprimary training	0.182	0.107	0.117	0.552	0.562	0.000	0.169	0.418
Higher level	0.309	0.007	0.316	0.121	0.662	0.000	0.410	0.054
Previous professional experience	0.107	0.331	-0.287	0.036	0.164	0.136	-0.241	0.083
Working experience in past year	-0.199	0.012	0.054	0.645	-0.141	0.080	0.041	0.731
Constant	5.517	0.000	6.637	0.000	5.754	0.000	6.284	0.000
Lambda	-0.918	0.022	-1.138	0.041	-0.914	0.021	-1.175	0.044

Probability of working

Probecat—School-based	0.018	0.842	0.211	0.046	0.075	0.312	0.291	0.004
Probecat—In-service	0.207	0.308	0.455	0.001	-0.038	0.061	0.033	0.407
Aged between 15 and 25	0.892	0.000	0.541	0.187	1.073	0.000	0.116	0.819
Aged between 16 and 55	0.810	0.000	0.482	0.245	0.937	0.000	-0.047	0.927
Primary education completed	0.041	0.813	0.574	0.003	0.241	0.274	0.469	0.014
Secondary or postprimary training	-0.043	0.796	0.191	0.286	0.106	0.637	-0.007	0.971
Higher level	-0.083	0.620	0.420	0.024	0.049	0.821	0.218	0.253
Previous professional experience	0.108	0.426	0.175	0.182	0.068	0.611	0.122	0.343
Working experience in past year	0.561	0.000	0.058	0.599	0.523	0.000	0.017	0.875
Household head	0.165	0.063	0.312	0.009	0.174	0.048	0.198	0.069
Married individual	0.039	0.655	-0.145	0.069	0.070	0.421	-0.167	0.013
Number of children			-0.023	0.635			-0.028	0.492
Number of children squared			0.000	0.978			0.002	0.674
Constant	0.700	0.299	-2.573	0.004	-1.001	0.324	-1.636	0.085
Number of observations	2,167		948		2,160		947	
Log likelihood	-3,044		-1,332		-3,020		1,328	

Source: Authors' estimation from pooled Probecat and ENEU panel surveys (1993–94). Thirteen state-level control variables are included in the regression but not shown in the table. See text for more details.

instead of being positive. While the levels of significance differ according to the method, these results at the least shed doubts on the positive impact of Probecat observed on earnings in past evaluations.

Conclusion

During the last 15 years, Probecat has been implemented by the Mexican government as a training program for the unemployed. Past evaluations of the program suggest that it is effective in reducing the length of unemployment and increasing earnings for participants. It could be, however, that these results were obtained because of inadequate consideration of the problem of sample selection. Using the data of the last evaluation of Probecat conducted by the Mexican Ministry of Labor, we have proposed another methodology for assessing impacts. According to our results, Probecat does not have large positive effects for participants. From a policy point of view, this finding suggests that the program may not be delivering its promise. From a scientific point of view, our results point to the sensitivity of evaluation results to the methodologies used to generate the results, which is of concern when these results are used for policy recommendations.

New initiatives have been taken in recent years to try to improve the functioning of Probecat. This includes the implementation of the PILEOT module since 1995, which is targeted at economically disadvantaged communities. The main requirement for participation in PILEOT is that the applicant must have basic literacy and numeracy skills, and be unemployed or underemployed. The module provides training for individuals and groups who intend to engage in self-employment or community-based productive activities. The training contents are demand-driven. It will be important to evaluate this new module rigorously, and to test the sensitivity of the evaluation results to the assumptions made and the techniques used in the evaluation process.

References

Carlson, S. 1991. "Mexico Labor Retraining Program: Poverty Alleviation and Contribution to Growth." Report No. 6. World Bank, Latin America and the Caribbean Technical Department, Regional Studies Program, Washington, D.C.

Dar, A., and I. S. Gill. 1998. "On Evaluating Retraining Programs in OECD Countries." *World Bank Research Observer* 13:79–101.

Fleck, S., and C. Sorrentino. 1994. "Employment and Unemployment in Mexico's Labor Force." *Monthly Labor Review*, November: 3–31.

Foley, P. 1992. "Local Economic Policy and Job Creation: A Review of Evaluation Studies." *Urban Studies* 29(3–4):557–98.

Goldberger, A. 1983. "Abnormal Selection Bias." In T. Amemiya and I. Olkin, eds., *Studies in Econometrics, Time Series and Multivariate Statistics*. San Diego, London, and Toronto: Academic Press.

Heckman, J. 1979. "Sample Selection Bias as a Specification Error." *Econometrica* 47(1):54–61.

Manski, C. 1996. "Review of the Probecat Program Evaluation Study." World Bank, Washington, D.C.

Ravallion, Martin, and Q. Wodon. 1998. *Evaluating a Targeted Social Program When Placement Is Decentralized*. Policy Research Working Paper 1945. World Bank, Washington, D.C.

———. 2000. "Does Child Labor Displace Schooling? Evidence on Behavioral Responses to an Enrollment Subsidy." *Economic Journal* 110(462):C158–75.

Revenga, A., M. Riboud, and H. Tan. 1994. "The Impact of Mexico's Retraining Program on Employment and Wages." *World Bank Economic Review* 8(2):247–77.

Rosenbaum, P., and D. Rubin. 1983. "The Central Role of the Propensity Score in Observational Studies for Causal Effects." *Biometrika* 70:41–55.

———. 1985. "Constructing a Control Group Using Multivariate Matched Sampling Methods That Incorporate the Propensity Score." *American Statistician* 39:35–39.

STPS (Secretaría del Trabajo y Previsión Social). 1995. *Evaluación del Programa de Becas de Capacitación para Desempleados*. Mexico, D.F.: STPS.

The Impact of Access to Urban Potable Water and Sewerage Connection on Child Mortality: City-Level Evidence, 1993

Anqing Shi

Abstract

Using a city-level database of Global Urban Indicators, this article finds that it is not economic development alone that could lead to a lower child mortality regime. Rather, other aspects of the city are equally important, such as inequality among city incomes, infrastructure, and strength of financial resources. As this article shows, higher child mortality is attributable to problems found in urban areas worldwide—inadequate access to potable water and sewerage connections, higher percentage of households below the poverty line within a city, and lack of sufficient revenue from the central government. It is particularly true that increasing income inequality in the city keeps the poor from accessing potable water and sewerage connections, which in turn leads to a high child mortality.

Mortality among children under age 5 varies greatly around the world, ranging from 0.8 per 1,000 live births in Rennes, France, to 320 per 1,000 live births in Luanda, Angola, in 1993 (Flood 1997). Although the effects of nutrition, education, and health programs on child mortality in

I am grateful to Gerard Caprio, George Clarke, Bob Cull, Lionel Demery, Shantayanan Devarajan, Halsey Rogers, Lyn Squire, and referees for very helpful comments.

rural areas are well documented, the roles of access to potable water and sewerage connection in reducing child mortality in urban areas have not been well researched.

During the last two decades, vigorous efforts have been made to improve access to potable water and sewerage connection in urban areas. The United Nations General Assembly proclaimed 1981–90 as the International Drinking Water Supply and Sanitation Decade. Many member countries assumed a commitment to improving the quality of and access to potable water and the sewerage system by the year 1990. At the end of the 1980s, however, the situation had not improved greatly. Global Urban Indicators data show that in many cities around the world, one-quarter of households did not have access to potable water within 200 meters of their living places in 1993 (Auclair 1998), and most poor people do not have an adequate disposal system (Briscoe 1992). The problem will become more serious in the years to come as city populations continue to grow rapidly. It is projected that by year 2030, the world's urban population will grow to 3.3 billion, over 90 percent of which will accrue to cities in developing countries (UNCHS 1997).

In this context, this article examines how access to potable water and sewerage connections affect child mortality in cities worldwide, using 1993 city-level data available from Global Urban Indicators, a product of the United Nations Centre for Human Settlements (Flood 1997). As evidenced from this study, higher child mortality is also attributed to the problems found in urban areas worldwide—inadequate access to potable water and sewerage connections, income inequality within a city, and lack of sufficient revenue from the central government. It is particularly true that increasing income inequality in the city keeps the poor from accessing potable water and sewerage connection, which in turn leads to a higher child mortality.

This article is organized as follows: in the next section, I briefly review the literature on the roles of access to potable water and sewerage connection on child mortality, and the impact of urban management on child mortality. This is followed by a description of the data, the empirical model, construction of variables, and major findings. The final section will highlight major conclusions for policy formation.

Literature

The literature on the determinants of child mortality has suggested a strong inverse correlation between access to urban water and sewerage connection on the one hand and child mortality on the other (Feachem 1984; Schultz 1980; WHO 1978). The macrolevel studies suggest that increases in the amount of water used and wide coverage of sewerage connections contribute to better hygiene and to the elimination of bacteriological contamination. Puffer and Serrano (1973) studied infant and child mortality in several Latin American cities and found that a high proportion of households reporting infant deaths lacked adequate sources of water. In a study of regional variation of infant and child mortality in Sri Lanka, Patel (1981) found that differences in the supply of well water and presence of latrines explained substantial regional variation in mortality.

The microlevel studies also show that the quality or availability of water or in the disposal of excreta could significantly improve the health outcomes. In a study on the variation of mortality in urban Brazil, Merrick (1985) found that access to piped water in a household was likely to be of most direct benefit in lowering child mortality by reducing exposure to waterborne diseases, particularly diarrhea. After reviewing 67 microlevel studies from 28 countries, Esrey, Feachem, and Hughes (1985) and Esrey and others (1990) found that improvements in water access and sanitation had great impacts on diarrheal diseases. The median reduction in diarrheal morbidity rates was 22 percent from all studies and 27 percent from a few better-designed studies; all studies of the impact on total mortality rates showed a median reduction of 21 percent.

Although there is a continuing interest in studying the effects of urban water supply and sewerage connections on child mortality, recent research on child mortality differentials has focused on the impact of the political economy of cities, with particular focus on the possible impacts of urban resources for revenue and urban management on child mortality (Cheema 1992; Minujin 1995; Stren 1995). The economic restructuring in many countries and the world financial crises since the 1980s have affected the well-being of residents in major cities, mainly through declining public expenditure on municipal services and city infrastructure (Demery and Squire 1996; Gilbert 1993). Brockerhoff and Brennan (1998) used the level of infant mortality to compare well-being across cities of 1 million or more residents and smaller settlements within developing regions. They found that the pronounced advantage of early infant survival of big city residents in Latin America and the Caribbean declined steadily since the late 1970s and was no longer apparent by the early 1990s. The reason was that these big cities, where finance and trade were concentrated, had been exposed to volatile capital outflows. Sharp reductions in expenditure led to a worsening of nutritional levels and to an exclusion from access to public utilities such as water access and sanitation. As a result, the earlier infant survival advantage was substantially reduced. The unequal income distribution within the city further aggravated this situation. Studies showed that child mortality rates were several times higher in slums and periurban areas than in more privileged neighborhoods (Harpham, Lusty, and Vaughan 1988; Stephens 1996; Timaeus and Lush 1995).

Infant and child survival rates were affected not only through reduced public expenditure on city infrastructure, but also indirectly through the way in which the urban infrastructure was managed. A household-level study on the determinants of diarrheal disease in Jakarta (Alberini and others 1996) found that the frequency of water interruptions caused by the utility company had an impact on diarrheal disease, and that the poor often used vendors or public hydrants and rarely had household connections, whereas in wealthy households, the situation was reversed. The higher price usually charged by vendors kept the poor from access-ing potable water. A recent country study by the World Bank (1998) shows that in India the distribution of access to water and sanitation varies across income categories; the wealthier have far better access to piped and other exclusive sources of water than the poor.

Another important aspect that may affect child survival rates through city infrastructure management is the provision and delivery of water and access to the sewerage system. Recent urban studies suggest that, to implement service provision effectively, it is necessary to have em-powered coordinating bodies at the local level that incorporate indig-enous urban institutions into a program (McCarney, Halfani, and Rodriguez 1995; Werna 1996). In addition, active involvement by the private sector in bridging supply-and-demand discrepancies in city ser-vices is also considered a necessary step to ensure the welfare of the city population (Briscoe 1992).

By taking these prevailing views into consideration, this article pro-poses two hypotheses to be examined: (a) access on the part of a higher percentage of the population to potable water or sewerage connections in the city would lower the child mortality rate; and (b) equally impor-tant, a city with lower poverty, with sufficient financial resources, and with effective involvement in implementing services provisions could facilitate better delivery of water and sewerage services, which in turn would lead to lower the child mortality.

Data

Data used in this study come from the Global Urban Indicators of 1993, which were collected for 237 cities in 110 countries by the United Na-tions Centre for Human Settlements (UNCHS) in 1993. They provide a global picture of urban conditions. About three-quarters are in developing countries. There are 46 key indictors in eight modules: demographic data, socioeconomic development, infrastructure, transportation, environmental management, local government, housing affordability and adequacy, and housing provision. A good range of city sizes is represented in the data: 34 percent are cities of fewer than 0.3 million people, 29 percent are cities with 0.3–1.0 million people, and 37 percent are cities with more than 1.0 million people (Auclair 1998).

City information was gathered by data collectors assigned by Global Urban Observatory of UNCHS who were asked to make best use of secondary sources for indicators wherever possible, or otherwise to make use of an expert focus group, conducting an impromptu survey, or using other estimation techniques (Auclair 1998). Many of the data provided were of surprisingly good quality, particularly from the poorer countries, which are often considered to have a low capacity for data collection (Flood 1997). Because of missing values on some variables in various model specifications, the usable samples of this study range from 92 to 51 observations, depending on the model specifications. A list of 92 cities included in this study is in appendix A. A full data set appears in appendix C.

Empirical Model and Variables Construction

I modeled the level of child mortality as a function of access to potable water or sewerage connection, and constructed a set of controlled variables. The basic specification takes the following form:

$$M_i = a + bP_i + cX_i + dS_i + u_i$$

Where M_i is the child mortality rate, P_i is either the percentage of city residents with access to potable water in city or the percentage of households with sewerage connections in the city, X_i is a set of control variables. To address the concern over the possibility that the results were driven by the systematic differences among different regions of the world (Frankel and Romer 1999), I included a series of dummies for four regions, denoted by S_i, and with a residual of u_i. The coefficients were estimated using ordinary least squares (OLS) regression, and White's (1980) procedure for calculating standard errors was used to correct for heteroskedasticity.

The set of control variables is as follows: (a) level of economic development, measured by household's income per capita in constant U.S. dollars (1993), (b) level of health service facilities, measured by the number of people per hospital bed, (c) city poverty level, measured by the percentage of households below the locally defined poverty line, and (d) strength of city revenue resources, measured by the percentage of city total revenue coming from central government transfers.

One concern, as suggested in the recent literature and specified in the second hypothesis, is that the level of access to potable water and household sewerage connections might be endogenous in their child mortality equations, and treating them as exogenous variables could incur a simultaneity bias in the estimations. To address whether such biases have driven our estimations, I also ran two-stage least squares (2SLS) regressions in which the access to potable water and household sewerage connection were treated as endogenous variables. The instruments included (a) city poverty level, (b) sufficiency of city financial resources, (c) regional dummies, (d) type of service providers, and (e) the extent to which local government has the authority to set service use fees without the permission of the central government.

To construct the variable of type of service providers, I used the information provided by Global Urban Indicators on water and sewerage service provisions, respectively. In some countries, local government has very few responsibilities, and instead parastatal and private providers are heavily involved, while in others it is the local government that is virtually responsible for a whole range of local services, including the management of access to potable water and sewerage connections. I used this information to create a variable of type of service providers, which is captured by a series of dummies: (a) the private sector, including the parastatal sector, as the providers (coded as the reference group), (b) local government alone as the provider, (c) central government alone as the provider, (d) both local and central governments as the providers, and (e) a mixture of private and public sectors as the providers.

Global Urban Indicators also include information on local government's authority in setting service use fees without the permission of the central government. I used this information to create a variable to address the issue of whether the extent to which local government is able to set up service use fees has any impact on water access or sewerage connection. The variable ranges from 0 for the least and 2 for the most. The definitions of all variables are given in table 1.

Findings: Descriptive Results

The descriptive statistics for all variables used in this study are presented in table 2 for the water access equation and in table 3 for the

TABLE 1. VARIABLES USED IN THE STUDY, 1993

Variable	Definition
Child mortality	Number of children dead before reaching the age of 5 per 1,000 live births
Access to potable water	Percentage of households with access to potable water within 200 meters of their housing
Households with sewerage connections	Percentage of households connected to the sewerage system
Household income per capita	Household income per capita in 1993 U.S. dollars (in 100s)
Population per hospital bed	Population per hospital bed (in 10s)
Households below poverty line	Percentage of households below the locally defined poverty line
Strength of city financial resource	Percentage of city revenue coming from central government transfers
Type of water or sewerage service providers	Providers are dummy variables: • Local government alone • Central government alone, including regional government • Combination of local, regional, and national governments • Private sector, including parastatal sector (reference group) • Mixture of types of providers
Local government has the authority to set service use fees without permission of central government	Ranging from 0 for the least to 2 for the most

sewerage connection equation. The child mortality rate is 55.5 per 1,000 live births on average for the cities in the sample. The average level of access to potable water in this sample is 86.9 percent; 53.6 percent of households have a sewerage connection.

The child mortality rate is inversely correlated with access to potable water ($r = -0.68$) and sewerage connection ($r = -0.66$). As expected, cities with higher household income per capita have lower child mortality ($r = -0.39$), while the percentage of households below the poverty line in the city is positively correlated with child mortality ($r = 0.36$).

The lack of health services facilities (measured by a higher number of persons per hospital bed) is also associated with higher child mortality ($r = 0.40$); however, the strength of a city's financial resource measured by the percentage of local revenue from central government transfers is not significantly associated with the child mortality rate.

Tables 2 and 3 further show that access to potable water or sewerage connections varies with the level of city poverty and local government involvement in the provision of services. A higher percentage of households below the poverty level within a city is significantly associated with a lower rate of water access and sewerage connection, although their associations are weak. The extent to which local government has authority in setting service use fees is inversely associated with access to potable water in the city ($r = -0.36$), but not associated with sewerage connections.

Findings: Regression Results

This bivariate relationship between access to potable water and sewerage connections on the one hand and child mortality on the other was further examined in regression models in table 4 and table 5, respectively. Specification 1 of table 4 includes only the water access variable, two control variables, household income per capita, population per hospital bed, and regional dummies. The results confirm an inverse relationship between access to potable water and child mortality. Also, as expected, the higher household income per capita was associated with lower child mortality, whereas the inadequacy of health services in the city (more people per hospital bed) was correlated with higher child mortality. The regional variation in child mortality was also clearly revealed. In contrast to African and Middle Eastern countries (the reference group), other regions all have lower child mortality.

I further examined this inverse relationship between the access to potable water and child mortality by introducing another variable, the percentage of households under the poverty line (specification 2).[1] Findings suggested that the city poverty level does have an independent effect on child mortality: a higher poverty level is associated with a

---

1. A better measurement of income inequality in a city is the household income disparity (Q5/Q1), a ratio of the income of highest quintile over lowest quintile. I tried to use this variable; however, the coefficient turned out to be insignificant. The simple correlation also suggests that this variable does not significantly correlate with child mortality. Hence, I dropped this variable.

higher child mortality level. It is important to note that the inverse association between access to potable water and child mortality remains when the poverty variable is introduced, but the magnitude of this inverse association is somewhat reduced. This suggests that the effect of access to potable water on child mortality is contingent upon the income inequality within a city, and that access to water could be endogenous in the child mortality equation.

In specification 3, the strength of city revenue resources is further brought into the model. The result further confirms a significant inverse relationship between access to potable water and child mortality even though the association is reduced a little bit further. Specifically, the estimated coefficient implies that a one standard deviation increase (17.5 percent) in access to potable water would decrease child mortality by nearly 18 per 1,000. In addition, city revenue resources do exhibit an effect on child mortality: a higher percentage of city revenue from central government transfers is associated with a lower child mortality.

To check whether the access to potable water could be endogenous in the child mortality equation, I further ran a two-stage least squares regression. The last two columns of table 4 report the instrumental variable (IV) estimates of the equation where the access to potable water is treated as endogenous, and the instruments include a constant, the percentage of population under the poverty line, share of city revenue from central government transfers, local government's authority in setting service use fees, and the type of providers of city water services. The coefficient on access of potable water rises sharply (coefficient = −1.97), and is significant ($t = 3.23$). This suggests that examining the link between access to potable water and child mortality using IV could yield a better estimation of the effect of access to water access. The estimated coefficient implies that a one standard deviation increase (17.5 percent) in access to potable water would decrease child mortality by nearly 34 per 1,000 rather than 18 per 1,000 in the OLS estimation.

Moving from OLS to IV, nevertheless, decreases the estimated impact of poverty on child mortality. It is also interesting to see that the poverty's impact is clearly revealed in the equation on access to water. The coefficient (−0.17) suggests that a higher income inequality within a city is associated with a lower level of access to potable water. In addition, a service use fee set up by the local government tends to greatly reduce the access to potable water. Finally, it appears that public involvement, either by local or national government, in the provision and delivery of water service tends to facilitate a higher level of access to water than through nonpublic providers, such as parastatal and pri-

TABLE 2. THE MEANS AND STANDARD DEVIATIONS AND CORRELATION OF VARIABLES USED IN EQUATION FOR ACCESS TO POTABLE WATER, 1993

	Child mortality	(1)	(2)	(3)	(4)	(5)	(6)	(7)	(8)	(9)	(10)	(11)
(1)	-0.3851 (0.0002)											
(2)	0.4015 (0.0001)	-0.2006 (0.055)										
(3)	-0.6814 (0.0001)	0.3256 (0.0015)	-0.3201 (0.0019)									
(4)	0.3627 (0.0009)	-0.2253 (0.0431)	0.2579 (0.0201)	-0.2294 (0.0394)								
(5)	-0.0655 (0.5614)	0.0910 (0.4221)	0.1828 (0.1047)	0.0970 (0.3921)	0.2501 (0.0328)							
(6)	0.2338 (0.0588)	-0.0822 (0.5116)	0.0997 (0.4259)	-0.3642 (0.0026)	0.2247 (0.0791)	0.0593 (0.6473)						
(7)	-0.2218 (0.0336)	0.1836 (0.0799)	0.0428 (0.6856)	0.1750 (0.0953)	-0.0481 (0.6696)	-0.0346 (0.7604)	-0.1520 (0.2231)					
(8)	-0.0561 (0.5953)	-0.1780 (0.0896)	-0.0618 (0.5583)	-0.0407 (0.7003)	-0.2273 (0.0413)	-0.1490 (0.1873)	0.0970 (0.4383)	-0.3834 (0.0002)				
(9)	-0.0123 (0.9071)	-0.1140 (0.2794)	-0.0257 (0.8079)	0.0577 (0.5847)	0.1500 (0.1814)	0.3157 (0.0043)	-0.0085 (0.9460)	-0.2133 (0.0412)	-0.2192 (0.0358)			

(10)	0.2581	-0.0027	0.0445	-0.0201	0.1152	-0.0959	0.0262	-0.1753	-0.1801	-0.1002	-0.1111	
	(0.0130)	(0.9797)	(0.6737)	(0.8498)	(0.3058)	(0.3977)	(0.8349)	(0.0947)	(0.0858)	(0.3419)	(0.2915)	
(11)	0.0689	-0.1384	0.0573	-0.0769	0.2408	0.2227	0.0570	-0.2366	-0.2431	-0.1353		
	(0.5142)	(0.1883)	(0.5876)	(0.4665)	(0.0303)	(0.0471)	(0.6494)	(0.0232)	(0.0196)	(0.1986)		
Mean*	55.5163	17.80	42.10	86.8920	27.8004	20.2589	1.3485	0.3125	0.3250	0.1250	0.0875	0.1500
Std. dev.	52.5405	35.20	61.81	17.5665	22.8479	25.1500	0.5682	0.4664	0.4713	0.3328	0.2843	0.3593
N	92	92	92	92	81	81	66	80	80	80	80	80

* Mean for dummy variables of water access providers are the proportions of number observations of each category in total sample.

Note: P values are shown in parentheses.

(1) Household income per capita
(2) Population per hospital bed
(3) Household's access to potable water
(4) Household below poverty line
(5) Percentage share of total revenue from central government
(6) Local government has the authority to set service use fees
(7) Local government alone as water service provider
(8) Central government alone as water service provider
(9) Both local and central governments
(10) Private sector, including parastatal sector, as water service provider
(11) Mix of all types of providers

Table 3. The Means and Standard Deviations and Correlation of Variables Used in Sewerage Equation, 1993

	Child mortality	(1)	(2)	(3)	(4)	(5)	(6)	(7)	(8)	(9)	(10)	(11)
(1)	-0.3851 (0.0002)											
(2)	0.4015 (0.0001)	-0.2006 (0.055)										
(3)	-0.6560 (0.0001)	0.4606 (0.0001)	-0.2981 (0.0041)									
(4)	0.3627 (0.0009)	-0.2253 (0.0431)	0.2579 (0.0201)	-0.1040 (0.3584)								
(5)	-0.0655 (0.5614)	0.0910 (0.4221)	0.1828 (0.1047)	0.0349 (0.7615)	0.2501 (0.0328)							
(6)	0.2338 (0.0588)	-0.0822 (0.5116)	0.0997 (0.4259)	-0.0156 (0.9024)	0.2247 (0.0791)	0.0593 (0.6473)						
(7)	-0.2576 (0.0137)	0.1403 (0.1848)	-0.0029 (0.9786)	0.2726 (0.0089)	0.0228 (0.8407)	-0.0011 (0.9924)	-0.1080 (0.3958)					
(8)	0.0540 (0.6113)	-0.1184 (0.2638)	0.0017 (0.9872)	0.0109 (0.9187)	-0.2221 (0.0477)	-0.1282 (0.2633)	0.0678 (0.5944)	-0.3722 (0.0003)				
(9)	0.2332 (0.0261)	-0.1382 (0.1915)	0.0367 (0.7295)	-0.1565 (0.1385)	0.2041 (0.0694)	0.1826 (0.1096)	0.0030 (0.9813)	-0.2464 (0.0185)	-0.1865 (0.0767)			

	(1)	(2)	(3)	(4)	(5)	(6)	(7)	(8)	(9)	(10)	(11)
(10)	-0.1146	0.0557	-0.0904	0.0668	0.0972	0.2010	0.0792	-0.1504	-0.1138	-0.0753	-0.0619
	(0.0261)	(0.5997)	(0.3940)	(0.5292)	(0.3909)	(0.0776)	(0.5340)	(0.1548)	(0.2828)	(0.4778)	(0.3387)
(11)	0.0162	-0.0989	-0.0469	0.0006	0.1439	-0.1323	-0.0342	-0.2024	-0.1532	-0.1014	0.0845
	(0.8789)	(0.3510)	(0.6590)	(0.9956)	(0.2029)	(0.0634)	(0.2485)	(0.7471)	(0.0543)	(0.1471)	(0.2801)
Mean*	55.5163	17.80	42.10	53.6058	27.8004	20.2589	1.3281	0.2958	0.3239	0.1127	0.0986
Std. Dev.	52.5405	35.20	61.81	37.9837	22.8479	25.1500	0.5650	0.4596	0.4713	0.3184	0.3002
N	92	92	92	91	81	80	64	71	71	71	71

* Mean for dummy variables of sewerage connection providers are the proportions of number observations of each category in total sample.

Note: P values are shown in parentheses.

(1) Household income per capita
(2) Population per hospital bed
(3) Household's sewerage connection
(4) Household below poverty line
(5) Percentage share of total revenue from central government
(6) Local government has the authority to set service use fees
(7) Local government alone as sewerage connection provider
(8) Central government alone as sewerage connection provider
(9) Both local and central governments
(10) Private sector, including parastatal sector, as sewerage connection provider
(11) Mix of all types of providers

TABLE 4. THE OLS REGRESSION OF CHILD MORTALITY ON ACCESS
TO POTABLE WATER AND OTHER VARIABLES, 1993

Variables	OLS[a] 1	OLS[a] 2	OLS[a] 3	2SLS Child mortality	2SLS Water access
Constant	197.29[b]	175.11[b]	176.68[b]	259.37[b]	102.22[c]
	(24.62)	(22.60)	(20.13)	(57.65)	(6.43)
Household income	−0.14[b]	−0.07	−0.01	−0.05	
per capita	(0.04)	(0.05)	(0.06)	(0.16)	
Household below		0.33[b]	0.39[d]	0.12	−0.17[c]
poverty line		(0.21)	(0.21)	(0.22)	(0.07)
Population per hospital	0.13[b]	0.10[c]	0.14[b]	0.11[d]	
bed	(0.05)	(0.05)	(0.05)	(0.04)	
Access to potable water	−1.29[b]	−1.11[b]	−1.03[b]	−1.97[b]	
	(0.27)	(0.25)	(0.23)	(0.61)	
City revenue from				−0.40[b]	0.09
central government				(0.14)	(0.06)
Local government setting					−11.41[b]
service use fees					(2.75)
Providers of city water services[e]					
Local government alone					4.52
					(5.75)
Central government					3.39
alone					(5.70)
Both local and central					8.69
governments					(6.65)
Mixture of types of					5.06
providers					(6.29)
Region[f]					
European and developed	−49.39[b]	−55.33[b]	−64.39[b]	−52.14[b]	10.72[c]
countries	(9.08)	(8.78)	(8.76)	(14.47)	(4.29)
Latin American	−43.35[b]	−46.08[b]	−49.28[b]	−51.08[b]	4.21
countries	(9.41)	(9.63)	(9.35)	(13.58)	(4.72)
Asian countries	−52.03[b]	−48.56[b]	−54.33[b]	−59.70[b]	−6.85
	(9.95)	(9.67)	(9.26)	(11.86)	(4.15)
R^2 (%)	68.52	70.56	76.46	61.46	51.53
Number of observations	92	81	73	59	59

a. Heteroskedasticity-consistent standard errors are shown in parentheses.
b. Significant at $p < 0.01$.
c. Significant at $p < 0.05$.
d. Significant at $p < 0.10$.
e. The omitted category is the private sector provider, which includes the parastatal sector.
f. The omitted category is African and Middle Eastern countries.

vate providers. Their contrasts, however, do not turn to be statistically significant.

Table 5 shows the findings on the impact of sewerage connection on child mortality. Specification 1 includes only the sewerage connection variable, two control variables, household income per capita and population per hospital bed, plus regional dummies. The inverse relationship between the level of household sewerage connection and child mortality is confirmed. The estimated coefficient implies that a one standard deviation increase (38 percent) in sewerage connection would decrease child mortality by nearly 24 per 1,000. The impacts of income per capita and population per hospital bed are all in the expected direction.

In specifications 2 and 3, I further examine the relationship between sewerage connection and child mortality by introducing a city poverty level variable and a revenue share variable sequentially. The results suggest that the inverse relationship between sewerage connection and child mortality remains, although the magnitude of this relationship is reduced somewhat when these two variables are controlled for, especially the city poverty level variable. This suggests that the role of sewerage connection on child mortality is contingent upon the income inequality within a city, and that sewerage connection could be endogenous in the child mortality equation as well.

The last two columns of table 5 also report the IV estimates of the equation where sewerage connection is treated as endogenous. The coefficient on sewerage connection rises sharply (coefficient = −1.43) and is significant ($t = 2.55$). This again suggests that examining the link between sewerage connection and child mortality using IV could reach a better estimation of the effect of sewerage connection. The estimated coefficient implies that a one standard deviation increase (38 percent) in sewerage connection could decrease child mortality by nearly 54 per 1,000.

Moving from OLS to IV decreases the estimated impact of poverty on child mortality. Nevertheless, note that poverty's impact is clearly revealed in the sewerage connection equation; the coefficient (−0.30) suggests that a higher poverty level within a city is associated with a lower level of sewerage connection. In addition, a higher percentage revenue share from the central government tends to increase the sewerage connection, but its effect is not statistically significant. Finally, in contrast to parastatal and private providers, public providers—either local government or central government or both—tend to have a higher level of sewerage connection, but again their contrasts are not statistically significant.

TABLE 5. THE OLS REGRESSION OF CHILD MORTALITY ON SEWERAGE
CONNECTION AND OTHER VARIABLES, 1993

| | OLS[a] | | | 2SLS | |
Variables	1	2	3	Child mortality	Sewerage access
Constant	113.64[b]	103.54[b]	112.17[b]	149.04[b]	45.00[c]
	(9.98)	(9.48)	(9.02)	(29.41)	(18.34)
Household income	−0.13[c]	−0.04	0.07	−0.00	
per capita	(0.06)	(0.07)	(0.08)	(0.17)	
Household below		0.32	0.37	0.05	−0.30[d]
poverty line		(0.26)	(0.27)	(0.24)	(0.16)
Population per hospital	0.18[b]	0.14[b]	0.18[b]	0.19[b]	
bed	(0.05)	(0.06)	(0.05)	(0.07)	
Sewerage connection	−0.63[b]	−0.54[b]	−0.50[b]	−1.43[c]	
	(0.15)	(0.13)	(0.14)	(0.56)	
City revenue from			−0.51[b]		0.22
central government			(0.17)		(0.16)
Local government setting					−8.41
service use fees					(6.33)
Providers of city sewerage system[e]					
Local government alone					12.08
					(13.74)
Central government alone					11.40
					(15.23)
Both local and central					20.01
governments					(16.85)
Mixture of types of					8.91
providers					(16.75)
Region[f]					
European and developed	−35.89[b]	−46.72[b]	−56.16[b]	−8.31	50.45[b]
countries	(10.30)	(10.06)	(10.66)	(28.08)	(10.58)
Latin American	−38.81[b]	−39.90[b]	−41.70[b]	−15.76	36.62[b]
countries	(10.64)	(8.87)	(8.72)	(22.22)	(12.05)
Asian countries	−59.35[b]	−56.00[b]	−64.07[b]	−73.65[b]	−5.47
	(9.18)	(9.00)	(8.76)	(12.84)	(10.47)
R^2 (%)	67.42	68.05	75.14	66.01	58.02
Number of observations	91	80	71	51	51

a. Heteroskedasticity-consistent standard errors are shown in parentheses.
b. Significant at $p < 0.01$.
c. Significant at $p < 0.05$.
d. Significant at $p < 0.10$.
e. The omitted category is the private sector provider, which includes the parastatal sector.
f. The omitted category is African and Middle Eastern countries.

Table 6. Predicted Child Mortality by Access to Potable Water and Sewerage Systems, African and Middle Eastern Countries, 1993

Percentage of water access or sewerage connection	Predicted child mortality rate per 1,000	
	Water access equation	Sewerage connection equation
10	175	113
20	165	108
30	155	103
40	145	98
50	134	93
60	124	88
70	113	83
80	103	78
90	93	73
95	88	71
100	83	68
Mean	97[a]	90[b]

Note: The predicted child mortality rates are calculated from column 3 of table 4 and table 5, respectively, holding all other variables at their means.
a. The mean percentage of access to potable water is 86.89.
b. The mean percentage of sewerage connection is 53.61.

To examine the impact of water access and sewerage connection on child mortality more clearly, the predicted rates of child mortality for African and Middle East countries are calculated from OLS specifications (column 3 of table 4 and table 5) for parsimony. The predicted rates are calculated for different levels of access to water and sewerage connection by holding all other variables constant at their means. The results are shown in table 6. They suggest that if coverage of access to potable water increased from a level of 70 percent, which is true for most cities in Africa, to 80 percent, the child mortality rate would decline from 113 per 1,000 to 103 per 1,000. Similarly, an increase in household sewerage connections is also associated with a decline in child mortality. For example, if the level of sewerage connection were as low as 20 percent, which is the average level for most African countries, the child mortality would be 108 per 1,000. If the level of sewerage connection increased to 53.6 percent, which is the mean level of the sample, child mortality rate would fall to 90 per 1,000.

Robustness

To check the robustness of these results, I was concerned about a potential problem with sample selection. Because of the missing values on variables I used in this study, the sample is relatively small, ranging from 92 to 51, depending on the specifications. Thus, efforts were made to increase the sample size to see if the relationship between access to potable water and sewerage connections on one hand and child mortality on the other still held. I took comparable statistics on urban water access, urban sanitation access, and income per capita (in constant U.S. dollars) from the World Bank data source (World Bank 2000) to substitute for the missing values. As a result, 48 cities were added (see appendix B).

Regression results for the extended sample are presented in table 7. The inverse association between access to water and child mortality remains firm, as does the association between sewerage connection and child mortality. The results for other variables remain more or less the same as revealed in the previous sections: the high poverty level in the cities is associated with higher child mortality, a lack of health facilities is associated with higher child mortality, and a higher percentage share of revenue from central government transfers is associated with lower child mortality. Thus, sensitivity analyses through expanding the sample size demonstrate the robustness of the original results.

Conclusion

The *World Development Report 1990* (World Bank 1990) claimed that urban poverty would become the most significant and politically explosive problem of the next century. Therefore, there is an urgent need to study the current living conditions in urban areas. In this context, this article examined one of the dimensions of well-being in cities, child mortality, which can be compared across highly diverse urban populations worldwide.

The findings of this article do not suggest that narrowly economic development alone, as measured by household income per capita, could lead to a lower child mortality regime. Rather, other aspects, such as city infrastructure, strength of city financial resources, and income inequality, are equally important. As evidenced in this article, higher child mortality is also attributed to the problems found in urban areas worldwide—inadequate access to potable water and sewerage connections; income inequality within a city, and lack of sufficient revenue from the

TABLE 7. THE OLS REGRESSION OF CHILD MORTALITY ON ACCESS
TO POTABLE WATER AND SEWERAGE CONNECTIONS, 1993

	Extended sample			
	Water access equation		Sewerage connection equation	
Variables	1	2	1	2
Constant	194.27[a]	177.36[a]	116.54[a]	107.51[a]
	(21.56)	(20.87)	(7.71)	(11.39)
Household income	−0.08[a]	−0.04	−0.07	0.00
per capita	(0.02)	(0.16)	(0.06)	(0.17)
Household below		0.38[b]		0.47[b]
poverty line		(0.18)		(0.18)
Population per hospital	0.11[b]	0.12[c]	0.13[a]	0.15[b]
bed	(0.05)	(0.06)	(0.05)	(0.07)
Access to potable water	−1.19[a]	−1.02[a]	−0.43[b]	−0.34[b]
and sewerage connection	(0.23)	(0.24)	(0.19)	(0.17)
City revenue from central		−0.16		−0.30[c]
government		(0.16)		(0.17)
Region[d]				
European and developed	−57.77[a]	−69.02[a]	−59.15[a]	−71.12[a]
countries	(9.35)	(12.51)	(16.52)	(16.31)
Latin American countries	−49.99[a]	−54.95[a]	−47.97[a]	−50.34[a]
	(9.29)	(11.51)	(15.21)	(14.59)
Asian countries	−55.73[a]	−61.02[a]	−62.37[a]	−67.40[a]
	(9.52)	(10.50)	(10.50)	(11.20)
R^2 (%)	64.85	67.63	60.63	62.62
Number of observations	140	102	137	101

Note: Heteroskedasticity-consistent standard errors are shown in parentheses.
a. Significant at $p < 0.01$.
b. Significant at $p < 0.05$.
c. Significant at $p < 0.10$.
d. The omitted category is African and Middle Eastern countries.

central government. It is particularly true that increasing income inequality in the city keeps the poor from accessing potable water and sewerage connections, which in turn leads to a high child mortality. These findings confirm a view shared by the 1996 U.N. Global Conference on Human Settlements, and recent urban theorists who point to the adequacy of access to water, as well as sewerage connections, a lower poverty rate, and the efficiency of urban management as the critical components affecting child mortality in urban areas (Mills and Becker 1986; Prud'homme 1994).

Appendix A. City Sample: 92 Cities

Abidjan (Côte d'Ivoire)
Amman (Jordan)
Amsterdam (Netherlands)
Arusha (Tanzania)
Assiout (Egypt)
Atlanta (United States)
Baku (Azerbaijan)
Bandung (Indonesia)
Bangalore (India)
Banjarmasin (Indonesia)
Barbados (Barbados)
Bedfordshire (United Kingdom)
Bobo-Dioulasso (Burkina Faso)
Bogota (Colombia)
Bombay (India)
Brasilia (Brazil)
Bratislava (Slovak Republic)
Brest (France)
Budapest (Hungary)
Bujumbura (Burundi)
Bulawayo (Zimbabwe)
Cairo (Egypt, Arab Rep. of)
Chennai (India)
Chisinau (Moldova)
Chittagong (Bangladesh)
Colombo (Sri Lanka)
Copenhagen (Denmark)
Cotonou (Benin)
Cuenca (Ecuador)
Curitiba (Brazil)
Dakar (Senegal)
Dar es Salaam (Tanzania)
Delhi (India)
Djibouti (Djibouti)
Foshan (China)
Freetown (Sierra Leone)
Gharbeya (Egypt, Arab Rep. of)
Guatemala City (Guatemala)
Guayaquil (Ecuador)
Gulbarga (India)
Harare (Zimbabwe)
Hefei (China)
Hubli-Dharbad (India)
Ibadan (Nigeria)
Jakarta (Indonesia)
Kaoloack (Senegal)
Koper (Slovenia)

Kostroma (Russian Federation)
La Paz (Bolivia)
Labe (Guinea)
Lahore (Pakistan)
Libreville (Gabon)
Lima (Peru)
Ljubljana (Slovenia)
Lucknow (India)
Maribor (Slovenia)
Medan (Indonesia)
Melbourne (Australia)
Moscow (Russian Federation)
Mysore (India)
Niamey (Niger)
Nizhny Novgorod (Russian
    Federation)
Nouakchott (Mauritania)
Novgorod (Russian Federation)
Onitsha (Nigeria)
Ouagadougou (Burkina Faso)
Paris (France)
Porto Novo (Benin)
Rabat (Morocco)
Recife (Brazil)
Rio de Janeiro (Brazil)
Ryazan (Russian Federation)
San Miguel (El Salvador)
San Salvador (El Salvador)
Sana'a (Yemen)
Santa Ana (El Salvador)
Santiago (Chile)
Seattle (United States)
Semarang (Indonesia)
Stockholm (Sweden)
Surabaya (Indonesia)
Tambacounda (Senegal)
Tangail (Bangladesh)
Toronto (Canada)
Tumkur (India)
Tunis (Tunisia)
Ulan Bator(Mongolia)
Varanasi (India)
Windhoek (Namibia)
Yerevan (Armenia)
Zagreb (Croatia)
Ziguinchor (Senegal)

Appendix B. Additional 48 Cities in Extended Sample

Addis Ababa (Ethiopia)
Almaty (Kazakhstan)
Amman (Jordan)
Antananarivo (Madagascar)
Athens (Greece)
Bamako (Mali)
Bangui (Central African Republic)
Bhiwandi (India)
Cajamarca (Peru)
Cardiff (United Kingdom)
Cologne (Germany)
Dhaka (Bangladesh)
Donetsk (Ukraine)
Duisburg (Germany)
Dunkirk (France)
Erfurt (Germany)
Freiburg (Germany)
Gaborone (Botswana)
Georgetown (Guyana)
Jinja (Uganda)
Kampala (Uganda)
Khartoum (Sudan)
Kigali (Rwanda)
Koudougou (Burkina Faso)

Leipzig (Germany)
Lilongwe (Malawi)
Lomé (Togo)
Lyon (France)
Mbale (Uganda)
Mbarara (Uganda)
Mbeya (Tanzania)
Mwanza (Tanzania)
Mzuzu (Malawi)
Nairobi (Kenya)
N'Djamena (Chad)
Pokhara (Nepal)
Prague (Czech Republic)
Quito (Ecuador)
Riga (Latvia)
Seychelles (Seychelles)
Sofia (Bulgaria)
Suva (Fiji)
Tallin (Estonia)
Tbilisi (Georgia)
Tirana (Albania)
Trujillo (Peru)
Vilnius (Lithuania)
Wiesbaden (Germany)

Appendix C. City-Level Data, 1993

City name	Population per hospital bed	Potable water access (%)	Households below poverty line (%)	Child mortality rate (per 1,000)	City population growth rate (per 1,000)	Revenue from local tax. (%)	Revenue from central gov. transfers (%)	Household sewerage connection (%)	Household income per capita (100s of US$)	Type of water service provider	Type of sewerage service provider
Abidjan	1,027.0	61.70	36.50	37.00	50.00	—	—	45.00	4.01	6	6
Amman	390.0	100.00	16.20	39.00	36.00	28.50	0.11	79.00	11.25	2	2
Amsterdam	114.7	100.00	20.50	5.20	6.00	5.00	95.00	100.00	99.00	1	1
Arusha	1,190.0	60.00	23.00	110.00	95.00	—	—	16.00	0.63	3	3
Assiout	631.0	92.90	53.00	94.00	26.00	8.70	77.40	30.00	3.28	3	3
Atlanta	71.3	100.00	24.60	12.00	7.50	35.53	16.59	97.70	101.65	—	—
Baku	69.0	100.00	87.10	19.50	10.30	91.40	0.00	79.30	1.80	3	3
Bandung	771.0	86.30	10.96	54.00	27.60	9.57	1.74	27.00	2.86	1	1
Bangalore	270.0	80.90	12.00	9.00	41.40	67.28	9.47	35.30	2.37	2	2
Banjarmasin	403.0	93.70	12.53	74.00	20.90	36.00	0.00	0.00	2.45	6	
Barbados	133.0	100.00	—	2.00	5.00	—	—	4.50	51.21	—	—
Bedfordshire	270.0	98.00	15.00	0.10	5.20	16.00	71.00	93.00	94.02	5	5
Bobo-Dioulasso	594.0	81.07	11.40	162.00	71.00	57.80	0.00	0.00	2.62	2	3
Bogota	634.0	97.00	22.91	65.00	20.90	58.83	11.49	98.82	10.04	1	1
Bombay	398.0	96.40	17.00	17.50	20.40	42.65	0.94	51.40	1.96	1	1
Brasilia	339.0	89.20	18.50	28.70	28.30	22.30	51.10	74.44	16.28	2	2
Bratislava	86.0	100.00	2.20	2.00	5.00	—	—	96.00	14.36	2	2
Brest	80.0	100.00	—	0.20	0.60	36.30	13.50	99.00	100.48	—	—
Budapest	66.0	100.00	36.60	24.00	-17.10	20.60	43.50	90.00	17.25	3	1
Bujumbura	188.0	93.00	42.30	106.00	57.00	69.60	0.00	29.00	3.26	4	6
Bulawayo	263.0	100.00	—	11.20	70.00	—	—	98.00	1.60	3	1

City											
Cairo	373.0	97.90	42.90	69.00	16.10	18.80	46.30	91.00	3.66	3	3
Chennai	137.0	59.90	18.50	22.30	21.10	75.21	5.86	37.20	1.64	2	2
Chisinau	54.6	100.00	92.00	29.70	−2.80	84.00	16.00	86.00	2.88	1	1
Chittagong	5,240.0	72.10	78.00	129.00	53.40	29.71	59.46	53.31	0.60	1	1
Colombo	110.0	98.00	13.91	29.10	4.90	68.00	18.00	60.00	0.82	2	1
Copenhagen	98.0	100.00	—	7.50	3.00	41.90	20.80	100.00	131.18	1	1
Cotonou	370.0	60.00	27.90	111.00	40.50	89.20	0.00	1.30	4.81	2	6
Cuenca	500.0	100.00	37.60	36.40	30.80	15.50	25.11	89.00	7.81	1	1
Curitiba	204.0	97.20	5.70	29.80	22.70	25.10	36.75	75.40	1.85	2	2
Dakar	1,682.0	92.00	12.50	110.50	34.00	83.60	0.60	24.70	2.43	4	2
Dar es Salaam	345.0	60.00	23.00	110.00	43.00	12.00	67.00	6.00	0.92	3	3
Delhi	372.0	91.50	17.00	19.00	31.90	48.72	28.78	39.60	2.18	1	1
Djibouti	328.0	69.00	—	156.00	61.00	0.00	100.00	15.00	7.10	6	2
Foshan	125.0	100.00	0.65	3.00	5.20	—	—	100.00	8.82	—	—
Freetown	443.0	53.00	80.00	252.00	30.10	65.60	1.40	0.82	0.45	4	2
Gharbeya	543.0	99.40	45.00	57.00	19.00	8.60	78.00	90.50	3.60	3	3
Guatemala City	810.0	63.90	79.90	122.00	32.00	26.00	20.00	—	2.14	6	1
Guayaquil	322.0	85.00	31.30	47.00	30.60	—	—	55.00	6.44	2	3
Gulbarga	209.0	90.40	17.44	32.40	27.50	39.59	0.23	13.90	1.38	2	2
Harare	180.0	97.00	—	7.70	60.00	30.00	—	93.00	1.86	1	1
Hefei	100.0	100.00	0.30	14.00	6.60	—	—	56.60	3.58	—	—
Hubli-Dharbad	721.0	88.70	12.82	22.90	23.30	35.95	0.00	37.40	1.95	2	2
Ibadan	2,091.0	70.20	62.10	62.00	30.00	13.90	80.20	0.05	0.19	6	—
Jakarta	611.0	92.64	8.50	33.00	21.10	43.60	29.95	0.00	3.89	2	—
Kaoloack	478.0	55.90	35.10	170.20	35.00	44.60	8.70	3.00	0.97	—	—
Koper	106.2	100.00	2.70	8.30	8.00	60.30	10.00	98.00	39.18	1	1
Kostroma	74.2	100.00	20.00	22.00	17.00	68.00	0.00	91.00	8.81	6	6

(Appendix C continued.)

City name	Population per hospital bed	Potable water access (%)	Households below poverty line (%)	Child mortality rate (per 1,000)	City population growth rate (per 1,000)	Revenue from local tax. (%)	Revenue from central gov. transfers (%)	Household sewerage connection (%)	Household income per capita (100s of US$)	Type of water service provider	Type of sewerage service provider
La Paz	326.0	89.80	62.23	62.00	17.80	21.87	35.84	58.18	6.10	6	6
Labe	568.0	80.00	—	148.00	35.00	70.00	0.00	0.00	1.50	—	—
Lahore	509.0	90.00	30.00	91.90	35.90	40.18	12.02	74.00	3.67	—	—
Libreville	311.0	100.00	—	114.00	47.00	96.60	0.00	0.00	17.06	4	3
Lima	198.0	86.90	29.40	24.00	27.00	64.40	11.00	68.80	3.57	4	4
Ljubljana	36.0	100.00	3.60	8.30	18.00	87.40	0.00	99.00	37.89	1	1
Lucknow	460.0	88.20	22.00	41.70	40.40	34.50	30.88	30.00	1.33	1	1
Maribor	47.5	99.50	14.40	8.10	-2.00	68.00	19.00	58.00	28.06	1	1
Medan	256.0	93.75	8.70	50.00	19.50	28.64	26.41	19.00	2.54	2	—
Melbourne	312.0	100.00	—	7.00	11.00	49.00	7.00	98.90	86.55	2	2
Moscow	80.1	100.00	15.00	20.70	-9.00	76.70	9.90	99.70	10.35	6	4
Mysore	156.0	89.90	5.51	29.20	36.40	67.23	0.94	60.00	2.25	2	2
Niamey	522.0	76.80	42.00	111.00	48.00	40.15	3.66	0.00	1.51	4	3
Nizhny Novgorod	100.0	100.00	24.00	20.00	-29.00	69.00	0.00	94.70	9.24	6	6
Nouakchott	1,084.0	68.00	25.00	120.00	80.00	80.90	0.00	4.00	2.59	2	2
Novgorod	58.7	100.00	18.00	26.00	0.00	64.90	0.00	96.00	9.09	2	2
Onitsha	109.9	95.00	87.00	63.00	47.00	12.90	77.10	0.00	0.53	6	5
Ouagadougou	833.0	74.70	11.40	150.00	94.00	63.46	0.00	0.00	2.87	2	2
Paris	117.0	100.00	—	9.10	5.70	41.00	15.00	98.00	60.62	—	—
Porto Novo	714.0	76.00	31.70	110.00	23.10	58.30	1.57	1.40	2.22	2	1
Rabat	365.0	100.00	7.00	60.00	37.00	35.60	0.00	95.00	11.55	1	2
Recife	131.0	94.70	34.80	38.50	6.90	21.10	42.00	37.50	0.88	2	—

Rio de Janeiro	165.0	97.60	18.50	31.80	6.70	26.81	20.15	87.10	19.57	3	1
Ryazan	74.2	100.00	36.00	20.00	20.00	73.30	6.70	91.50	7.27	1	1
San Miguel	249.0	56.20	50.00	46.00	35.10	26.00	7.00	46.00	5.52	2	1
San Salvador	259.0	90.50	40.10	45.00	39.10	41.00	8.00	80.10	6.71	2	2
Sana'a	520.0	60.00	—	122.00	88.30	—	—	12.00	0.26	6	1
Santa Ana	225.0	82.20	49.50	46.00	16.70	59.00	17.00	56.60	5.31	2	6
Santiago	310.0	97.80	21.60	17.00	18.00	—	—	91.70	12.35	6	2
Seattle	169.5	100.00	7.40	12.00	20.40	37.00	8.40	99.50	140.39	—	—
Semarang	465.0	88.17	6.80	53.00	15.10	14.35	32.80	0.00	2.29	1	1
Stockholm	90.0	100.00	0.30	5.80	8.60	42.00	13.00	100.00	131.86	1	1
Surabaya	516.0	99.03	4.50	52.00	17.30	12.39	21.00	0.00	3.17	1	—
Tambacounda	571.0	12.90	44.00	182.70	42.00	67.60	0.00	2.40	1.53	—	—
Tangail	143.0	51.00	37.00	106.00	33.70	42.93	10.39	—	0.32	1	1
Toronto	177.0	100.00	23.00	1.80	7.50	38.00	29.00	99.50	165.98	1	1
Tumkur	486.0	86.20	24.60	29.20	40.40	64.24	2.53	0.00	1.26	1	1
Tunis	360.0	96.30	6.30	43.00	27.00	35.00	39.00	72.70	7.75	2	2
Ulan Bator	78.0	49.00	12.40	11.30	17.00	79.20	0.00	51.00	0.69	1	1
Varanasi	372.0	84.50	28.27	43.10	22.70	24.28	49.34	40.65	0.85	2	1
Windhoek	97.7	98.00	30.00	87.00	54.40	16.00	0.00	75.00	15.66	1	1
Yerevan	98.0	98.00	80.00	50.00	-0.20	—	—	93.40	1.22	1	1
Zagreb	113.0	90.00	6.10	10.20	8.70	53.10	19.10	80.00	11.49	3	1
Ziguincho	1,323.0	29.50	26.60	194.90	49.00	52.70	0.00	1.90	1.02	—	—

— Not available.

Note: Coding for type of providers is as follows: (1) local government only, (2) national and regional government only, (3) local, regional, and national government, (4) parastatal, (5) private, (6) mix of public and private providers.

Source: UNCHS Global Urban Indicators Database 1993.

References

Alberini, Anna, Gunnar S. Eskeland, Alan Krupnick, and Gordon McGranahan. 1996. "Determinants of Diarrheal Disease in Jakarta." *Water Resources Research* 32(7):2259–69.

Auclair, Christine. 1998. "Urban Indicators Programme." United Nations Centre for Human Settlements (Habitat), New York. Unpublished.

Briscoe, John. 1992. "Poverty and Water Supply: How to Move Forward." *Finance & Development* 29(4):16–19.

Brockerhoff, Martin, and Ellen Brennan. 1998. "The Poverty of Cities in Developing Regions." *Population and Development Review* 24(1):75–114.

Cheema, G. Shabbir. 1992. "Issues in Urban Management." In Nigel Harris, ed., *Cities in the 1990s: The Challenges for Developing Countries*. New York: St. Martin's Press: 110–12.

Demery, Lionel, and Lyn Squire. 1996. "Macroeconomic Adjustment and Poverty in African: An Emerging Picture." *The World Bank Research Observer* 11(1):39–59.

Esrey, Steven A., R. G. Feachem, and J. M. Hughes. 1985. "Intervention for the Control of Diarrhoeal Diseases among Young Children: Improving Water Supplies and Excreta Disposal Facilities." *Bulletin of the World Health Organization* 63(4):757–72.

Esrey, Steven A., James B. Potash, Leslie Roberts, and Clive Shiff. 1990. "Health Benefits from Improvement in Water Supply and Sanitation: Survey and Analysis of the Literature of Selected Disease." Water and Sanitation for Health (WASH) Technical Report 66. U.S. Agency for International Development, Washington, D.C.

Feachem, Richard G. 1984. "Interventions for the Control of Diarrhoeal Diseases among Young Children: Promotion of Personal and Domestic Hygiene." *Bulletin of the World Health Organization* 62:467–76.

Flood, Joe. 1997. *Indicators Programme 1994–96: Report Prepared for the UNCHS for Human Settlements*. New York: United Nations Centre for Human Settlements (Habitat).

Frankel, Jeffrey, and David Romer. 1999. "Does Trade Cause Growth?" *The American Economic Review* 89(3):379–99.

Gilbert, Alan. 1993. "Third World Cities: The Changing National Settlement System" *Urban Studies* 30(4/5):721–40.

Harpham, Trudy, Tim Lusty, and Patrick Vaughan. 1988. *In the Shadow of the City: Community Health and the Urban Poor*. Oxford: Oxford University Press.

Harrison, Paul. 1982. *Inside the Third World*. Harmondsworth, U.K.: Penguin.

Kennedy, Paul. 1993. *Preparing for the Twenty-First Century*. New York: Random House.